A NEW GUIDE TO RATIONAL LIVING

BOOKS BY ALBERT ELLIS

The Folklore of Sex
Sex, Society and the Individual (with A. P. Pillay)
Sex Life of the American Woman and the Kinsey Report
The American Sexual Tragedy
The Psychology of Sex Offenders (with Ralph Brancale)
How to Live with a Neurotic
Sex Without Guilt
The Art and Science of Love
The Encyclopedia of Sexual Behavior (with Albert Abarbanel)
Reason and Emotion in Psychotherapy
If This Be Sexual Heresy . . .
The Origins and Development of the Incest Taboo
Sex and the Single Man
The Intelligent Woman's Guide to Manhunting
Nymphomania: A Study of the Over-sexed Woman (with Edward Sagarin)
Homosexuality
The Case for Sexual Liberty
Suppressed: Seven Key Essays Publishers Dared Not Print
The Search for Sexual Enjoyment
The Art of Erotic Seduction (with Roger O. Conway)
Is Objectivism a Religion?
How to Raise an Emotionally Healthy, Happy Child (with Janet L. Wolfe and
      Sandra Moseley)
Growth Through Reason (with Ben. N. Ard, Jr., John M. Gullo, Paul A.
      Hauck, Maxie C. Maultsby, Jr., and H. Jon Geis)
Executive Leadership: A Rational Approach
How to Master Your Fear of Flying
The Civilized Couple's Guide to Extramarital Adventure
The Sensuous Person: Critique and Corrections
Humanistic Psychotherapy: The Rational-Emotive Approach

BOOKS BY ROBERT A. HARPER

Marriage
Problems of American Society (with John F. Cuber and William F. Kenkel)
Psychoanalysis and Psychotherapy: 36 Systems
45 Levels to Sexual Understanding and Enjoyment (with Walter Stokes)
The New Psychotherapies

BOOKS BY ALBERT ELLIS AND ROBERT A. HARPER

Creative Marriage (paperback edition title: *A Guide to Successful Marriage*)
A Guide to Rational Living

A NEW
GUIDE TO
RATIONAL LIVING

Albert Ellis, Ph.D. and
Robert A. Harper, Ph.D.

PRENTICE-HALL, INC.
Englewood Cliffs, New Jersey

A New Guide to Rational Living
by Albert Ellis, Ph.D. and Robert A. Harper, Ph.D.

Copyright © 1975, 1961, by Institute for Rational Living, Inc.

This book is based on the work *A Guide to Rational Living*

Printed in the United States of America

Prentice-Hall International, Inc., London
Prentice-Hall of Australia, Pty. Ltd., Sydney
Prentice-Hall of Canada, Ltd., Toronto
Prentice-Hall of India Private Ltd., New Delhi
Prentice-Hall of Japan, Inc., Tokyo

10 9 8 7 6 5 4 3 2

Library of Congress Cataloging in Publication Data

Ellis, Albert.
    A new guide to rational living.

    Published in 1961 under title: A guide to rational
living.
    Bibliography: p.
    Includes index.
    1. Rational-emotive psychotherapy.   I. Harper,
Robert Allan, joint author.   II. Title.
RC489.R3E444   616.8'914   75-4961
ISBN 0-13-614909-X

ACKNOWLEDGMENTS

We gratefully acknowledge the helpful contributions of Dr. Raymond J. Corsini, Dr. Frances Harper Corbett, Rhoda Winter Russell, and Brooking Tatum, who read the original draft of the manuscript of this book and who made valuable critical comments and suggestions. We also acknowledge the unusual contributions of Robert H. Moore to the revised edition of the book, since without his exceptional encouragement and help the translation of the work into E-prime would probably never have gotten completed. Full responsibility for the contents of the book, however, remains with the authors.

FOREWORD

In the first chapter of this extraordinary book, Drs. Albert Ellis and Robert A. Harper express the hope that readers of *A New Guide to Rational Living*—because the English language has limitations—will not "jump to the conclusion that we hand out the same old hackneyed, Pollyannaish message that you may have long ago considered and rejected as having no practical value."

Because they use such words as "creativity," "happiness," "love," "maturity," and "problem-solving" (all terms used superficially by "positive thinking" and other "utopian" credos), they feel alarmed that people will accuse them of adding one more book to the already superfluous list of those promised to make everyone rich, happy, and powerful, to say nothing of emotionally mature.

They need not worry. Drs. Ellis and Harper have refreshing humility in this era of dogmatic formulas for living, and they see that constant happiness remains as illusive as moonbeams. As proof of this conviction, they have termed the chapter dealing with happiness "Refusing to Feel Desperately Unhappy." What a far cry from the super-positive pseudo-philosophies of the "inspirational" books!

Actually, their associates had to talk these two prominent psychologists into doing a book about the "rational-emotive psychotherapy" they practice, and they had to feel it would truly help others before they wrote a word. They still believe intensive individual therapy desirable in serious cases, but they have come to believe a book can help a certain percentage of people who have the capacity for honest self-evaluation.

This book, like no other you have read, employs none of the jargon usually associated with psychology or psychiatry, and it may well prove the best book on psychotherapy for laymen ever written. It can provide emotionally disturbed individuals with many answers they seek.

The authors use a unique method of projecting their answers to common problems. Thus, they point out that the individual who feels inadequate and insecure suffers from, for example, "Irrational Idea No. 2: *The idea that you must prove thoroughly competent, adequate, and achieving.*"

Drs. Ellis and Harper use ten such ideas to bring out the scope of their psychotherapy, with answers far more subtle and helpful than those devised by laymen in the field. This seems only natural. All of them have shown proven results in a clinical setting.

Unlike laymen who undertake to write books outlining the steps to take toward emotional adequacy, the writers of this book have training and a host of case histories, taken from their office charts, to buttress their advice. This not only makes for a more interesting book but creates confidence in the reader concerning the techniques suggested.

Probably many readers will remember Dr. Ellis as a sexologist who has done so much valuable work in this area that critics frequently compare him to the other Ellis, Havelock, a pioneer in sexual research. His books in this field have done an incalculable amount of good, particularly in freeing people of feelings of guilt stemming from their environments.

Dr. Harper has a similar background, and he possesses added knowledge of anthropology and sociology, both disciplines desirably supplemental to psychology. He has collaborated with Dr. Ellis previously and has worked on other books in the area of rational therapy.

Those readers can most appreciate this book who have read a large number of euphoric and so-called inspirational books without the success so glowingly described by their authors. I have the firm opinion that, although it makes no promises, it will help them more than all the others put together.

I find it difficult not to sound lyrical about this unusual book. After two decades of reading manuscripts which profess to have all the virtues which this one *actually* possesses, I feel that all the midnight oil I have burned has not burned in vain. This book will remain a classic in the field.

Drs. Ellis and Harper dissect the main emotional problems which humans tend to have. They present their ideas in a brilliant and all-encompassing manner—so brilliant, in fact, that I believe the reader will find more answers than he or she would in the average vis-à-vis confrontation. I say this despite the disclaimers of both authors who ethically point out the limitations of "absent" therapy.

For one thing, the book proves not as maddening as many personal visits to therapists who subscribe to the passive, nondirective method still used by most psychologists and psychiatrists. In this type of therapy all questions get answered by, "You tell me."

Drs. Ellis and Harper make it clear they do not practice as the "orthodox psychoanalyst . . . with whom we respectfully but wholeheartedly disagree." Rather than maintain the traditional Freudian silence, both therapists, in the early part of the treatment, indicate where the "emotionally disturbed individual . . . seems off the beam."

Their direct, get-to-the-heart-of-the-problem methods show wide variance with most orthodox treatments that drag on interminably with clients never quite knowing where they stand. As far as I can see, here certainly lies, along with group therapy, the direction psychotherapy will take if it intends to make a real contribution to comprehensive health.

If you feel you have the rigorous honesty necessary to conduct self-analysis, this book will prove the most important one you have ever read. And it will seem a boon to those who cannot pay the high fees charged for individual treatment.

I find so many excellent techniques explored in this book that I should like to mention a great deal more. I feel deterred only by the fact that the authors speak very well for themselves.

You have my best wishes in reading a book that I think will remain the standard for years to come.

Melvin Powers

INTRODUCTION TO THE REVISED EDITION

We view *A Guide to Rational Living* as a somewhat revolutionary book. When it first appeared, in 1961, it presented to the reading public one of the first books by reputable, experienced psychotherapists that showed people how to deal effectively with their own problems. This occurred a few years before Eric Berne's *Games People Play* came out; and a long time before such popular books as *I'm OK, You're OK* and *How to Be Your Own Best Friend.*

Even a little earlier, we had anticipated the trend to popular self-help books, since one of us (A.E.) had brought out *How to Live with a Neurotic* in 1957 and *The Art and Science of Love* in 1960, and we had jointly authored *Creative Marriage*—just before writing *A Guide to Rational Living* in 1961. These former books, however, only dealt with certain aspects of human disturbance and did not cover the wider range of emotional problems. Moreover, they only partly presented the new system of rational-emotive therapy (RET), which got started around the beginning of 1955. The *Guide* (as thousands of readers and hundreds of therapists have affectionately come to call it during the last decade and a half) easily preempted our earlier writings and developed into the most authoritative and widely quoted work on RET for the general public. Along with *Reason and Emotion in Psychotherapy* (aimed largely at the professional therapist) it has evolved, we feel happy to state, into a classic in the field. Over the years, we have received literally thousands of letters and oral communications testifying to its helpfulness with many moderately and seriously disturbed individuals. Great numbers of psychotherapists seem to employ it as supplementary reading with their clients. Many of its main tenets and formulations have got copied or paraphrased with or without due acknowledgment, in others' writings. Good! For our purpose continues: to take the best wisdom about "human nature" from the past and present—and particularly from the somewhat neglected philosophic writings of Epictetus, Marcus Aurelius, John Dewey, and Bertrand Russell—and to make it widely available, with suitable revisions and additions, to present-day troubled people.

We also believe, as part of rational-emotive theory and practice, in the *educative* aspects of psychotherapy. RET doesn't exactly follow the usual medical model of disturbance, which essentially holds that emotional problems consist of diseases or aberrations, curable by an *outside* person's (a therapist's) authoritarianly telling people what they have to do to improve. Nor does it follow the somewhat similar conditioning model (held in common by both psychoanalysts and classical behaviorists), which claims that humans get *made* disturbed by early influences, and that they therefore have to get restructured or reconditioned by an outside, parentlike therapist who somehow forces them into new patterns of behaving. It follows, instead, the humanistic, educative model which asserts that people, even in their early lives, have a great many more *choices* than they tend to recognize; that most of their "conditioning" actually consists of *self*-conditioning; and that a therapist, a teacher, or even a book can help them see much more clearly their range of alternatives and thereby to *choose* to reeducate and retrain themselves so that they surrender most of their serious self-*created* emotional difficulties. In consequence, RET keeps trying to develop a wide range of educative methods of showing people how they behave self-defeatingly and how they can get themselves to change.) From the start, it has employed the usual methods of individual, face-to-face, and small group therapy. But it also makes notable use of large workshops, lectures, seminars, public therapy demonstrations, tape recordings, films, stories, books, pamphlets, and other mass media presentations to *teach* people what they unfortunately do to needlessly upset themselves and what they can do, instead, to help themselves emotionally.

Although hundreds of therapists in the United States and elsewhere now largely or partly employ RET methods with their clients, and although these therapists have helped benefit thousands of people during the last two decades, it seems likely that five or ten times this number of individuals have significantly changed during this same period of time by reading the *Guide* and other pamphlets and books on RET. Again: good! If we and other authors can keep up this helpful pace, and if we eventually put psychotherapists out of business (an unlikely result for the near future, as we indicate a little later on in this book), we would find that result great. Meanwhile, we intend to keep trying to contribute to it.

Back to this *new* edition of the *Guide*. We have tried to add to it another notable, and we think highly revolutionary, aspect. From the start—as perusal of the first edition of the work will show—RET has emerged as a form of "semantic therapy." Dr. Donald Meichenbaum and other researchers have emphasized this aspect of it; and we agree. Uniquely, we have pointed out from the start that, unlike lower animals, people *tell themselves* various sane and crazy things. Their beliefs, attitudes, opinions, and philosophies largely (though hardly exclusively) take the form of *internalized sentences* or *self-talk*. Consequently, one of the most powerful and elegant modalities they can use to change themselves, and particularly to modify their self-defeating emotions and sabotaging behaviors, consists of their clearly seeing, understanding, disputing, altering, and acting against their internal verbalizations. This theory seemed most revolutionary when we espoused it in the first edition of the *Guide*. Since that time, it has gotten confirmed by literally hundreds of research studies—largely by clinical, experimental, and social psychologists, many of whom have little to do with psychotherapy—almost all of which demonstrate that when we directly or indirectly induce people to change their beliefs or philosophies about something, their emotions and their behaviors also significantly change.

Fine! But after practicing RET for about a decade and after our friends in the general semantics movement pointed out to us that we had developed a technique of applying some of the teachings of Alfred Korzybski more effectively than others had done, we reread the leading general semanticists and quickly discovered the truth of this view. RET *does* take over where Korzybski left off and advocates that therapists (and writers on therapy) employ semantic methods that often prove most helpful in minimizing emotional disturbances. Once we discovered this, we increasingly and more consciously helped our clients to change their semantic usages so as to concomitantly change their thinking, emoting, and behaving.

For example? Well, let us present a few common cases in point.

When clients (in individual or group therapy) state, "I *must* work harder at the office," or "I *should not* hate my mate," we frequently interrupt them with: "You mean, "*It would prove better* if you worked harder at the office," or "You *preferably* should not hate your mate."

When clients state, "I can't stop worrying," or "I find it impossible to diet," we try to get them to change their sentences to "I *can* stop worrying, but so far I haven't," and "I find it exceptionally difficult to diet—but hardly impossible!"

When people say "I *always* do badly *every* time I go to a social affair," we try to get them to change this to "I *usually* [or *often*] do badly *most* of the time I go to a social affair."

When individuals insist, "It would prove *awful* if I lost my job!" or "How *terrible* to get rejected!" we try to ge them to say and think, instead, "I would find it highly *inconvenient* if I lost my job," or "I view it as distinctly disadvantageous when I get rejected."

When clients state that "*I* am a *bad person* for acting so incompetently," or "I am a *worthless individual* for treating Smith so badly," we help them to say, instead, "It remains highly unfortunate when I act incompetently but it does *not* make me a bad person." And: "I behave immorally and badly when I treat Smith so badly, but *I* cannot get legitimately rated, as either a worthwhile or a worthless individual for any of my actions."

When people believe and state, "I *am* an animal," we show

them (as Korzybski indicated), "You more accurately mean, 'I copy animals in some respects, but I largely act as a human and not entirely as a lower animal.' " And when they say, "I *am* no good at arithmetic," we get them to say, instead, "Up to the present time, I have done poorly at arithmetic. But that doesn't mean that I cannot possibly do better at arithmetic in the future."

When humans think and declare, "He *is* a murderous black." or "He *is* a rotten American," we try to show them that they could much more accurately say, "Born and raised as a black, he sometimes acts murderously, while others who got born and raised as blacks never seem to act murderously." And: "He grew up in America and often, perhaps related to his upbringing, acts crummily; but others who grew up in the same area and much the same way as he tend to act much less crummily."

When clients claim, "I *need* love!" we attempt to get them to say, instead, "I *want* love very much, but I do not absolutely *need* it and can survive and feel reasonably happy without it." When they contend, "I *must* have a high standard of living and *can't stand it* when I don't," we try to get them to believe, "I would very much *desire* or *like* a high standard of living and I'll find it damned inconvenient if I don't. But I certainly can stand it!"

When clients hold that "I'm *supposed to* think rationally," we help them to change to "*I would most likely feel better* if I thought rationally." When they make commands like, "Thou *shalt* not steal," we try to get them to revise these into "*It usually turns out much better* if you do not steal, once you decide to remain a member of a social group, because you would not want others to steal from you and you would tend to get into serious trouble if you did steal."

When people say that "*That* makes me anxious," or "*You* made me angry," we help them see that "*I* made myself anxious about that" and "I angered myself about your behavior."

When clients use language like "I'm OK, you're OK," we try to get them to say, instead, "I choose to accept the fact that I remain alive and can enjoy myself, even though I make many errors; and I accept the fact that you remain alive and have the right to exist and keep yourself happy, even though you will at times act badly and perform deeds I don't like." When people say, "I like myself," we show them they could preferably and more realistically say something like, "I like the state of remaining alive and I choose to continue to exist and to avoid needless pain and to seek maximum short-range and long-range pleasure."

As you can see from the above examples, RET continually (among other things) stresses a semantic approach to understanding and minimizing human disturbance. Logically, therefore, we have thought for several years of extending its efficacy by rewriting some of its basic texts (as well as writing some new ones) in E-prime. Alfred Korzybski recommended, in *Science and Sanity* (originally published in 1933), that we avoid the "is" of identity and the "is" of predication—even though, throughout his writings, he did not avoid such forms of speech himself! For when we make a statement like, "The rose *is* red," we strongly imply that (1) redness constitutes the "natural" or usual color of *all* roses; (2) this particular rose we keep talking about has *total* redness; (3) it will *always* remain completely red; (4) it has some intrinsic *essence* of redness; and (5) if it does not have redness, we could not possibly or legitimately call it a rose.

When, Korzybski said in *Science and Sanity*, we employ the "is" of identity, "we must somehow copy animals in our nervous processes. Through wrong evaluation we are using the lower centres too much and cannot 'think' properly. We are 'over-emotional'; we get easily confused, worried, terrorized, or discouraged; or else we become absolutists, dogmatists." Quite a revolutionary statement for 1933! And probably quite right.

Encouraged by the example of Robert H. Moore, a staff member of the Florida Branch of the Institute for Rational Living, Inc., at Clearwater, and in collaboration with him (he has painstakingly gone over every word in this revised edition at least twice), we have revised this edition of the *Guide* in E-prime, a form of English invented by D. David Bourland, Jr., following Korzybski's suggestions. The name E-prime comes from the semantic equation: *E* prime = *E* minus *e*: where *E* represents all the words of standard English and *e* represents all the forms of *to be*: such as *is, was, am, has been, being*, etc. Although Bourland, who seems to remain somewhat allergic to putting his ideas in published form, has not yet come out with anything extensive on E-prime, he has, in a brief article, noted that its adoption leads to certain advantages:

1. When we use E-prime, we get rid of certain silly and essentially unanswerable questions, such as "What *is* my destiny?" "Who *am* I?" (If you think about it, you will see that Bourland hits the nail on the head here. while you can sensibly answer the question "What do I like?" or "What thoughts and feelings do I have?" you cannot very well answer a vague question like, "Who *am* I?")

2. We eliminate, by using E-prime, some misleading elegant abbreviations, such as "We know this is the right thing to do." Such abbreviations involve the "is" of predication.

3. We reveal, by employing E-prime, some normally hidden humans who express certain information and feelings. If we say, "It has been found that," we hardly know *who* has found it that ... We'd better say, instead, "Jones, in his study of polar bears, found that...." If we say, "That's where it's at," we put forth something exceptionally vague or meaningless. Better: "I believe

that if you keep coming in late to work, your boss will most probably fire you."

4. When we use E-prime, we tend to help expand our awareness of our *linguistic* environment and we more easily find means for improving conditions in that environment. "My parents were the source of all my troubles and still are" serves as a cop-out for your past and present behavior. If you acknowledge, instead, "My parents kept criticizing me severely during my childhood, and I kept taking them too seriously and thereby kept upsetting myself. Now I *still* down myself when I hear them criticize me, and I consequently still feel worthless," you strongly imply what you can and had better do to interrupt and change your own self-downing tendencies.

5. When we employ E-prime, we eliminate the degree of completeness, finality, and time independence that we state or imply when we use the verb "to be." We thereby forgo the "is" of predication and the use of such misleading statements and over-generalizations as "Roses are red"—which strongly implies that all roses at all times have to possess redness.

6. When we stick to E-prime and avoid all forms of *to be*, we get rid of absolutistic self-fulfilling prophecies, such as "I am a failure." For this non-E-prime sentence implies (1) I have always failed; (2) I will only and always fail in the future; and (3) the universe has a horror of my failing and will consequently punish and damn me, perhaps for eternity, for failing.

Although Korzybski didn't specifically advocate the use of E-prime, he did see its potential usefulness in minimizing what he called insanity and what we today generally call emotional disturbance. He also invented the structural differential method, closely related to E-prime. Using his method, Dr. John G. Lynn, in 1935, reported on the successful treatment of two chronic alcoholics with general semantics teachings. Wendell Johnson, a professor of psychology and a specialist in overcoming speech pathology, also pioneered in the use of general semantics to help people with emotional problems. We have used related methods in RET since the 1950's, including our stress on changing internalized sentences in the first edition of the *Guide*—as Donald Mosher pointed out in *Etc., a Review of General Semantics* in a 1966 paper, "Are Neurotics Victims of Their Emotions." Dr. Maxie C. Maultsby, Jr., an outstanding practitioner of RET and rational behavior therapy, has also emphasized semantic teaching for emotionally disturbed people for the last several years.

As a logical extension of this process, and to aid the development of Korzybski's structural differential in people's thinking, we have consistently employed E-prime in this revision of the *Guide*. As I (A.E.) noted in my recent revision of *How to Live with a "Neurotic,"* the use of E-prime itself does not completely rid writing of *all* kinds of overgeneralizations. But it goes a long way in this direction and tends to prove most helpful! Whether, when people get used to thinking and speaking in this kind of language, they will tend automatically to do significantly less over- and underemotionalizing and to behave more sensibly and less self-defeatingly, we cannot at the moment prove. But that remains our hypothesis!

Many other important revisions of RET get included in this volume: so many, in fact, that we list the major ones in a special extra chapter of the *Guide*. Let us just say briefly here that in numerous instances, in the course of this revision, we eliminate the absolutistic kind of statements (including many *shoulds* and *musts*) that we carelessly let stand in the original edition. We significantly modify the RET concepts of human worth and worthlessness. We clearly distinguish inappropriate from appropriate forms of emotions. We notably sharpen our distinctions between blaming or condemning certain of your behaviors and damning or devil-ifying *yourself* for engaging in those poor behaviors. We stress, much more than we did in the first edition of the *Guide*, both thinking and activity homework assignments. And we include a good many newly developed rational procedures, such as the rational-emotive imagery techniques originated by Dr. Maxie C. Maultsby, Jr., that seem to greatly add to the effectiveness of RET.

In many ways, then, this adds up to a notably updated, significantly developed, and extensively revised edition of *A Guide to Rational Living*. We believe that virtually all the effective teachings of the original version remain. But a whale of a lot has gotten added! Read on—and see for yourself.

ALBERT ELLIS, Ph.D., Executive Director, Institute for Advanced Study in Rational Psychotherapy, New York City

ROBERT A. HARPER, Ph.D., Psychologist and Psychotherapist, Washington, D.C.

CONTENTS

1 HOW FAR CAN YOU GO WITH SELF-ANALYSIS?

People often say to us, "Look, let's suppose that your principles of rational-emotive therapy actually work. Let's suppose that you really can, as you claim, teach any intelligent human not to feel desperately unhappy about practically anything. If you find this true, why don't you just put your theories in a book and let us read them? That way, we'd save a whale of a lot of time, trouble, and treasure going for psychotherapy."

We usually demur.

Self-analysis, we point out, has distinct limitations. No matter how clearly one states the principles of self-help, people often misunderstand or distort them. They read into these principles what they *want* to read—and ignore some of their most salient aspects. They oversimplify, edit out most of the ifs, ands, and buts and cavalierly apply cautiously stated rules of disturbance to almost any person in any situation.

Worse yet, thousands of readers give vast lip service to psychological, moral, social, and other principles in which they stoutly *say* they believe. "I just don't know how to thank you," they keep saying and writing, "for having written that wonderful book! I keep rereading it all the time and have found it the *greatest* of help." But when we correspond or speak with them further, we find that they often have done nothing along the lines painstakingly described in our "wonderful book"—or that their actual behavior diametrically opposes our advocacies.

Intensive psychotherapy has this unique advantage over almost any other form of reconstructive teaching: it provides for systematic and periodic check on whether the therapist's message really gets home to the client. Somewhere in the early part of treatment, the active-directive, rational psychotherapist (quite unlike the passive orthodox psychoanalyst or the nondirective therapist, with whom we respectfully but wholeheartedly disagree) clearly indicates to you that not only do you have problems, but that if you want to get on a saner course you'd better see that you think and act in irrational ways and had better forcefully challenge your illogical assumptions and begin to think and act more rationally and less self-defeatingly.

"Very well," you say after a fairly short period of rational-emotive therapy (RET), "I think I pretty much see what you mean. I'm going to try to do as you say and challenge my own nonsense by which I keep creating my emotional disturbance." And you do try, and soon (perhaps even the very next session) come back to report significant progress. You report, for example (as one of our clients stated), "Say, I find this really great! I did exactly what you told me to do. Instead of groveling before my wife, as usual, when she laid me out for having come to see you, supposedly telling tales about her, and spending money for treatment, I remembered what you said. 'What does she think she gains,' I asked myself, 'from her anger? I'll bet that, just as the doctor said, she really has covered-up weaknesses, and perhaps tries to feel strong by jumping on me. But this time I refuse to take her so seriously and upset myself about her weakness.' And I didn't. I didn't let it bother me at all."

"Fine!" I (A.E.) said, feeling that perhaps this client really had begun to learn how to question his own assumptions regarding himself and his wife and to act more rationally. "And then, when you didn't let it bother you, what did you do, how did you behave toward your wife?"

"Oh, that seemed easy!" said the client. "I just said to myself again—just like you told me to, Doctor—'Look, I won't let this sick-thinking female get away with this kind of stuff any longer. I've taken it for much too long now. I've had enough!' And I really let her have it. I didn't feel afraid, as I usually do, and I told her exactly what I thought of her, how goddamn stupidly she behaved, how you agreed with me that she kept giving me too hard a time, and how if she kept up that kind of stuff any longer I'd push her goddamn teeth in and make her swallow them. Oh, I really let her have it! Just like you told me."

"I did? I told you *that*?" I asked, appalled. And for the next few sessions, by careful repetition and the use of the simplest examples tailored to order for his level of understanding, I helped him—finally—to see what I really meant. Yes, he would better learn to question his wife's motives, and not take her disapproval too seriously. But he could *also* learn not to condemn her (or anyone else) for acting the way she did, and try to accept and forgive her shrewishness and sympathetically help her, if possible, to overcome it. Eventually (actually, after three and a half months of weekly rational-emotive therapy), he learned to think and act more rationally. But only after persistent repetition by me, backsliding on his part, more explanations, his renewed experimental attempts to apply his perceptions of my instructions, and still more corrections.

One of the main advantages of intensive psychotherapy lies in its repetitive, experimenting, revising, practicing nature. And no book, sermon, article, or series of lectures, no matter how clear, can fully give this. Consequently, we, the authors of this book, intend to continue doing individual and group therapy and to train other psychotherapists. Whether we like it or not, we cannot reasonably expect most people with serious problems to rid themselves of their needless anxiety and hostility without some amount of intensive, direct contact with a competent therapist. How nice if easier modes of treatment prevailed! But let us face it: they rarely do.

Now for a look at the other side of the fence. While *most* emotionally disturbed individuals only benefit to a limited extent by reading and hearing material designed to help them combat their disturbances, *some* do derive considerable help, like the fifty-year-old engineer who visited me (A.E.) after reading my book *How to Live with a Neurotic*. This man had a wife with obvious psychotic difficulties, with whom he had had a most difficult time for the twenty-eight years of their marriage. He reported that, until he read the book, he had continually felt angry at her because of her behavior. After reading it twice, almost all his anger vanished and he lived peaceably, though not entirely happily, with her and devoted himself more effectively to protecting their three children from some of the effects of her erratic behavior.

"One passage in the book particularly helped me," he reported. "After I read and reread that passage several times, almost all my anger against my wife seemed to melt away, as if by magic. It really impressed me."

"And what was that passage?" I asked.

"In your chapter on how to live with a person who has severe disturbances, you say, 'All right. So Jones gets drunk every night and acts noisily. How do you expect a drunk to act—sober?' That really hit me. And I asked myself: 'How do you expect your crazy wife to behave—sanely?' That did it! Ever since then, would you believe it? I've acted a heck of a lot differently—and more sanely."

As far as I could see, he had acted much more rationally since he took this passage to heart—even though, technically, both he and the book made wrong statements. For no such person as a drunk exists—only a person who frequently drinks or behaves drunkenly. And no one "is" crazy—we only have humans who *behave* crazily. When we use terms like *a drunk* and *a crazy person*, we make slipshod overgeneralizations. We imply that an individual who drinks too much will *always* and *only* do so, and that a person who behaves crazily will *inevitably* behave that way. False! "Drunks" can sober up—sometimes for good. And "crazy people" can train themselves to behave much more sanely.

Anyway, the reader of *How to Live with a Neurotic* began to see one thing clearly: that we'd better not expect people who consistently act drunkenly to maintain sobriety; nor expect those who frequently behave crazily to keep acting sanely. If we expect otherwise, we ignore reality.

Another instance proves even more spectacular. An ex-client, whom we shall call Bob Smith, spent a year and a half in a state hospital with a diagnosis of paranoid schizophrenia. He has worked in the community for the past five years and does remarkably well. Not only has he taken care of his family, but he has also considerably helped many other somewhat disturbed individuals.

But Bob Smith has had his problems. For a couple of years he has not talked to his parents (who, expectably, have their own personality difficulties). He has verged on divorcing his wife. He has anxiously refrained from doing many things, such as approaching various people and discussing intimate or "embarrassing" situations with them. In many ways he has acted defensively and angrily.

Came the dawn: several weeks after running across the article "An Impolite Interview with Albert Ellis," in the iconoclastic magazine *The Realist*, and tracking down some of the main papers on rational-emotive psychotherapy published in professional journals, Bob Smith went through mental mood changes "the likes of which I never felt before." He suddenly learned a simple fact: "People and things do not upset us. Rather, we upset ourselves by believing that they can upset us."

This main tenet of what Bob Smith refers to as the "anti-unhappiness formula," constituting his own simplified restatement of principles presented in the first major paper on RET, remarkably changed his life. Almost immediately, he began talking to his parents, getting along much better with his wife, and discussing with people the things he had fearfully refrained from voicing for years.

Not only did he effect some almost incredible unblockings in his own thinking and doing, but Bob Smith also began talking to others, sending out leaflets, writing letters, and doing a host of other things that he hopes will lead to a "chain reaction" of interest in rational living. He believes that by continuing this chain, and by inducing important people and statesmen to think sanely and stop upsetting themselves with the belief that other people and events upset them, unusual strides toward world peace will occur. Whether right or wrong about this, he has certainly helped himself to think straight and now leads a more productive and peaceful existence.

So you *can* do it. With or without prior psychological know-how, you can read or hear about a new idea, forcefully set about applying it to your own thought and action, and carve amazing changes in your own life. Not everyone, of course, can or will do this. But some can; and some will. Will you?

History gives us several outstanding instances of those who changed themselves and helped change others by hardheaded thinking. Zeno of Citium, for example, who flourished in the third century B.C., and founded the Greek Stoic school of philosophy. The Greek philosopher Epicurus; the Phrygian Epictetus; the Roman emperor Marcus Aurelius; the Dutch Jew Baruch Spinoza. These and other outstanding rational thinkers, after reading about the teaching of still earlier thinkers (Heraclitus and Democritus, among others), and doing some deep thinking of their own, enthusiastically adopted philosophies radically different from their original beliefs. More to the point for purposes of our present discussion, they actually began to *live* these philosophies, to *act* in accordance with them.

All this, mind you, without benefit of what we today would call formal psychotherapy. Granted, of course, these individuals performed outstandingly—and held rare places in human history. But they did see the light of another's reasoning and use it for their own saner living.

Can basic personality change, then, really result from anything except intensive psychotherapy? Most modern authorities strongly say no. Thus, Sigmund Freud, Otto Rank, Wilhelm Reich, Carl Rogers, and Harry Stack Sullivan all stoutly contend that certain therapeutic conditions must exist and continue over a period of time for basic personality change to occur. But this unanimity of opinion hardly proves anything than that the quoted authorities agree.

Our own position? People with personality disturbance *usually* have such deep-seated and long-standing problems that they *often* require persistent psychotherapeutic help. But this by no means *always* holds true. Profoundly changed attitudes and behavior patterns follow from no single condition. Many conditions, such as those listed by the therapists mentioned in our last paragraph, may prove highly desirable. But improvement can occur as long as a troubled person *somehow* undergoes significant life experiences, *or* learns about others' experiences, *or* sits down and thinks for himself, *or* talks to a therapist who helps him reconstruct his basic attitudes toward himself and others.

Let us, then, not put down self-analysis, for all its limitations. We rarely find those who complete it. But they do exist; they can effectively employ it.

In one sense, indeed we require self-analysis for *all* basic personality change. For even when people receive competent, adequate therapeutic help, unless they *add* persistent and forceful self-analysis, they will tend to obtain superficial and nonlasting results. As we often explain to our psychotherapy and marriage counseling clients, our instruction and advice help them overcome their emotional upsets mainly because of what they *do* with what we say.

More concretely: Although effective therapists teach their clients to think straight, they cannot at any time really think for them. Even though we may advise them what to do in a given life situation, and although they may benefit thereby, we strive to get them to think for themselves—otherwise, they may always remain dependent upon us or others.

This means that therapy, in essence, largely involves teaching clients effective self-analysis: how to observe their own feelings and actions, how to evaluate them objectively instead of moralistically or grandiosely. Also: how to change, by consistent effort and practice, so that they may achieve the things that they most want to do while not needlessly interfering with the preferences of others. Clients find self-analysis not merely important but virtually necessary for successful therapy.

In RET in particular, we induce individual and group therapy clients to do considerable work in between sessions. We give them concrete homework assignments—such as risk-taking, imagining failing and not upsetting themselves about this failure, or changing their thinking in some important ways. We also teach self-management techniques: methods of reinforcing or rewarding themselves for good behavior and penalizing (but not damning) themselves for poor behavior. We show them how to dispute irrational thinking on many occasions during the week, not merely during therapy sessions. RET (like many other therapies) consequently *includes* self-work and self-analysis, and makes this kind of activity an integral part of the therapeutic process.

Which brings us to one of the main purposes of writing this book. We hope that it will reach many individuals who have never had (though many of them well could use some) therapeutic help, and that it will help some of them to think more clearly and act more effectively in regard to their personality problems. We also hope that it will serve as useful supplementary readings for the millions of Americans who have had some therapy.

Continually, as we practice psychotherapy and marriage and family counseling, clients ask us: "What can we read that will help us while we undergo therapy? Have you any kind of a reading list to supplement our work with you?" In answer to these questions, we try to suggest some suitable reading and have included some references for this purpose in the bibliography at the end of this volume.

Since, however, we do a particular kind of treatment (RET), and since most of the published material in the area of self-analysis only partially includes some of its principles, we have written (and revised) the present volume to provide a book that goes beyond our two earlier and less comprehensive books in this area—*How to Live with a Neurotic* and *Creative Marriage*. We comprehensively discuss rational-emotive therapy in such books as *Reason and Emotion in Psychotherapy*, *Growth Through Reason*, and *Humanistic Psychotherapy: The Rational-Emotive Approach*. In the present book, we shall mainly outline its principles and give some concrete descriptions of its self-help aspects.

To those who want to get specific personal help from this book, let us again sound a warning: No book, including this one, can cure all your emotional problems. Since you always have something unique about your individual makeup and situation, a book cannot substitute for personalized counseling. A good book, however, may nicely supplement or reinforce therapy. And it can encourage highly beneficial self-analysis.

Still another *caveat*. Remember that every language has its limitations. Because we, like other writers in the field of mental health, use words such as "creativity," "happiness," "love," "maturity," and "problem-solving," do not jump to the conclusion that we hand out the same old hackneyed, pollyannaish message that you may have long ago considered and rejected as having no practical value. Superficially, some of the things we say may sound like "positive thinking," let-us-pray-for-the-best-ism, orthodox stoicism, or other utopian creeds. Actually, no! Try reading the anti-unhappiness principles we present in this book; then try thinking and acting on them. We confidently expect that you, like many of our clients, will find that we've "got something there."

Here, then, we present our plan for straight thinking and rational living. Read it carefully and with all due allowances for our limitations—and yours! No matter how good the rules of living that we set before you, what reads easily and simply may prove quite difficult and complicated to believe and to act upon. Do not assume that because you have read and understood some of our practical *suggestions* for improving your life functioning that *that remains that*. That doesn't. To change, you still have before you the great task of seeing, challenging, and blocking out old self-defeating behavior patterns and learning new, self-fulfilling ways of thinking, perceiving, feeling, and doing.

Well, happy thinking!

2 YOU FEEL THE WAY YOU THINK

"What you say, Dr. Harper, seems on the surface plausible and sensible. And it would delight me if people actually worked as simply as you indicate they do! But, frankly, what you and Dr. Ellis call your theory of rational therapy sounds to me, when you probe a little into it, very superficial, antipsychoanalytic, and like a few pages out of the how-to-lift-yourself-by-your-bootstraps school of slick magazine psychology."

The speaker, Dr. B., attended my lecture to a group of educators to whom I had set out to describe the tenets of rational-emotive therapy. And his views had some truth. Some of our ideas on RET *do* sound superficial. And they definitely oppose the views of orthodox psychoanalysis—though they overlap with the teachings of Alfred Adler, Karen Horney, Harry Stack Sullivan, Erich Fromm, Eric Berne, and the psychoanalysts who stress "ego psychology."

Still, I couldn't help taking my heckler somewhat to task—not because I thought I could change his mind, for who can unfreeze the prejudices of a trained psychotherapist?—and not because I itched to put him in his place (for the luxury of venting one's spleen on others holds, as we shall show later in this book, little reward for the rationally inclined person), but because I thought that his objections might demonstrate one of the main principles of RET for the rest of my audience.

"You presumably object," I said, "to our view that human feelings significantly overlap with thoughts, and you believe that they cannot get changed, as I have just said they could, mainly by changing one's thinking. Do I grasp your main point?"

"Yes. We have fifty or a hundred years' history of experimental and clinical findings that prove otherwise."

"Perhaps so. But suppose we forget this hundred years of history for a moment and concentrate on the history of the last few moments. Just a short while ago, as I gave my talk on RET, you experienced some intense feelings, did you not?"

"I certainly did! I felt that you acted idiotically and should not go on spouting such nonsense."

"Fine," I said, as the rest of my audience gleefully howled. "But you also," I persisted, "had another emotion, just before you stood up to speak against me, did you not?"

"I did? What kind of an emotion do you mean?"

"Well, I would say that judging from the high and uneven pitch of your voice as you just spoke, you had at least a little bit of anxiety about getting up among your peers here and voicing your anti-Harperian opinion. Do I judge incorrectly about this?"

"Uh . . ." My antagonist hesitated for several long seconds (while the knowing smiles of the members of the audience changed in my favor). "No—. I guess you don't judge totally incorrectly. I did have some anxiety just before speaking and during the first part of my words; though I don't have it now."

"All right. Just as I imagined, then. You had two emotions while I spoke: anger and anxiety. And now, at this present moment, you seem to have neither? Correct?"

"Definitely. I no longer feel anxious or angry—though perhaps I feel a littly pity for you for still holding to an untenable position." Touché! Again the smiles backed him.

"Good. Maybe we'll examine the feeling of pity for me a little later. But let's, for a moment, get back to the anxiety and anger. Do I wrongly assume that behind your anger lay some chain of sentences such as: 'That idiot, Harper—along with that other nincompoop colleague of his, Ellis—mouths utter hogwash! They ought to outlaw his boring us to tears with this kind of stuff at an otherwise highly scientific meeting'?"

"Precisely! How did you guess?" Again the chorus of snickers pretty solidly supported him. I continued:

"My clinical intuition! Anyway, you did have such a thought, and by it you made yourself angry. Our thesis in rational therapy holds just that: From your thought—'Dr. Harper not only mouths hogwash but he *shouldn't* do so'—comes the real source of your anger. Moreover, we believe that you do not, at this present moment, still feel angry, because you have replaced the original thought with quite a different one, namely: 'Oh, well, if Dr. Harper wrongly believes this nonsense, and if the poor fellow wants to keep believing it, let him have this problem.' And this new thought, Dr. Ellis and I would contend, lies at the heart of your present state of feeling, which you accurately describe, I think, as 'pity.' "

Before my opponent could say anything further, another member of the audience interjected: "Suppose you rightly see the origins of Dr. B.'s feelings of anger and now pity. What about his anxiety?"

"According, again, to the theories of rational-emotive psychology," I replied, "his anxiety occurred as follows. As I spoke, and as he incited himself to anger by telling himself how badly I behaved—and *should* not behave—Dr. B. also said to himself something along these lines: 'Just wait till Harper stops talking! Boy, have I something to say that will show everyone how idiotically he acts (and how cleverly I come across for showing him up before everyone!). Let me see, now, how shall I squelch him, when I get the chance?'

"And then, I further suggest, Dr. B. tested several opening sentences in his mind, rejected some of them quickly, thought others might do, and kept looking for still better ones with which to annihilate my views. Not only, however, did he try to discover the best set of phrases and sentences he could use against me, but he also kept saying to himself: 'What will the other members of the group think? Will they think I act just as foolishly as Harper? Will he sway them by his charm? Will they think I feel jealous of his and Ellis's success with clients and with their writings? Will it *really* do me any good to open my big mouth against him?'

"These self-created sentences of Dr. B.'s, I hypothesize, caused him to feel anxious. True, Dr. B.?"

"Not entirely wrong," my opponent acquiesced, with more than a shade of embarrassed redness of his face and nearly bald pate. "But doesn't everyone, do not all of us, say things to ourselves like this before we get up to talk about almost anything in public?"

"We most certainly do," I heartily agreed. "And, believe me, I use your internalized beliefs as an example here only because they illustrate what virtually all of us do. But that precisely covers my main point: that exactly because we keep telling ourselves these kinds of sentences, we feel anxious before speaking in public. Because we tell ourselves (a) 'I might make a mistake and fall on my face before this group of my peers' and, much more importantly, tell ourselves (b) 'And I have to think it *awful* if I do make a mistake and fall on my face in public.'

"Precisely because we tell ourselves these catastrophizing sentences, we almost immediately begin to *feel* anxious. Otherwise, if we told ourselves only sentence (a) and instead of (b), said to ourselves quite a different sentence, which we might call (b́), namely, 'Too bad! If I make a mistake and fall on my face, I won't think it great, but I still don't have to view it as *awful*'—if we told ourselves *this* at (b), we would practically never feel anxious."

"But suppose," asked the same educator who had asked about Dr. B.'s anxiety, "you correctly see, Dr. Harper, how B. created his anxiety. How do you explain its later disappearance, in terms of your theory of RET?"

"Very simply again. Having screwed up sufficient courage to speak in spite of his self-created anxiety, Dr. B. found that even though he did partly fall on his face, the world did *not* come to an end, and no actual horror occurred. At worst, he found that I kept standing up to his assault and that some of the members of the audience remained on my side, although perhaps some also sided with him. So he changed his internalized beliefs to something like:

" 'Oh, well. Harper still doesn't really get my point and see his errors. And several others still side with him. Too damned bad! You can always fool some of the people, and I just can't expect anything different. I'll just bide my time, continue to present my view, and even if I don't win everyone over, I can still hold it myself.'

"With these new, anti-awfulizing beliefs, Dr. B. has dispelled the anxiety he previously caused himself and now feels, as he again has probably accurately reported, more pitying than angry. Correct?"

My opponent again hesitated a moment; then replied, "I can only repeat that you may prove partially right. But I still don't feel entirely convinced."

"Nor did I expect that you would. I just wanted to use your own example to induce you to give this matter some additional thought, and to encourage the members of this audience to do likewise. Maybe rational psychotherapy has, as you say, superficiality and slickness. I only ask that you professionals give it an honest try to see for yourself whether it really works."

As far as I know, I have not yet convinced my heckler of the soundness of my position. But several other members of my audience now enthusiastically see that human emotions do *not* magically exist in their own right, and do *not* mysteriously flow from unconscious needs and desires. Rather, they almost always directly stem from ideas, thought, attitudes, or beliefs, and can usually get radically changed by modifying our thinking processes.

When we first began thinking and writing about rational-emotive therapy, in the latter half of the 1950's, we could cite little research material to back up the idea that humans do not *get* upset, but that they *upset themselves* by devoutly convincing themselves, at point B, of irrational Beliefs about what happens to them (the Activating Events or Activating Experiences of their lives) at point A. The field of cognitive psychology, then in its formative stages, only included rare psychologists, such as Magda

Arnold, who viewed emotions as linked with thinking. Since that time, hundreds of experiments have clearly demonstrated that if an experimenter induces, by fair means or foul, individuals to change their thoughts, they also profoundly change their emoting and behaving. Evidence that we feel the way we think keeps accumulating, steadily reaffirmed by the work of many experimenters, including Rudolf Arnheim, Richard S. Lazarus, Donald Meichenbaum, Stanley Schachter, and numerous others.

All of which brings us back to the paramount thesis of this book: namely, that people can live the most self-fulfilling, creative, and emotionally satisfying lives by disciplining their thinking. All the pages that follow will, in one way or another, bear testimony to this central rational-emotive view.

3 FEELING
WELL BY
THINKING STRAIGHT

"What do you mean by a person's intelligently organizing and disciplining his thinking?" our clients, friends, and professional associates often ask.

Answer: "Exactly that. Just what we say."

"But when you say that by rationally and realistically organizing and disciplining his or her thinking a human can live the most self-fulfilling, creative, and emotionally satisfying life, you make that 'life' sound like a cold, intellectual, mechanical and, candidly, rather unpleasant affair."

"Maybe so. But doesn't it *sound* that way because our parents, teachers (and therapists!) propagandize us to believe that we can 'live it up' and 'get the most out of life' only through highly 'emotional' experiences? Haven't novelists and dramatists, by rationalizing some of their own 'emotional' excesses, often spread the dubious notion that unless we roller-coast from deep depression to manic joy and then down to the bogs of despair again, we can't claim we really 'live'?"

"Oh, come now! Don't you exaggerate?"

"Yes, probably. But don't *you*?"

"No. Surely you don't, in your own personal lives, always behave like cold-blooded, big-brained, emotion-squelching individuals who never *feel* any sorrow, pain, joy, elation—or *anything*?"

"We hope we don't. And we can get affidavits from sundry past and present wives, sweethearts, friends, and co-workers to prove that we don't. But whoever proved well-organized, rational thinking incompatible with intense emotion?"

"It still sounds that way. And as yet you rational therapy boys haven't done a thing to disprove this. How can you disprove our feeling that rationality makes us too cold?"

"We don't have to disprove *your* hypothesis. According to the first principles of science, the individual who hypothesizes had better prove the theory and not expect anyone who doubts to disprove it. You assume that just because reason *may* interfere with intense emotion (and we definitely grant that it *may*) it *must* so interfere. When and how will you prove *that*?"

"A good point," our questioners often admit. "Reasoning *need* not interfere seriously with intense feeling, but doesn't it normally tend to do so?"

"Not that we've ever found. Reasoning normally blocks inappropriate, self-defeating, or disorganizing emotion. Indeed, we hold, as one of our main tenets of RET, that since thinking creates feeling, the more clearly the inappropriately emoting individual thinks, the less he continues to sustain his inappropriate state of feeling."

"Then you've practically admitted our charge," our questioners often interject at this point. "You've just said that rational thinking and intense emotion cannot coexist and that the former drives away the latter."

Nothing of the sort! You've illegitimately substituted the word 'intense'—which we did *not* use—for our words 'inappropriate, self-defeating, and disorganizing.' "

"What a silly quibble! Don't they mean the same thing?"

"Not necessarily. Intense emotion may appropriately and realistically follow the actualizing of some of your values. Thus, you may greatly desire to love, find a most suitable object (such as a member of the other sex) with traits you rate highly, and intensely love that person. You may then express your love quite constructively by treating your beloved affectionately and by inducing him or her to join you as your steady companion or mate. And your love may lead to fortunate results: inducing you to work harder at your profession. Self-defeating or disorganizing love, on the other hand, would rarely lead to these results."

"Your main point, then," interject our skeptics, "holds that although disorganizing emotion seems largely incompatible with rational thinking, *appropriate* emotion and rationality seem compatible. Right?"

"Yes. We contend that rational thinking in the long run results in increased feelings of pleasure. For human reason, properly used, helps people rid themselves of their disruptive feelings—and especially of disorganizing panic and rage. Then highly pleasurable emotions and pursuits tend to surface. Even unpleasant emotions—such as intense sorrow and regret—help us to feel happier and get more of what we want in life. For when we handle them properly, and use them as signals that something has gone wrong in our lives and had better get corrected, they help us rid ourselves of undesirable experiences and occurrences (such as failure and rejection) that instigate us to feel sorry and regretful."

"Very interesting. But this remains *your* hypothesis. And, as you so cleverly noted before, the onus now rests on *you* to prove your view valid."

"Right. And prove it we shall, in the remaining pages of this book, by presenting a mass of clinical, experimental, personal, and other data. But the most important and unique proof remains the one you'd better try for yourself."

"Who—*us?*"

"Yes—you. If you really want to see whether the theories we shall present have value for you, we would strongly advise you to keep your present appropriately skeptical frame of mind, but also experimentally to put it at times in abeyance and give yourself a chance to *try out* our rational viewpoint in your own life. Take some area in which you think you have needless misery—some shame, guilt, or grandiosity that keeps ravaging you—and try, really try, some of our thinking formulas to rid yourself of these damaging feelings. Don't accept what we say on faith. Try out our notions. *See* to what results they lead."

"Seems fair enough. Maybe we shall try."

"OK, then. Let's see if we can get on with some of the evidence to back our basic theories of rational thinking and *appropriate* emoting."

At this point, we generally outline some of the basic principles of rational living.

As noted, human feeling stems from thinking. Does this mean that you can—or should—control *all* your emotions by reason? Not exactly.

As a human, you have four basic processes, all indispensable to your survival and happiness: 1. You perceive or sense—see, taste, smell, feel hear. 2. You feel or emote—love, hate, fear, feel guilty or depressed. 3. You move or act—walk, eat, swim, climb, and so forth. 4. You reason or think—remember, imagine, hypothesize, conclude, solve problems.

Ordinarily, you experience none of these four basic processes in isolation. Take, first of all, perceiving. When you perceive or sense something (for example, see an apple), you also tend, at the very same time, to think about it (figure out its suitability for food); to have some feelings about it (to desire or not to desire it); and to do something about it (to pick it up or throw it away).

Similarly, if you move or act (say, pick up a stick), you also tend to perceive what you do (for example, to see and touch the stick); to think about your act (imagine what you might do with this particular stick); and to have some emotion about it (to like it or dislike it).

Again: If you think about something (for example, about a crossword puzzle), you simultaneously tend to perceive (see) it; to have feelings about it (react favorably or unfavorably to it); and to move in connection with it (use a pencil to write on it).

Finally, if you emote about something (say, hate other people), you will also tend to perceive (see, hear, touch) them; think about them (remember them, figure out how to avoid them); and take some kind of action in regard to them (run from them).

We function, then holistically—perceiving, moving, thinking, and emoting simultaneously. Our four basic modes of relating to the world do *not* work separately, each beginning where the others leave off. They all significantly overlap and denote different aspects of the same life processes.

Thus, thinking, aside from consisting of bioelectric changes in the brain and of remembering, learning, and problem-solving, also involves—and to some extent, has to involve—sensory, motor, and emotional behavior.

Instead, therefore, of saying, as we usually vaguely say, "Jones thinks about this puzzle," we could more accurately note that "Jones perceives-moves-feels-*and*—thinks about this puzzle. Because, however, Jones's motives in regard to the puzzle may *largely* focus upon solving it, and only *incidentally* on seeing, manipulating, and emoting about it, we may state that he thinks about the puzzle without specially mentioning that he *also* perceives, moves, and feels in relation to it. But we'd better not forget that Jones (like everyone else) doesn't really have the ability, except for a split second or two, *just* to think about the puzzle.

Question: Since we have four basic life processes and cannot truly separate thinking from perceiving, moving, and feeling, why do we give it top billing in rational-emotive therapy?

Answer: For reasons we shall shortly make clear. But let us first point out that emoting rather than thinking emerges as the main problem of human living today. Previously, in competition with other animals, humans had the problem of seeing, moving, and thinking better than they did, to ensure their survival. Today, after inventing eyeglasses, radar, aircraft, electronic calculators, and other perceiving-moving-thinking aids, humans rule supreme on this earth and literally seek other worlds to conquer.

Only in the emotional area have they as yet made remarkably few advances. In spite of amazing physical progress, they still show little more emotional maturity or happiness than in past centuries. Indeed, they act in some ways more childishly, emotionally uncontrolled, and mentally disturbed.

We have made some progress, of course. In the field of diagnosis and psychotherapy, considerable understanding of emotional disturbance has already occurred. In the biochemical realm, the use of drugs, neurological exploration, biofeedback methods, and other techniques add to our knowledge of how humans upset themselves and what we can do to help them regain their emotional equilibrium.

Nonetheless, our outstanding problem emerges as that of controlling or changing emotion and thereby alleviating almost universal disturbance. Which leads us to ask: *How* can we go about understanding emotion and make it better serve human ends?

4   HOW YOU CREATE
       YOUR FEELINGS

How the devil can we understand emotion?

Hundreds of profound books and articles have tried to answer this question—none of them, as yet, with anything close to certainty. Let us now, with something short of a perfect answer as our goal, see if we can shed some light on this puzzling question.

Emotion seems a life process involved with perceiving, moving and thinking. It emerges as a combination of several seemingly diverse, yet actually closely related, things. The famous neurologist Stanley Cobb has given this somewhat technical description, suggesting (as interpreted by John Reid):

> that we use the term "emotion" to mean the same thing as (1) an introspectively given affective state, usually mediated by acts of interpretation; (2) the whole set of internal physiological changes, which help (ideally) the return to normal equilibrium between the organism and its environment, and (3) the various patterns of overt behavior, stimulated by the environment and implying constant interaction with it, expressive of the stirred-up physiological state (2) and also the more or less agitated psychological state (1). [An emotion doesn't mean] a private mental state, nor a set of static qualities abstracted from such a state, nor a hypothalamic response with intense autonomic discharge, nor a pattern of behavior viewed in purely objective terms, nor a particular stimulus-situation, even though it has some emotogenic

*meaning for distinguishable things, nor the entire set of
them viewed as constituting a merely additive whole. An
emotion [constitutes] rather,* an acute disturbance, involving marked somatic changes, experienced as a more
or less agitated feeling. *There remain associated infer-
ences, of varying degrees of explicitness, as to the meaning of what happens. Both the feeling and the behavior
which expresses it, as well as the internal physiological
responses to the stimulus-situation, constitute a dynami-
cally interrelated whole, which* [constitutes] *the emotion. Thus,* an emotion [remains] at once physiological,
psychological, and social *since other persons usually
[emerge as] the most highly emotogenic stimuli in our
civilized environment.*

Question: Has Dr. Cobb's definition of emotion final and full
acceptance by all modern psychologists and neuropsychiatrists?

Answer: No. As Horace English and Ava English point out, in
their *Comprehensive Dictionary of Psychological Terms*, we cannot as yet define emotion without referring to several conflicting
theories. Most authorities agree, however, that emotion has no
single cause or result. Emotions arise through a three-way process:
first, through some kind of physical stimulation of the special
emotional center of our brains (called the hypothalamus) and the
nerve network of our bodies (called the autonomic nervous
system); second, through our perceiving and moving (technically
called our sensorimotor) processes; and third, through our desiring
and thinking (technically, conation and cognition).

Normally, our emotional centers as well as our perceiving,
moving, and thinking centers display a degree of excitability and
receptivity. Then a stimulus of a certain intensity impinges upon
and excites or damps them. We can directly apply this stimulus (in
rather unusual cases) to the emotional centers—for example, by
electrically stimulating parts of the brain or by giving the individual exciting or depressing drugs which act on parts of the brain or
autonomic nervous system. Or we can (more usually) apply the
stimulus indirectly, through the individual's perceiving, moving,
and thinking, thereby affecting the central-nervous-system and
brain pathways which, in turn, connect with and influence the
emotional (hypothalamic and autonomic) centers.

If you wish to control your feelings, then, you may do so in
three major ways. Suppose, for example, you feel highly excitable
and wish to calm down. You can directly influence your emotions
by electrical or biochemical means—such as by taking barbiturates
or tranquilizing drugs. Or, secondly, you can work through your
perceiving-moving (sensorimotor) system—for example, by doing
relaxation exercises, by dancing, by resorting to "primal screaming,"

or by yoga breathing techniques. Or, thirdly, you can counteract your excitability by using your willing-thinking processes—by reflecting, thinking, imaginatively desensitizing yourself, or telling yourself calming ideas.

Which combination of these three means of controlling your emotional state will prove most effective in any given instance will depend largely on how disturbed you feel and in what direction and how extensively you wish to change or control your feeling.

Question: If we have three effective methods of controlling one's emotions available, why do you emphasize one of them in RET and in rational living?

Answer: For several reasons. First, we do not specialize in medicine or biophysics, and therefore do not consider pharmacological, bioelectrical, or other physical methods our field. We at times refer clients to physicians, physiotherapists, masseurs, and other trained individuals who specialize in physical modes of treatment; and we see good reason to combine some of these methods with RET. But we don't especially consider them our thing.

Second, we do not doubt that certain physical means of reducing tensions and changing human behavior—such as yoga, bioenergetics, and Rolfing—at times have a beneficial effect. But we look with skepticism on the all-encompassing claims frequently made for these techniques. They largely consist of diversion, since they help people to focus on their bodies rather than on the nutty thoughts and fantasies with which they tend to plague themselves. Consequently, they bring palliation rather than cure, help people *feel* better instead of *get* better, and rarely produce elegant philosophic changes.

We think it highly probable that biophysical and sensorimotor techniques for affecting human emotions, unless combined with thinking-desiring methods, produce limited effect. People may get helped through a depression by the use of drugs or relaxation techniques. But unless they begin to think more clearly and to value their aliveness, they will tend to depress themselves again when they stop the drugs or exercises. For effecting *permanent* and *deep-seated* emotional changes, philosophic changes appear virtually necessary.

We particularly encourage people with disturbances to help themselves and not rely too much on what others (such as biochemists, physicians, or physiotherapists) can do for them. They'd better, in many instances, seek outside help to stop over- or underemoting. But the less dependent they remain on drugs or physical apparatuses, the better. Our rational-emotive methods of persuading them to think for themselves ideally lead to independence. Once they learn and persistently practice rationality for a while, they require little or no further outside assistance.

We do not, then, oppose controlling defeating emotions by

drugs, relaxation techniques (such as those of Edmond Jacobsen, or J. H. Schultz and W. Luthe), movement therapy, yoga exercises, or other physical approaches. We believe that these techniques may help. And we teach, as we shall show later, many emotive, dramatic, fantasy, self-management, and behavior modification methods. More than most other schools of therapy, RET employs a comprehensive, almost eclectic, multifaceted approach to treatment.

We mainly hold, however, that if you would make the most thoroughgoing and permanent changes in your disturbed feelings, you'd better use considerable reasoning and reality-testing. Because a huge element (though not the whole) of emoting directly stems from thought.

Question: Granted that bioelectrical, pharmacological, and sensorimotor approaches to emotional change seem limited. But has not the rational approach to conscious thought equal superficiality? Have not the psychoanalysts long ago established the fact that *un*conscious processes create much *emotional* behavior? How can we learn to control and change the thoughts that create our feelings, if we have these thoughts buried deeply in our unconscious minds?

Answer: A very good point! And one that we cannot answer in a word. As we shall keep showing throughout this book, what the orthodox Freudians and many other psychoanalysts keep referring to as "deeply unconscious thoughts" emerge, in the vast majority of instances, as what Freud originally called preconscious ideas. We don't have these thoughts and feelings *immediately* accessible to our awareness. But we can fairly easily learn to infer and observe them, by working back from the behavior which they induce.

We firmly believe that, whatever your emotional upsets, you can learn to perceive the cerebral self-signalings that invariably lie behind and motivate your emotions—and thereby succeed in deciphering the "unconscious" messages you transmit to yourself. Once you clearly see, understand, and begin to dispute the irrational beliefs that create your inappropriate feelings, your "unconscious" thoughts will rise to consciousness, greatly enhancing your power of emotional self-control.

Enough of our own promises! Let us note again that a large part of what we call emotion stems from a certain kind—a biased, prejudiced, or strongly evaluative kind—of thinking. What we usually label as thinking consists of a relatively calm appraisal of a situation, an objective comparison of many of its elements, and a coming to some conclusion as a result of this comparing process.

Thus, when you think, you may observe a piece of bread, see one part of it as moldy, remember that eating mold previously made you ill, and therefore cut off the moldy part and eat the rest of it. When you inappropriately emote, however, you will tend to observe the same piece of bread and remember so violently or prejudicially your previous experience with the moldy part that you may feel nauseated, throw away the whole piece of bread, and go hungry.

When you emote, in this instance, you do as much thinking as when you merely think about the bread. But you do a different *kind* of thinking—thinking so prejudiced about an unpleasant prior experience that you do it in a biased, overgeneralized, and ineffective way. Because you feel relatively calm when you "think," you use the maximum information available to you—the information that moldy bread brings unpleasant and nonmoldy bread good results. Because you feel excited when you "emote," you tend to use only part of the information available—that moldy bread has unpleasant qualities.

Thinking does *not* mean unemotional; nor does emotional mean unthinking. When you think, you usually find yourself less strongly biased by previous experience than when you feel "emotional." You therefore tend to employ *more* of the available information. You then act more flexibly about making decisions.

Question: Hadn't you better watch your step? After first making a four-way division of human behavior into the acts of perceiving, moving, thinking, and feeling, you now talk about a "thinking" and an "emotional" individual as if you had never made your previous distinctions.

Answer: Right! No exclusively thinking or emotional persons exist, since everyone simultaneously perceives, moves, thinks, *and* feels. However, to use our previous terms, some people perceive, move, *think*, and feel; while others perceive, move, think, and *feel.* The latter do a kind of thinking different from the former, and hence *predominantly* feel. While the others, with their calmer and less prejudiced type of cognition, *predominantly* think. All people, however, think *and* emote.

More important: We all feel, but many of us have inappropriate feelings much of the time, while others have largely appropriate feelings. For no matter how honestly and authentically you experience intense feelings, they don't prove holy; and the encounter movement that has achieved such popularity has often misled people in this respect.

You do not *merely* feel; nor do you *just* (for no reason) feel. You feel, rather, because you evaluate things as good or bad, favorable or disadvantageous to your chosen goals. And your feelings motivate—move—you to survive and feel happy (or unhappy) while surviving.

You feel, for example, good about living and bad about dying. So you avoid, because of these feelings, swimming too far out to sea, driving your car at ninety-five miles an hour, jumping off cliffs, and consuming poisonous foods. If you didn't have these feelings, how long would you survive?

You also feel, now that you have chosen to live, that you *prefer* different kinds of pleasures; that you *desire* productivity rather than idleness; that you *choose* efficiency instead of inefficiency; that you *like* creativity; that you *enjoy* absorption in long-range pursuits (such as building a business or writing a novel); and that you *desire* intimate relations with others. Notice that all the words in italics involve feelings and that without them, you would not experience pleasure, joy, efficiency, creativity, and love. Your feelings not only help to keep you alive; they also aid you to survive *happily.*

Feelings, then, have valuable goals or purposes—usually your survival and happiness. When they help you achieve these goals, we call them *appropriate* feelings. When they serve to block your basic goals, we call them *inappropriate.* RET shows you how to distinguish clearly between appropriate emotion, such as your feeling real sorrow or annoyance when you don't get what you want, and inappropriate or self-defeating emotions, such as your feeling depressed, self-downing, or enraged under the same conditions.

By the same token, RET helps you discriminate between rational and irrational thinking. It holds that rational thinking normally leads to appropriate and irrational thinking to inappropriate emoting. What do we label as rational thinking? That kind of thinking that assists you (1) to survive and (2) to achieve the goals or values you select to make your survival pleasurable, enjoyable, or worthwhile.

As Dr. Maxie Maultsby states, in his introduction to the pamphlet giving information on Associated Rational Thinkers (ART), a self-help group of individuals who want to learn and to teach their fellows the main principles of RET (which also stands for rational-emotive thinking):

> *Rational thinking has the following four characteristics: (1) It [bases itself] primarily on objective fact as opposed to subjective opinion. (2) If acted upon, it most likely will result in the preservation of your life and limb rather than your premature death or injury. (3) If acted upon, it produces your personally defined life's goals most quickly. (4) If acted upon, it prevents undesirable personal and/or environmental conflict.*

Maultsby also notes that rational thinking (5) minimizes your inner conflicts and turmoil.

Perhaps it will make things a bit clearer if we note that much of what we call *emotion* mainly seems to include (1) a certain kind of forceful thinking—a kind strongly slanted or biased by previous perceptions or experiences; (2) intense bodily responses, such as feelings of pleasure or nausea; and (3) tendencies toward positive or negative action in regard to the events that seem to cause the strong thinking and its emotional concomitants.

In other words: "Emotion" accompanies a kind of powerful, vigorous, or prejudiced thought; while "thinking" often involves a relatively calm, unbiased, reflective kind of discrimination. Thus, if we compare one apple with another, we may thoughtfully conclude that it has more firmness, fewer blemishes, and better color and therefore will more likely please. But if we have had very pleasant prior experiences with blemished apples (if we, for instance, successfully bobbed for one at a Halloween party and, as a prize, kissed an attractive member of the other sex); or if we have had unpleasant prior experiences with unblemished apples (if we ate too many and felt ill), we may excitedly, rashly, and prejudicially— meaning, *emotionally*—conclude that the blemished apple has advantages and may start eating it.

It would appear, then, that thinking and emoting closely interrelate and at times differ mainly in that thinking involves a more tranquil, less activity-directed mode of discrimination; while emoting comprises a less tranquil, more somatically involved, and more activity-directed mode of behavior.

Question: Do you really contend that *all* emotion directly follows thought and can under *no condition* exist without thinking?

Answer: No, we do not believe or say that. Emotion may *briefly* exist without thought. An individual, for instance, steps on your toe and you spontaneously, immediately get angry. Or you hear a piece of music and you instantly begin to feel warm and excited. Or you learn that a close friend died and you begin to feel sad. Under these conditions, you may feel emotional without doing any associated thinking.

Perhaps, however, even in these cases you do, with split-second rapidity, start thinking to yourself: "This person who stepped on my toe acts like a blackguard!" or "This music sounds wonderful!" or "Oh, how awful that my friend died!" Perhaps only *after* you have had these rapid-fire and "unconscious" thoughts you *then* begin to feel emotional.

In any event, assuming that you don't, at the very beginning, have any conscious or unconscious thought accompanying your emotion, you virtually never *sustain* an emotional outburst without bolstering it by ideas. For unless you keep telling yourself something on the order of "That blackguard who stepped on my toe shouldn't have done that!" or "How could he do a horrible thing like that to me!" the pain of having your toe stepped on will soon die and your emotional reaction will die with the pain.

Of course, you may keep getting your toe stepped on and the continuing pain may help sustain your anger. But assuming that your pain stops, you sustain your emotional response by some kind of thinking. Otherwise, by what magical process could it endure?

Similarly with pleasant feelings. By continuing to listen to certain music and having your sensations thereby prolonged, your feelings of warmth and excitement may get sustained. But even then you will have difficulty *perpetuating* your feelings unless you keep telling yourself something like: "I find this music great!"; "Oh, how I love those harmonies!"; "What a wonderful composer!"; and so on.

In the case of the death of one of your close friends or relatives, you will find it easy to make yourself depressed, since you have lost a relationship with someone truly dear to you. But even in this instance you will find it difficult to sustain your emotion of depression unless you keep reminding yourself: "Oh, how terrible that he has died!" or "How could she have died so young?" or something of that sort.

Even then, when thinking does not immediately precede or accompany feeling, *sustained* emotion normally requires repeated evaluative thought. We say "normally" because emotional circuits, once they have begun to reverberate to some physical or psychological stimulus, can also keep reverberating under their own power.

Drugs or electrical impulses can also keep acting directly on emotion-carrying nervous circuits (such as the cells of the hypothalamus and autonomic nervous system) and thereby keep you emotionally excited once arousal has started. Usually, however, continued direct stimulation of the emotion-producing centers does not occur. You *make* it occur by restimulating yourself with exciting *ideas.*

Question: Granting that thinking processes usually precede, follow, and sustain human feeling, must these thinking processes literally consist of words, phrases, and sentences that people "say to themselves"? Does *all* thinking consist of self-verbalizations?

Answer: Perhaps not. We certainly do not want to take an absolutist position. However, practically all of us, by the time we reach adulthood, seem to do most of our important thinking, and consequently our emoting, in terms of self-talk or internalized sentences.

Humans, as uniquely language-creating animals, begin to learn from early childhood to formulate thoughts, perceptions, and feelings in words, phrases, and sentences. They usually find this easier than to think in pictures, sounds, touch units, or other possible methods.

To illustrate this human propensity, let us take the example of a man who gets interviewed for a job (at point A, his Activating Experience). Before the interview, he will often start talking to himself (at point B, his Belief System) along the following lines:

"I wonder if I'll get this job. . . . I wish I didn't have to face the interview, because I don't enjoy it and they may reject me. . . . But if I don't face the interview, I certainly won't get the job. . . . Besides, what difference does it make if they do reject me? I really have nothing to lose thereby. . . . While if I don't try for the job, I may have a lot to lose. . . . I'd better, then, take the interview, get it over with, and see whether I get accepted."

By telling himself these kinds of sentences, this man thinks. For all practical purposes, his sentences *constitute* his thinking. And we may call his thoughts rational Beliefs (rB's) because they help him to get what he values or wants—the job which he seeks. He therefore feels appropriate emotional Consequences (at point C)—*determination* to get the job; positive *action* to go for the interview; and feelings of *disappointment* and *annoyance* if he gets rejected.

If, however, this same individual creates for himself inappropriate emotional Consequences (C), he does so by telling himself different sentences that include irrational Beliefs (iB's):

"Suppose I go for this interview, make a fool of myself, and don't get the job. . . . *That would make life awful!* . . . Or suppose I go for the interview, get the job and then prove incompetent. . . . *How horrible*! I would rate as a worm!"

By telling himself these kinds of sentences, and including the irrational negative evaluation *"That* would make life awful!" or "How horrible! I would rate as a worm!" this man changes his rational thinking into irrational evaluation of his job-seeking situation. We can see, then, that for all practical purposes, his evaluative internalized sentences *create* his emotional reactions. He feels in his gut, in his body; but he largely creates his feelings in his head.

It would appear, then, that positive human emotions, such as feelings of love or elation, often accompany or result from positive internalized sentences, such as "I find this good!" and that appropriate negative human emotions (like feelings of displeasure and disappointment) accompany or result from rational sentences, such as "I find this frustrating and bad," and that inappropriate negative emotions (like depression and anger) result from irrational sentences, such as "I find this awful! It makes me a worm!" Without employing—on some conscious or unconscious level—such strong sentences as these, we would simply not feel much emotions.

Question: If what you say holds true, why do so few people, including few members of the psychological profession, clearly see that thinking and emoting go together and that they largely stem from internalized sentences? Pure ignorance on their part?

Answer: In part, yes. Many people, including psychologists and psychiatrists, just don't bother to look very closely at so-called emotions and therefore remain ignorant of their ideological basis. Others look closely enough, but only in the light of some preconceived dogma, such as classical psychoanalysis. Some rigid Freudians will no more consider the possibility that you can understand and change your emotion by observing and changing the sentences that create it than will some religious fundamentalists consider anything other than their rigid interpretation of the Bible.

We unreligiously contend: You can change your thinking and the emotions associated with this thinking by observing and changing your strong beliefs that underlie them. We hold, more specifically, that you needlessly create inappropriate emotions—such as depression, anxiety, rage, and guilt—and that you can largely eradicate such sustained feelings if you will learn to think straight and to follow up your straight thinking with effective action.

Question: Can you eliminate *all* negative emotions by controlling your thinking?

Answer: Hardly. Many emotional outbursts, such as fits of grief or fear, almost spontaneously follow pronounced frustration or loss. Thus, if your beloved parent or child dies, you immediately tend to feel great sorrow or grief.

These kinds of emotions, based on distinct threats to your satisfactions, tend to have biological roots and probably have their source in primitive pleasure-pain processes. We could hardly survive without such negative feelings.

Certain negative emotions seem especially to aid survival. Thus, if you did not feel displeased, sorry, regretful, annoyed, irritated, frustrated, or disappointed when you suffered hunger, injury, or defeat, would you feel motivated to keep out of harm's way and to continue your existence? Or would you favorably compete with others who did feel *very* displeased when they didn't get their way?

Many emotions, moreover, add appreciably to human health and happiness. Your joy at hearing a beautiful piece of music, watching a lovely sunset, or successfully finishing a difficult task does not exactly preserve your life. But an existence bereft of feelings like these would indeed seem drab and nonrewarding.

Anyone, therefore, who attempts to control human emotions out of existence tackles a goal of dubious value. Succeeding at such a task helps dehumanize men and woman and makes their lives meaningless.

The ancient philosophers who wanted humans to achieve a state of pure "soul" or pure intellect, devoid of all "crass" emotions, actually asked us to behave as super-robots. If we achieved this "superior" state, we could, like some of our modern electronic computers, effectively solve certain problems but would not feel any pleasure or satisfaction. Who would want such a super-"human" existence?

Question: Then ridding the world of emotion, or substituting intellect for feeling, definitely does not send you? Correct?

Answer: Quite correct. If anything, we mainly want to help many inhibited and apathetic individuals to achieve *more* honest-to-goodness feeling, *higher* pitches of emotion. We definitely favor highly emotional experiencing. We merely oppose unduly negative, self-defeating, highly exaggerated emotionalizing that tends to sabotage the goals of survival and joyfulness.

We also favor your honestly, openly, and nonjudgmentally getting in touch with your feelings—as long as you forgo perfectionism. For what you *really* or *truly* feel you often cannot precisely determine. You make yourself angry, for example, at a friend who has let you down. Then you make yourself feel guilty because you hate him. Then you deliberately remember, again, the wrongs he has done you and thoroughly incense yourself at him, thereby covering up or driving away your guilt. What do you *really* feel in this case: anger? guilt? defensive hatred? What?

Who can, with absolute precision, say? Yes, you act, as a human, highly suggestibly. Yes, you can easily escalate or cover up your own feelings. Yes, your moods show susceptibility to alcohol, drugs, food, others' words and moods, and a host of other influences. These facts tend to prove that you can feel, from moment to moment, almost *any* way you choose to feel, and that *all* your feelings (just because you honestly feel them) have reality and authenticity. But none of them emerges as super-real or absolutely "true."

Anyway, you'd better recognize, as honestly and as accurately as you can, your basic feelings. Do you, at a given time, feel loving, hating, or indifferent? angry or determined? concerned, anxious, or unconcerned? How can you tell? Mainly by accepting yourself fully with whatever feelings you do have; by distinguishing clearly the "goodness" or "badness" of the feeling from the "goodness" or "badness" of *you.*

RET notably can help you get in touch with your feelings, and acknowledge their intensity, by helping you stop rating yourself for *having* (or *not* having) them. Using a rational philosophy, you first can choose to accept yourself *with* your feelings—even the crummy ones of depression and hatred. You can actually, then, show *interest* in and *curiosity* about your feelings. You can say to yourself: "How fascinating I find it" (instead of "How awful!") "that a basically intelligent person like me keeps acting so damned foolishly and negatively!" You can see that you choose to create your self-downing feelings, and that you can choose to *change* them if you really want to work at doing so.

You can also *discriminate* your appropriate (self-fulfilling) from your inappropriate (self-damning) feelings. You can see the difference between your healthfully feeling *displeased* with your acts and your unhealthfully feeling *horrified* about them. You can distinguish between your feeling *disappointed* with others' behavior and *asserting* your disappointment, and your feeling *angry* at their behavior and your *commanding* that they change it.

Rational-emotive thinking, in other words, helps you to more fully and openly observe your feelings, acknowledge that they exist, accept yourself with their existence, determine their appropriateness, and eventually choose to feel what you want to feel and what will help you get more of what you want out of life. Its highly rational methods, paradoxically enough, can put you more in touch with your feelings and help you react more emotionally than you ever could previously allow yourself.

5 THINKING YOURSELF OUT OF EMOTIONAL DISTURBANCES

Many psychotherapy clients make difficult customers, but this one abused the privilege. No matter how often I (A.E.) tried to show her that she had control over her own destiny, if only she believed that she had, she kept parrying my arguments with all kinds of excuses and evasions.

"I know you've shown many other clients how to handle their feelings," she said, "but I just can't seem to do it. Maybe I work differently. Maybe they've got something that I lack."

"Yes, maybe they have got something that you haven't," I agreed. "Recently acquired corks to plug the holes in their heads. And I've shown them where to get the corks. Now, how come I have so much trouble showing you?"

"Yes, how come you haven't shown me? God knows, I've tried to see what you keep telling me."

"You mean God knows you keep *thinking* you really try to see. But maybe the trouble lies there—you've convinced yourself that you keep trying to see how you bother yourself with the nonsense you keep drumming into yourself all the time. And having convinced yourself that you keep trying, you find no reason for actually trying. So you quickly give up and don't really try to see anything. Now, if I could only get you to *work* at observing and changing your own self-defeating internal sentences, your enormous feelings of anger against your mother and your brother would go away with surprising speed."

"But how can I *work* at a thing like that? I find it so indefinite."

"It only *seems* indefinite. Because you make little actual

effort to grasp it: to see your own beliefs and to examine the premises behind them. Actually, it works like playing the piano or playing tennis—which you once told me you do very well."

"Oh, but I find that much different. Playing tennis involves something physical. Not at all like thinking or getting angry or anything like that."

"Ah, now I think I've got you!" I exclaimed.

"What do you mean?" she asked. I found it almost laughable (had it not seemed so tragic) how fearful she felt about the thought that I *might* have her, and that she *might* have to surrender her neurosis.

"You say that playing tennis involves something physical. And on the surface, of course, it does. You make muscle movements with your eyes and your arms and your hands, and somehow the ball keeps going over the net. And, looking at your muscles moving and the ball flying, you think of the whole process as physical, almost mechanical."

"Do I view it wrongly?"

"You do! Suppose your opponent hits the ball to you. You try to hit it back over the net, preferably in a place where he or she won't easily reach and return it. So you run after the ball (using your legs), reach out for it (using your arms), swing at it (using your arms and wrist). But what *makes* you run this way or that way, stretch out or pull back your arms, turn your wrist to the left or right?"

"What makes me—? Well, I guess my eyes do. I *see* the ball over here or over there. I *see* where I want to place it, and I move accordingly."

"Fine. But do you see *by magic?* And do you somehow magically get your sight to direct your legs this way, your arms that way, your wrist still another way?"

"No, not by any magic. It results from—." My client stopped, troubled.

"Could you," I asked, "could you possibly do it by *thinking?* Could you see, as you say, your opponent's ball going over here or over there, and *think* it best to return it on this or that corner of the court, and you *think*, again, that you can reach the ball by stretching out your arm a little more in this direction, and your wrist in this other direction, and so on and so forth?"

"You mean, I don't act as mechanically and physically in my actions as I think I do; but I really direct these actions by my thinking? You mean I continually tell myself, while playing the game, to do this and that, and to stretch my arm out here or turn my wrist over this way? Do you mean that?"

"Well, *doesn't* that explain what really transpires while you play this so-called *physical* game of tennis? Don't you, during every single minute of the play, continually direct your arm to do this and your wrist to do that? And don't you accomplish this directing by real, hard, concerted thinking?"

"Come to think of it—and I must admit I never have thought of it that way before—I guess I really do. I never noticed! The whole thing—why, the whole thing seems really mental. Amazing!"

"Yes, amazing! Even this highly 'physical' game really works mentally. And you keep working at this game—and not only working by running, stretching, and turning your wrist, but working at *thinking* about what to do during the game. And this latter work, the work of thinking, really improves your tennis. Your main practice, in fact, in playing tennis consists of *thinking* practice. Right?"

"When you put it that way, I guess so. Funny! And I thought I only played physically. I guess I see now what you mean by *working* at changing my beliefs and changing my emotions. Just as in tennis, I work at changing my stance and my stroke and other things. And, as you say, I really work at thinking, and not just at mechanical changes."

"Exactly. Now if I can get you to apply the same method you use at tennis to changing the beliefs you use to create your disordered emotions, your game of life will begin to improve almost as quickly and as well as your game of tennis."

After this breakthrough, I had less difficulty inducing this previously stubborn client to work at changing her beliefs and emotions.

Back, now, to our main theme. Accepting human emotions as desirable, the important question remains: Do you have to endure inappropriate emotions, such as sustained anxiety or hostility?

Largely, no. You may occasionally feel appropriate sustained negative emotions: as, for example, when you suffer continuous discomfort or pain and you keep feeling sorry, regretful, or annoyed about this for a long period of time. Under such conditions, you would certainly not appropriately feel glad or indifferent.

Most sustained negative feelings, however illegitimately, follow imagined or self-escalated discomfort or pain. Your child dies, for instance, and for many weeks or months you appropriately sorrow about her death. But as these weeks and months go by, and as they turn into long years, you *keep* mulling over the unfortunateness of the child's death and you (more illegitimately) keep awfulizing about it. "How terrible," you keep telling yourself, "that my child died! No justice exists in the world, considering that an innocent youngster such as she has expired! How awful! She just shouldn't have died! I *can't stand* the thought of her no longer living!"

Naturally, in *these* circumstances, you never allow yourself to forget about the child's death. In fact, you keep reminding yourself incessantly that the child died, that *more* than misfortune has ensued, and that the world *must* not treat you as cruelly as it does. Not only, then, will you feel continually sad; but you will also make yourself depressed. *This* kind of sustained negative emotion you needlessly fabricate. It results from your own false and stupid beliefs about what *should* occur. You may therefore eliminate it by straighter thinking.

How do we reach this conclusion? Simply by extending some of the concepts of thinking and emoting which we have presented. For if sustained negative emotion results from your own thinking, you have *a choice* as to what you can think and how you can emote. That remains one of the main advantages of your humanness: you can *choose*, usually, to think one thing or another; and if you make your goal living and enjoying, one kind of thinking will aid this goal while another kind of thinking (and emoting) will sabotage it. Naturally, therefore, you'd better pick the first rather than the second kind of thinking.

You can, of course, choose to change, push aside, sweep under the rug, or repress practically *all* negative thinking. But would you then act wisely or rationally? You can choose to ignore the fact, for example, that an unnecessarily large amount of unemployment, pollution, or overpopulation exists in your community; and through such avoidance, you will choose not to feel sad, sorry, or frustrated by these unfortunate events (as long as they do not too directly affect you). But if you refuse to do the kind of negative thinking that would keep you feeling sad about truly unfortunate conditions, will you, especially in the long run, truly aid the survival and happiness of yourself and your loved ones, or of others in your community? We doubt it.

Many sustained negative thoughts and feelings, therefore, help you preserve and enjoy yourself. Others do not. Learn to discriminate the former from the latter, and to act accordingly.

Anyway, if sustained feelings usually result from your conscious or unconscious thinking (especially from your internalized sentences), you rarely feel glad or sad because of the things that occur from the outside. Rather, you make yourself happy or miserable by your perceptions, attitudes, or self-verbalizations *about* these outside events.

This principle, which we have recently rediscovered from the many therapy sessions with hundreds of clients, originally appeared in the writings of several ancient Greek and Roman philosophers, notably the famous Stoic Epictetus, who in the first century A.D. wrote in the *Enchiridion*: "Men feel disturbed not by things, but by the views which they take of them." William Shakespeare, many centuries later, rephrased this thought in *Hamlet*: "There [exists] nothing either good or bad but thinking makes it so."

As a case in point, let us turn for a moment to Geraldine, a highly intelligent and efficient thirty-three-year-old female client who came to see me (R.A.H.) about six months after she obtained a divorce. Although she had felt decidedly unhappy in her marriage to an irresponsible and dependent husband, she had gotten no happier since her divorce. Her husband had drunk to excess, run around with other women, and lost many jobs. But when she came to see me, she wondered if she had made a mistake in divorcing him. I said:

"Why do you think you made a mistake by divorcing your husband?"

"Because I consider divorce wrong," she replied. "I think when people get married, they should stay married."

"Yet you do not belong to a religious group that takes that position. You do not believe that heaven somehow makes and seals marriages, do you?"

"No, I don't even believe in a heaven. I just *feel* wrong about getting divorced and I blame myself for having gotten one. I have felt even more miserable since I got it than I felt when living with my husband."

"But look," I asked, "where do you think your feelings about the wrongness of divorce originated? Do you think you had them at birth? Do you think that humans have built-in feelings, like built-in taste buds, that tell them how to distinguish right from wrong? Your buds tell you what tastes salty, sweet, sour, or bitter. Do your feelings tell you what proves right or wrong?"

The young divorcée laughed. "You make it sound pretty silly. No, I don't suppose I have inborn feelings about right or wrong. I had to learn to feel as I do."

Seeing a good opening, I rushed in where less directive and less rational therapists often fear to tread. "Exactly," I said. "You had to learn to feel as you do. Like all humans, you started life with tendencies to learn, including tendencies to learn strong prejudices—such as those about divorce. And what you learned you can unlearn or modify. So even though you don't hold fundamentalist faith in the immorality of divorce, you could have easily picked up this idea—probably from your parents, schoolteachers, stories, or movies. And the idea that you picked up, simply stated, says:

" 'Only bad people get divorces. I got a divorce. So I must qualify as a bad person. Yes, I must acknowledge my real rottenness! Oh, what a no-good, awful, terrible person!' "

"Sounds dreadfully familiar," she said with a rather bitter laugh.

"It certainly does," I resumed. "Some such sentences as these probably started going through your mind—otherwise you would not feel as disturbed as you do. Over and over again, you have kept repeating this stuff. And then you have probably gone on to say to yourself:

" 'Because I did this horrible thing of getting a divorce, I deserve *damnation* and *punishment* for my dreadful act. I deserve to feel even more miserable and unhappy than when I lived with that lousy husband of mine!' "

She ruefully smiled, "Right again!"

"So of course," I continued, "you have felt unhappy. Anyone who spends a good portion of her waking hours thinking of herself as a terrible person and how much she *deserves* misery because of her rottenness (notice, if you will, the circular thinking involved in all this)—any such person will almost certainly feel miserable. If I, for example, started telling myself right this minute that I had no value because I never learned to play the violin, to ice-skate, or to win at tiddly-winks—if I kept telling myself this kind of bosh, I could quickly make myself feel depressed.

"Then I could also tell myself, in this kind of sequence, how much I *deserved* to feel unhappy because, after all, I had my chance to learn to play the violin or championship tiddly-winks, and I had messed up these chances. And what a real worthless skunk this made me! Oh, my God, what a *real* skunk!"

My client, by this time, seemed highly amused, as I satirically kept emphasizing my doom. "I make it sound silly," I said. "But with a purpose—to show you that *you* act just as foolishly when you start giving yourself the business about your divorce."

"I begin to understand what you mean," she said. "I *do* say this kind of thing to myself. But how can I stop? Don't you see quite a difference between divorce, on the one hand, and violin-playing or tiddly-winks, on the other hand?"

"Granted. But has your getting a divorce really made you any more horrible, terrible, or worthless than my not learning to play the fiddle?"

"Well, you'll have to admit that I made a serious mistake when I married such an irresponsible person as my husband. And maybe if I had behaved more maturely and wisely myself, I could have helped him to grow up."

"OK, agreed. You did make a mistake to marry him in the first place. And, quite probably, you did so because you behaved immaturely at the time of your marriage. All right, so you made a mistake, a neurotic mistake. But does this mean that you deserve punishment the rest of your life by having to live forever with your mistake?"

"No, I guess not. But how about a wife's responsibility to her husband? Don't you think that I should have stayed with him and tried to help him get over his severe problems?"

"A very lovely, and sometimes even practical, thought. But didn't you tell me that you tried to help him and he refused even to acknowledge that he had disturbances? And didn't you say that he strongly opposed your going for any kind of therapy during your marriage, let alone his going for help, too?"

"Yes, he did. The mere mention of the word *psychologist* or *marriage counselor* sent him into a fit of temper. He'd never think of going or even letting me go for help."

"The main thing you could have done, then, would have involved playing psychotherapist to him, and in your state, you'd hardly have proved effective at that. Why beat yourself down? You made a mistake in marrying. You did your best to do something to rectify it after marriage. You got blocked, mainly by your husband, but partly by your own feelings of severe upset, on both counts. So you finally got out of the marriage, as almost any reasonably sane person would have done. Now what crime have you committed? Why do you *insist* on blaming yourself? You think, erroneously, your unhappy situation makes you miserable. But does the situation—or what you keep telling yourself *about* this situation?"

"I begin to see your point. Although my marital situation never has felt good, you seem to say that I don't *have* to give myself such a hard time about it. Quite a point of view you have there!"

"Yes, I like it myself—and often use it in my own life. But now if we can only help you to make it *your* point of view, not because *I* hold it but because you figure out that it really will work better for you, not even a poor marriage and an as yet difficult divorce situation will faze you. In fact, if I can really help you to adopt this viewpoint, I can't imagine anything that will ever bother you too much."

"You really mean that, don't you?"

"Mean it, hell—I *believe* it!"

And so, to some extent, did this young divorcée, after another few months of rational-emotive therapy. Whereas she previously kept telling herself how far from ideally and how horribly she behaved for not achieving this ideal, she now began to substitute problem-solving, internalized sentences for her old self-beatings. In one of her last conferences with me, she said: "You know, I looked into the mirror yesterday morning and said to myself, 'Geraldine, you behave like a happy, fairly bright, increasingly mature, growingly efficient kid. I keep getting mighty fond of you.' And then I laughed with real joy."

"Fine," I said. "But don't lead yourself up the path of rating you, Geraldine, highly because you act so much better. For then you will have to rate yourself lowly, once again, if and when you act worse. Try to stick to: 'I like *behaving* so much better' rather than 'I like *me* for doing this good behavior!' "

"Yes, I see what you mean," she replied. "I feel glad you

warned me about that. Rating *myself* I unfortunately do most easily. But I'll fight it!''

This client discovered that her feelings did not derive from her unsuccessful marriage or her divorce but from her evaluations of *herself* in regard to these "failures." When she changed the kinds of thoughts (or internalized sentences) she fed herself, her emotions changed from depression and despair to sorrow and regret—and these *appropriate* negative feelings helped motivate her to change the conditions of her life. Not all clients, like Geraldine, see so quickly that they cause their own depressed feelings about divorce and *decide* to accept themselves. Sometimes they may require months or years of therapy before they come to this decision. But persistence, on their and their therapist's part, certainly helps!

If humans theoretically can control their negative thoughts and feelings, but in actual practice they often refrain from doing so and keep experiencing unnecessary misery, the question arises: Why? What blocks them from thinking effectively and emoting appropriately?

The main barriers to effective thinking and emoting include these: (1) Some people have too much stupidity to think clearly. Or (2) they possess sufficient intelligence to think straight, but just do not know how to do so. Or (3) they have enough intelligence and education to think clearly but act too disturbedly or neurotically to put their intelligence or knowledge to good use. As we have noted in two of our previous books, *How to Live with a Neurotic* and *Psychoanalysis and Psychotherapy: 36 Systems*, neurosis essentially consists of stupid behavior by nonstupid people.

Otherwise stated: People afflicted with neurotic behavior have potential capabilities but do not realize how self-defeatingly they act. Or they understand how they harm themselves but, for some irrational reasons, persist in self-sabotaging behavior. Since we assume that such people have potential capabilities, rather than have inborn stupidity, we also assume that their emotional problems arise because either they do not know how to, or know how but do not try to think more clearly and behave less self-defeatingly.

If so, what can they do? In the next chapter we shall try to show how to recognize and attack neurotic behavior.

6 RECOGNIZING AND ATTACKING NEUROTIC BEHAVIOR

Clear thinking, we contend, leads to appropriate emoting. Stupidity, ignorance, and disturbance block straight thinking and result in serious degrees of over- or underemotionalizing. When people function inhibitedly or practically foaming at the mouth, and when they do *not* appear stupid, we usually call them neurotic. Let us consider a couple of examples.

A twenty-two-year-old male says that he does not want to finish his dental training because he dislikes some of his subjects and has a difficult time studying them. In consequence, he concludes, he would just as soon go into business.

When we probe his motivations more deeply, we soon discover that he really would like dentistry but fights it because (1) his parents keep pressuring him to finish school and he loathes their pressuring; (2) he doesn't get along too well with his classmates and feels unpopular; and (3) he doubts that he has the manual dexterity and manipulative ability required of a good dentist.

This individual keeps sabotaging his own desires because he has no insight into, or seems ignorant of, his basic, unconscious motives. He starts with the conscious premise that he "naturally" dislikes certain of his subjects. But after some direct questioning (one of the main techniques of rational-emotive therapy) he quickly admits (first to the therapist and, more importantly, to himself) that he terribly fears domination by his parents, failing to win the esteem of his classmates, and ultimately failing as a dentist. His "natural" dislike for some of his subjects stems, therefore, from his highly "unnatural" underlying philosophy: "Oh, my Lord! What a weak poltroon I will always remain if I do not achieve outstanding independence, popularity, and competence!"

When, in the course of RET, this individual understands his irrational beliefs; and when, perhaps more importantly, he questions and challenges these fears, he usually decides to return to school and to work through his parental, social, and self-induced difficulties. Thus, this youth can ask himself: "*How* can my parents actually dominate me, if I refuse to let them do so? And why need I find it *awful*, why must I consider myself *a slob* if I continued to let them dominate me?" And he can dispute his horribilizing: "Why need I define it as horrible if I fail in popularity at school or never get acknowledged as the best dentist that ever existed? Granted, that might prove inconvenient, but what would make it horrible?" By this kind of disputing, challenging, and questioning of his own irrational (and empirically unconfirmable) beliefs, he can stop his stupid thinking and the overemotionalized reactions—such as his needless anxiety and flight—to which it leads.

A female client had a similar problem but more insight. This twenty-year-old woman knew that she wanted to teach and also knew that she had made no effort to do so because she had thought she couldn't. She also suspected that she often tried to punish herself for some promiscuous sex activity in which she had engaged a year previously. Even though she presumably had insight into her underlying beliefs, she continued to defeat herself and to behave in a neurotic manner.

This client did *not* realize that her self-downing and her sex guilt stemmed from ignorance and faulty thinking. She originally put herself down because she accepted the hypercritical views of her older sister, who jealously did not want her to think well of herself. Then the client, working on the unquestioned assumption that she had little scholastic ability, began to avoid her schoolwork and thereby to "prove" to herself that she actually had none—thus reinforcing her original sister-aided lack of confidence.

This woman's sexual promiscuity, moreover, largely stemmed from her same lack of confidence. Feeling worthless and that boys would not care for her, she took the easiest way of winning them by bartering her body for their attentions. She based her guilt about her promiscuity on the arbitrary notion, also taken over from her sister, that she would prove wicked for having premarital relations and would commit a particularly heinous offense if she behaved promiscuously.

Even though she seemed to know that she condemned herself for her sex behavior and therefore sabotaged her desire to teach, she actually had only partial insight into her neurosis. She did not see her two basic premises and realize their falseness and irrationality: (1) that she could not do well scholastically and that all people who do poorly in this area have no worth; and (2) that she deserved punishment for wickedly engaging in promiscuity.

A fuller understanding of her self-defeating behavior led to far-reaching changes in her thoughts and actions. First, I (A.E.) helped her to question the connection between scholastic success and so-called personal worth and to see that no such connection really exists. She began to understand that we have no way of accurately rating the totality, the essence, of a human; and that, in making such a global rating, we harm rather than help ourselves. Thus, she could accept herself (merely because she *decided* to do so) *whether or not* she succeeded at school. And she could enjoy herself considerably even when she failed. Ironically, as usually happens, seeing and acquiring this kind of unconditional self-acceptance helped her to concentrate much better on her school-work (since she still found it *desirable* though not *necessary* to do so) and to achieve better grades.

Secondly, I helped my client to challenge the so-called wickedness of her promiscuity and to understand that although she may have made mistakes (by having affairs with males whom she did not really enjoy as lovers), this hardly made her a *louse* who deserved damnation for these errors. By surrendering her philosophy of lousehood and self-condemnation, she removed her remaining motives for sabotaging her own endeavors and helped herself work toward her goal of teaching.

The case of this client, as perhaps of most individuals who come for therapy, exemplifies the differences between what we call Insight No. 1, Insight No. 2, and Insight No. 3. We mean by Insight No. 1 the fairly conventional kind of understanding first clearly postulated by Freud: knowledge by the individual that he or she has a problem and that certain antecedents cause this problem. Thus, the young dentist in training whose case we observed at the beginning of this chapter knew that he had a problem with his career, but thought it stemmed from his dislike of certain subjects and not from his anxiety about social and vocational failure. Not knowing the antecedents of his problem, he did not really have any reasonable amount of "insight."

The young teacher in training had more insight, since she not only recognized her failure at her chosen career, but also knew or suspected that (1) she lacked confidence and (2) she kept trying to punish herself for her previous sexual promiscuity. Knowing, therefore, some of her motives for her ineffective behavior, she had a considerable amount of "insight"—or what we call Insight No. 1. She only vaguely, however, had Insight No. 1, since she *knew* that she lacked confidence but didn't clearly see that this lack of confidence consisted, more concretely, of her telling herself: "My older, hypercritical sister views me as inadequate. How absolutely terrible if she correctly sees me this way! Perhaps she does. In fact, I feel sure she sees me correctly and that I never *can* perform adequately!"

This young woman also knew that she felt guilty and self-punitive about her previous premarital affairs. But she did not specifically see that her guilt and self-punishment resulted from her internalized sentences: "Many people view promiscuity as wicked. I have behaved promiscuously. Therefore I must see myself as wicked." And: "People often agree that those who do mistaken acts deserve punishment for their sins. I have committed such acts by having sex with males for whom I did not really care. Therefore I should punish myself by not trying to succeed in the career, teaching, in which I would like to succeed."

Although, then, this client definitely had a good measure of Insight No. 1, she had it in such a vague and indefinite manner that we could well call it only partial insight. As for Insight No. 2, she had little. For Insight No. 2 consists of seeing clearly that the irrational ideas that we create and acquire in our early lives still continue, and that they largely continue because we keep reindoctrinating ourselves with these ideas—consciously and unconsciously work fairly hard to perpetuate them. Thus, this client kept telling herself, over and over again, "I *should not* have had those promiscuous relations. And in order to expunge my sins and lead a happy life today, I *have to* keep punishing myself for behaving the way I did and thereby continue to cleanse myself." Without this kind of constant self-reinforcement, her early ideas (including those taken over from her sister) would almost certainly extinguish themselves. So Insight No. 2—which she did not have to any degree at the start of her therapy with me—consisted of her clearly seeing that she had not let herself go through this extinguishing process and that she still actively blocked it.

Insight No. 3 remained far from this client's horizon. For No. 3 consists of the wholehearted belief, "Now that I have discovered Insights No. 1 and 2, and fully acknowledge the self-creation and continued reinforcement with which I keep making myself believe the irrational ideas that I have believed for so long, I will most probably find no way of eliminating my disturbances than by steadily, persistently, and vigorously working to change these ideas."

More concretely, when my client acquired Insight No. 1 and No. 2, she could then go on to No. 3: "How fascinating that I have kept convincing myself that I *should not* have had promiscuous sex and that I *have to* keep punishing myself for my errors. As long as I keep believing this hogwash, how can I feel anything *but* self-downing and depressed? Well, I'd better keep strongly disputing and challenging these nutty beliefs until I give them up!" She and I working together in therapy helped her to achieve these three important insights; and by using them and following them up with other hard therapeutic work during the next year, she finally solved her main problems. She not only got a teaching job and did quite well at it during this period but also continued to have the kind of nonmarital sex for which her sister severely criticized her, to enjoy it considerably, and to feel no guilt about it.

We contend, in other words, that almost all neurotic or self-sabotaging behavior results from some kind of basic ignorance or lack of insight on the part of the disturbed individual. Although humans may behave neurotically because of certain biophysical conditions (such as severe hormonal imbalances or by their going sleepless for many nights on end), they don't often do so purely for these reasons. Under more usual conditions, they create their disturbances by their own *ideas*, which they may consciously or unconsciously hold.

Thus, as in the two cases cited in this chapter, people may know that they resist going to school because they fight against parental pressure. Or they may unconsciously resist going to school without clear awareness that rebellion against parental pressure lies at the bottom of this resistance. Or they may know they punish themselves for some sex guilt. Or they may punish themselves without realizing they do so because of this kind of guilt.

In any event, whether or not people consciously know their irrational ideas, they would hardly act neurotically without such ideas. Thus, in the instances given in this chapter, if the young dental student had not made himself so irrationally fearful of parental domination and vocational failure that he gave up studying and flunked out of school, we would find nothing inappropriate in his wanting to leave school and would conclude that he clearly saw the facts of life and acted in sane accordance with them. And if the student of education *rationally* accepted her sister's view of her worthlessness and *sensibly* kept punishing herself for her promiscuity, we would conclude that she had better give up teaching and practice, say, prostitution.

But we cannot justify pronounced feelings of failure, beliefs in worthlessness, unthinking acceptances of others' condemnation, and self-damning tendencies. Not because they emerge as absolutely wrong or wicked, or because they contradict the laws of God or the universe. But simply because, on good pragmatic grounds, they almost always prove self-defeating and needlessly prevent us from getting many of the things we desire.

Moreover, self-downing beliefs and emotions stem from unrealistic overgeneralizations that we cannot scientifically verify. They contain magical, demonizing formulations that remain definitional and unprovable. If you say to yourself, for example, "I have failed at this task [e.g., winning the love of another person or succeeding at a job] and I find that disadvantageous and unfortunate," you make a statement (or hypothesis) that you can empirically validate or disprove: for you (and others) can observe whether you really have failed and what disadvantages (in regard to certain of your personal goals) will probably follow from your failing.

If you say to yourself, however, "Because I have failed at this task, I find it *awful* and it makes me a *rotten person*," you make a statement (or hypothesis) that you cannot empirically validate or disprove. For *awfulness*, an essentially undefinable term, does not really mean *very disadvantageous*. It means *more than* 100 percent disadvantageous, unfortunate, obnoxious, or inconvenient. And how can anything in *that* category really exist? Your finding it *awful* when you fail, moreover, means that you *can't stand* failing and that you *shouldn't* fail. But, of course, you *can* stand failing; and the universe hardly insists that you *should* not or *must* not fail!

The hypothesis, again, that failing makes you a *rotten person* means that (1) you unfortunately have failed; that (2) since you have intrinsic, essential rottenness, you will *always* and *only* fail; and that (3) you deserve damnation (roasting in some kind of hell) for failing. Although we can empirically substantiate the first of these three meanings, the second and third meanings seem unprovable—except by arbitrary definition.

Although, therefore, we can confirm your *failing* at something (or at many things), we cannot confirm your all-inclusive label as *a failure*. You may devoutly call yourself a failure (even with a capital F!). But that label constitutes a misleading, pernicious overgeneralization.

Stated differently: Inappropriate, self-destructive emotion— such as your feeling severe anger, depression, guilt, or anxiety— results from your (consciously or unconsciously held) prejudiced, childish, senseless ideas and almost inevitably leads to inefficient, self-sabotaging behavior which we call neurosis. When you display neurotic behavior, you can employ several palliative methods to help overcome your disturbance. Thus, you can change your job or your marital status; take a vacation; develop a vital interest in some area; work at succeeding at professional or avocational pursuits; consume sufficient quantities of alcohol, marijuana, heroin, tranquilizers, psychic energizers, or other drugs; devote yourself to a new church or creed; or try various other diversionary approaches.

Almost any or all of these kinds of diversions may temporarily work. For they essentially induce you, when irrationally attached to some set of disturbance-provoking ideas (which we may call x), to divert yourself to some other set of ideas (which we may call y). As long as you keep thinking of y instead of x ideas, you may not feel too troubled.

Unfortunately, this kind of diversion rarely solves your basic problems. For no matter how vigorously or often you may divert yourself to y ideas, you still really believe in and have not given up x ideas. So you strongly keep tending to return to the neurotic behavior caused by x ideas.

Take Mrs. Janus, for example. People viewed her, at the age of thirty-eight, as a still beautiful and talented woman. When she did not lie in bed all day with a horrible migraine headache or did not fight viciously with her husband and two teen-age children, she showed herself as a charming companion, hostess, and club-woman. So, to keep herself unangry and relatively free from migraine, Mrs. Janus drank heavily, gobbled tranquilizers, and passionately devoted herself to a New Spiritism group which believed in reincarnation and taught that life in this sorry vale of tears serves as a prelude to an infinity of Real Lives to come.

It almost worked. Getting half crocked most of the time, and intently proselytizing for her spiritist views, Mrs. Janus found relatively little time to upset herself, to act terribly angry at others, and to retreat into her migraine headaches. But when the liquor lost some of its effectiveness, and she found life in the afterworld wanting in solving her problems in this world, Mrs. Janus's neurotic symptoms returned full blast. In fact, she felt so unable to contain her anger against her associates that even her newly found spiritist friends began to look askance at her behavior and to ease her out of some of the high positions that they at first delighted in giving her. Seeing even this new group desert her, Mrs. Janus grew angrier and began to verge on a complete breakdown.

Came the dawn. And, more by brute force than gentle persuasion, her husband dragged Mrs. Janus into therapy by telling her that unless she did something to help herself, he and the children would pack and leave. It required only a few sessions to reveal that she profoundly believed that because her parents had both acted strictly and punitively during her childhood, the rest of the world owed her a completely opposite kind of living. All her close associates, especially her husband and children, she thought absolutely *should* lean over backward to make life easy for her—and thereby compensate for her unduly hard life during childhood.

When, in the normal course of human events, Mrs. Janus found that her close relatives and friends somehow did not feel the way she did about catering to her, she felt inordinately angry, viewed them as treating her unethically, and did her best to ram their "rank injustices" down their throats. When everything went her way—which of course it rarely did—she felt fine. But when balked or frustrated, she felt miserable and tried to divert herself by making others equally miserable.

Alcohol and tranquilizers often made Mrs. Janus "feel good" for a short while—at which time all life's "injustices" would not seem so unjust. And her spiritistic views, which promised her the best of all possible afterworlds, also temporarily diverted her from her injustice collecting. But such diversions, naturally, could not last. Nor did they change her devout beliefs that the world *should* prove a kinder, easier place and that her close associates *should* make up for the horrors of her past by catering to her in the present.

In the course of a year and a half of both individual and group rational psychotherapy, I (R.A.H.) helped Mrs. Janus first acquire Insight No. 1: namely, that her extreme hostility and migrainous upsets stemmed from her own behavior, rather than that of others, and followed from the irrational philosophy: "Because I suffered in the past, people *should* treat me with utter kindness today."

After helping Mrs. Janus to see the real causes of her neurotic behavior, I then (with the help of the members of her therapy group) led her to Insights No. 2 and 3: "Now that I see that *I* create my disturbances with *my* often-repeated internalized sentences about the 'injustice' of it all, I'd better keep disputing, questioning, challenging, and changing these sentences. For I not only keep convincing myself that people treat me unkindly and unfairly—which at times they really may—but that such unfairness *shouldn't* exist and I find it *horrible* when it does. Well, what *makes* it horrible? Nothing, of course. Unfortunate, yes—because I don't keep getting what I want. But horrible? Only if I define it so!

"And why *shouldn't* people treat me the unkind way they often do? I can see no reason why they shouldn't—though I can think of many reasons why I would like them not to! If people don't cater to me the way I prefer, tough! But I'd better convince myself that I can still lead a good and happy existence, mainly by catering to myself!"

When she began to get Insights No. 2 and 3—that she kept reiterating her demanding philosophy and that she'd better keep working at changing it and the damaging emotions to which it led, Mrs. Janus reduced her drinking to a cocktail or two a day, threw away her tranquilizers and felt remarkably unangry, with her husband, children, and friends, even when (as fallible humans) they *did* act unjustly or unfairly to her. The more she accepted reality, and refused any longer to *make* it as grim as she had made it, the less spiritistic and devoutly believing in reincarnation she grew. As she said at one of her closing therapy sessions: "Why do I have to worry about highly hypothetical afterlives when I now know how to make *this* life so enjoyable?"

ADDITIONAL THOUGHTS ON RECOGNIZING
AND ATTACKING NEUROTIC BEHAVIOR
by Robert H. Moore
Florida Branch, Institute for Rational Living, Inc.
Clearwater, Florida 33516

Does neurotic behavior always consist of illogical thinking? Not exactly. In many ways, you behave quite *logically*, even though you may act neurotically.

How so? Well, even substantially neurotic behavior seldom results from completely illogical thinking. You generally do *what you believe* serves your best interest. As a member of the human race, when you react to a particular set of conditions you do essentially what we all do: At point A (your Activating experience), you gather, with all your sensory apparatus, as much relevant information as you can. At point B (your Belief system), you process that information, weigh it, consider it, think it over. At point C (your emotional or behavioral Consequence), you react with your gut and tend to take some action about your Activating experience.

As an example, I (R.H.M.) had a woman client, when I practiced psychology in Pennsylvania, who told me during one of her earlier sessions that her nineteen-year-old daughter had just written to her from a distant state to announce her pregnancy (point A). She and her husband then had sat up most of the evening arguing about whether or not the girl might have gotten pregnant before her wedding day, which had taken place several months earlier, and about how awful it would prove if such a premarital conception had occurred (point B). My client got herself into a considerable lather about it all and prepared to write her daughter angry words about what people do who take marriage vows so lightly (point C).

Now, did my client react *logically*? She most certainly did. Given her daughter's pregnancy a few months after marriage, and given the values through which she processed this information, how could she have "logically" reacted other than she did? I used her reaction to point out that even disturbed feelings (like moral condemnation of or anger toward her daughter) *logically* stem from the evaluative process (at point B). My client very clearly *believed* premarital sex wrong—and this belief *determined* that she react as she did to her suspicion about her daughter's pregnancy. For her to have *believed differently*—for instance, that premarital sex has a legitimate place in the lives of young lovers—would have caused her, again *logically*, to react quite differently to the very same suspicion about her daughter.

To get back to you: even when you behave from your "gut," or you prefer to rely upon what you call "intuition," or you act impulsively, without considering all the available evidence, you so behave because you have *judged*, rightly or wrongly, that you can allow yourself to react in these ways. You have *decided* that guessing seems better than careful consideration; and you therefore have chosen to act "intuitively" or "impulsively."

Virtually all your instantaneous or "spontaneous" emotional responses arise in the same way. At point A, you perceive what goes on around you. At B, you evaluate how likeable or dislikeable you find this situation at A. But you do your evaluations at B quickly, with the almost lightning speed that comes from your having rehearsed the scene many times before, if only in your mental imagery. *Then* you react emotionally at C.

Though you may not like to admit this, you basically remain a thinker, a calculator. And you devote much of your thinking to bringing about or preserving comfort, pleasure, or freedom from pain: to the pursuit of either short or long range hedonism. How, then, do you manage—in this seemingly "logical" manner—to behave, often, so neurotically? Have you inferior intelligence? Or have you suffered some brain impairment?

Not likely! Like other so-called neurotics, you rarely have innate retardation or brain impairment; and you can reason capably from premise to conclusion. Your fundamental premises, moreover, appear quite O.K.: for you probably start with the same basic values or goals that almost all humans start with—to stay alive and to feel reasonably happy and free from needless pain. Then you typically sabotage these basic goals (as Dr. Maxie C. Maultsby, Jr. has observed) in one or more of several important ways:

1. You perceive reality inaccurately.

2. You seriously jeopardize your own safety.

3. You impede your own progress toward your chosen goals.

4. You often experience more inner turmoil than you can comfortably bear.

5. You create needless conflict between yourself and other members of your community.

Look these criteria over carefully and they will help define for you self-defeating or neurotic behavior. But why do you, when you act neurotically, do these self-damaging things—especially if you think clearly and act so well in so many other respects? Who puts you up to this?

You do. How? In, again, several specific ways:

1. Regarding your inaccurately perceiving reality: In the exercise of your natural tendency to behave logically—meaning, to think things over, to draw conclusions, and to act in accordance

with these conclusions—you start with some "bad" data, or misinformation. You then unwittingly reason—straight as an arrow!—from a false premise to an almost inevitably faulty conclusion. Thus, by believing the false premise that someone close to you must always and only favor you, and by observing that he or she sometimes does not, you may erroneously conclude that this person intends to do you in, even to cause you bodily harm in some way. You thereby behave logically (self-preservingly), but at the same time unrealistically and neurotically when you defend yourself against this imagined "attack" against you.

Don't we all do this at times—jump from misinformation or false premises to wrong conclusions? Right! But then we usually discover our mistake, shift our gears, and recalculate. We unneurotically replace our faulty premise, correct our thinking, and revise our plan of action accordingly.

When you act as a real "neurotic," however, you change your behavior only with difficulty—because you generally accept little or no new information upon which to reason. Moreover, you often see reality in such a prejudiced light that you do not understand why everyone else does not reason as you do to reach the same conclusion. And you so successfully avoid a careful examination of some of your own false assumptions that you resist changing your behaviors even when their "logical" conclusions lead you to behave in obviously self-sabotaging ways.

When you behave neurotically, again, you "see" considerably more or less than an objective viewer would see on an instant replay of a perceived event. You view as fact what the rest of us speculate about—such as others' motives for their behaviors. You escalate probabilities into certainties. You often fail to distinguish a person, place, or thing from your evaluation of it. And you typically make dogmatic judgments about the goodness and rightness of many things that cross your path.

2. Regarding the neurotic jeopardizing of your own safety: When you appear seriously accident prone, smoke yourself half to death, overeat to the extent of taxing your heart and other vital organs, keep driving your car at speeds well above the traffic limits, or make an actual suicide attempt, you frequently exhibit foolish or neurotic behavior. Not that self-maiming or suicide always prove irrational or insane. Occasionally, they don't. But if your bents run strongly in these directions, you'd better at least seriously consider the *possibility* that emotional disturbance darkens your existence; and I'd advise you to beat a hasty path to the nearest rational-emotive therapist!

3. Regarding the impeding of your own progress toward your chosen goals: Does this kind of neurotic behavior have logical elements, too? Indeed, it does. For the unmitigated pursuit of achievement, or even of vital recreational pursuits, may prove

highly stressful; and your setting up some barriers to this kind of stress may indeed show some method in your "madness." When you act neurotically, however, you tend to set up such enormous barriers, in this respect, that you progress toward your important goals at something like a snail's pace—and completely forestall your reaching some of them.

I had a friend and colleague some years ago, Debbie P., who had earned a Phi Beta Kappa key at a major university—definitely a sign of ability and goal-orientation—but who thereafter organized her pursuits with the greatest difficulty. She not only had trouble establishing goals for herself, but she particularly sabotaged those goals related to her job as a social worker. Although ostensibly interested in building her skills in this area, her fears and anxieties so debilitated her that she often could not bring herself to schedule an interview at the clinic where she worked. She avoided having a social life and, when asked to address a group of people at a meeting, she went into a freeze. Once, in my presence, she bolted and ran, panic-stricken, from a room in which someone had "threatened" to take her picture with a camera.

Many neurotic individuals, like Debbie, weave for themselves such a consistent fabric of inactivity and inhibition that only with great difficulty can we ascertain that at one time they had notable goals and ambitions.

4. Concerning your experiencing more inner turmoil than you can comfortably stand: Instead of neurotically withdrawing from the goals, jobs, and relationships you get upset about, you may plunge into all these kinds of activities—but pay, as you plunge, a considerable (and unnecessary) toll in personal conflict and inner turmoil. Thus, while aspiring to a professorship or the presidency of a business concern, you can neurotically make yourself prone to constant feelings of quick anger, deep hurt, enormous anxiety, vicious hatred, profound anguish, and overwhelming depression.

Then, instead of expressing intense anxiety, anger, depression or other emotional upset, you may take out your disturbances on your body and may develop some psychosomatic condition—such as ulcers, high blood pressure, fainting spells, skin rashes, migraine headaches, allergic reactions, or debilitating fatigue. You can also rope yourself into the risky business of temporarily quelling your feelings of disturbance by getting yourself addicted to alcohol, pills of various sorts, temper tantrums, overabsorption in work, compulsive promiscuity, or various other forms of escapism.

5. In regard to your creating needless conflict between yourself and other members of your community: When you do, for any reason, feel upset emotionally, you tend to find it almost impossible to have such feelings in isolation, but almost always share them—all too willingly!—with your friends and associates.

Your mate, lover, and other intimates get involved with, and to some extent victimized by, your neurotic feelings and behaviors. Whereupon, disliking these behaviors, and often having emotional difficulties of their own, they interact poorly with you—and both you and they get penalized thereby.

When your family members and friends do get substantially involved with your problems, you often identify them as "causing" these problems. You tend to believe that your upset feelings or self-defeating behaviors flow directly from your interaction with them or from their "wrong" or "stupid" acts. You then commonly feel cheated or abused by them and conclude that your disturbances (depressions, anxieties, hostilities, etc.) got created by their "abusiveness." And even though you sometimes may correctly diagnose their neuroses, you foolishly believe that these difficulties give you a good excuse for acting disturbedly yourself.

"But how can I feel anything but depressed, with him out drinking all the time?" a young woman recently asked me. "If he didn't drink like that, I'd never get depressed!"

"Of course I drink," replied her husband. "Who wouldn't—when your wife flirts outrageously with other men right in front of you, with half the people we know in the community watching her do so? Wouldn't any man who cared for his wife so much and who kept getting treated like that by her take to drink—or even worse?"

The couple had come to me on the brink of separation, after fighting almost continuously through two of their three years of marriage. Both considered their reactions to the other's outlandish behavior perfectly "natural." She firmly believed that her husband's drinking caused her to get depressed. He believed that his wife's public flirtations drove him to drink. Each devoutly held that the other's performances would have to change in order that he or she feel or behave any differently. And, expectably, they had gotten heavily into damning each other for their own neurotic reactions. They felt almost doomed to divorce when they came to me for counseling.

Neither of these two recognized, before they came for rational-emotive help, that a partner's poor behavior can *not* actually reach out and command anyone to respond neurotically. Both had accepted the popular—but still highly erroneous—belief that *you* cause *my* emotional problems. And this belief put them, quite understandably, into regular conflict—a fairly typical example of neurotic behavior incorporating or feeding upon an element of its environment, in this case, a spouse.

Similarly, when you act neurotically you can easily blame non-human elements in your environment. When things don't work the way they presumably *should*. When planes don't take off on schedule. When your car that you have just spent a great deal of money on suddenly, for no good reason, sputters and balks. When the Internal Revenue Service refuses to accept your indubitably proper explanation for taking a large business or health deduction. When music blares out in public places in spite of your allergy to such noises. In all these instances, and in many more, you can cavalierly condemn the fates or powers above for their totally unfair attitudes toward you. And when you do, you neurotically not only upset yourself about some original hassles, but also make yourself so irate and temper-ridden that your reaction itself actively increases your difficulties with others and often gets you into much more trouble than the first problem that presented itself.

Neurosis, then, commonly strikes you in many different forms and shapes. If you recognize its various manifestations *as* neurotic, and fully accept the fact that you (and not others, social conditions, or the unkind fates) *make yourself* disturbed, you have an excellent chance of understanding and undoing your disturbance, instead of lamely excusing or needlessly living with it. Copping out proves easy. Coping with neurosis seems a damned sight harder—but also infinitely more rewarding.

7 OVERCOMING
THE INFLUENCES
OF THE PAST

"This stuff about people making themselves emotionally sick by their poor philosophies of life sounds all very well," many of our critics often say. "But how about the important influences of the past, over which we had no control whatever? How about, for instance, our childhood-imbibed Oedipus complexes or the fact that we may have suffered severe rejection by our parents? Didn't *these* things make us disturbed to begin with? And how can we overcome them now, if we merely concern ourselves about changing our *present* philosophies?"

Good questions, these, but fairly easy to answer in the light of our rational-emotive approach to personality change.

Let us take the Oedipus business first. Let us suppose the Freudians at least partly right in their belief that some individuals, if not all, have Oedipus complexes during their childhood and do get emotionally maimed. Can we still, by purely rational assaults on such people's current philosophies, overcome the pernicious effects of their early family romance?

Indeed we can. Let us, before we give any details here, first see how a so-called Oedipus complex comes about. A young male child, Harold, lusts after his mother, hates his father, feels guilty about his sex desires for his mother, and fears his father wants to castrate him. Consequently, he fears older men for the rest of his life and either refuses to compete with them (as, say, in business) or makes enormous efforts to ingratiate himself with them and thereby gain their favor (as, say, by acting as a passive homosexual). Obviously, such an individual has a rather classical Oedipus complex.

Let us even suppose, with the orthodox Freudians, that this individual originally acquired his Oedipal feelings because his sexual instincts (his id) inevitably pushed him in the direction of lusting after his mother and then, because of his superego (conscience), forced him to feel guilty about his incest feelings and hate both himself and his father. Even if this occurs (and often in our society it does not, since many boys apparently do not lust after their mothers or get jealous of their fathers), the question remains: Does the boy's Oedipal *attachment* mean the same thing as his Oedipus *complex?* Answer: By no means.

A so-called complex consists of a chain of negative ideas about an unfortunate set of facts. Thus, if John appears physically weaker than Henry, we may say that he has an inadequacy or inferiority. But if John has an inferiority *complex* we mean (1) that he notes his weakness, when he compares himself to Henry, and (2) that he views himself as a fairly *worthless person* for having this weakness. While (1) seems a statement of fact, (2) constitutes an overgeneralization *about* the fact. John's complex equals (2) rather than (1).

So with the Oedipus complex. Harold may "naturally" and "normally" lust after his mother and feel somewhat jealous of his father. But if he, while feeling lust and jealousy, does not at the same time *believe he has low value as a person* because of his feelings, he will only have an Oedipal *attachment* rather than a *complex.*

If Harold does have a full-blown Oedipus complex, we may feel pretty sure that, in addition to admitting his lust for his mother, he believes (1) that his mother, father, and other people must approve of him; (2) that he has done a terrible thing to lust after his mother; (3) that if people discover his lust, they will severely criticize him; (4) that if he actually has sex relations with his mother, the crime of incest, one of the most heinous known, will lead to serious legal and other difficulties; (5) that even if he never commits incest, his mere contemplation of such an act constitutes a horrible offense against his parents and humanity; (6) that if his father ever discovers his lust for his mother, he may make grim reprisals against Harold, such as castrating him; and (7) that if any of these things happen, he turns into a horrible *person.*

Whether Harold's beliefs about his lust for his mother prove true or not doesn't matter, as long as he strongly holds the kind of beliefs just listed. Thus, he may not need his parents' or others' approval and may get along very well without such approval. Nor may having sex with his mother get him into serious trouble. Nor may his father castrate him if he discovers his incestuous ideas. No matter. As long as Harold *believes* and *accepts* these "truths," he will tend to get seriously upset.

Although, then, Harold's Oedipal *attachment* or *desires* may have a biological base (or may, as the Freudians say, spring from his id), his Oedipus *complex* does not arise from these desires but from his *ideas* and *attitudes* about the desires. And these ideas and attitudes he partly learned, depending on the kind of community in which he got raised.

If, therefore, Harold wishes to overcome his Oedipus complex and the neurotic symptoms (such as fear of other males) to which it may lead, he does not have to change his incestuous desire (which he would find almost impossible) but to modify his ideas. He does not have to give up lusting after his mother but to surrender his notions of how *horrible*, how *criminal*, such lusting makes him.

More importantly, Harold, in order to rid himself of his Oedipus complex, does not have to change or even to understand fully his *past* ideas about his Oedipal attachment, but he'd better acquire Insights No. 1, 2, and 3 into his *present* or *still-existing* attitudes toward incest. Suppose, for example, that he once lusted after his mother and, weak and unable to stand up for himself against the other boys in his neighborhood, he feared his father's "castrating" him—not because of his committing the horrible crime of incest, but because he felt that he "deserved" punishment for his weakness. And suppose that, later in his life, having grown bigger and taller, he no longer feels intimidated by the boys in his neighborhood, and therefore no longer fears his father's "castration" in terms of his original fear of his "undeservingness" or "weakness."

Under these conditions, if Harold *now* gained insight into his *past* castration fears and Oedipus complex, he would learn little useful information about himself: since his *original* complex no longer exists in the old form, and he might view the details of its origins as cold and meaningless potatoes today. If, however, Harold *still* to this very day, has remnants of his old Oedipus complex, then we can guess that he *still* has some of the irrational ideas that originally caused him to acquire this complex.

And if we can bring to Harold's attention these *remaining* notions and get him to acquire Insights No. 1, 2, and 3 about *them*, it hardly matters whether he fully remembers, understands, or works through his *original* irrationalities (as, in Freudian theory, he must do to get cured).

No matter how we slice it, therefore, if *any* complex still exists to the extent that it bothers a male in his current life, we can suspect that he still harbors some senseless ideas in connection with it. These *present* ideas have importance, whatever the original ideological sources of his complex. This explains why so many non-Freudian psychoanalysts—such as Alfred Adler, Erich Fromm, Karen Horney, Otto Rank, and Harry Stack Sullivan—emphasize analyzing clients' present problems, ideas, and relationships, rather than the gory details of their past histories.

As another case in point to show how our past experiences hardly prove vital to our understanding and attacking present disturbances, let us take an instance of maternal rejection. Let us assume that a female child continually experiences criticism and rejection by her mother; that she "consequently" feels loathsome and inadequate; that she therefore refuses to attempt certain tasks; and that she ends up feeling more inadequate.

Such an individual will display serious disturbance. But will she feel disturbed because of the *fact* of her mother's rejection or because of her *ideas* about it?

Largely, the latter. For the bare *fact* of maternal rejection does not necessarily prove noxious, as shown by the observation of Dr. Norman Garmezy, Dr. Lawrence Casler, and others that in our society all rejected children do not turn out too badly, and as also shown by reports that in other societies children get severely criticized and rejected by their mothers without growing up disturbed. Lili E. Peller writes in this connection:

> *I have had the opportunity to observe children—Arab children in rural areas of Palestine and Egypt—where there [exists] almost no consideration for their welfare, where they experience the effects of the changing moods of adults; considerations of their wishes and needs [have] no importance and they seem a nuisance. Should [they get spared] any brutality by their parents, plenty of siblings and hardly-older uncles and aunts provide it. Yet these children do not [develop neurosis] for lack of love.*

What does prove harmful about maternal rejection in our society lies not in the rejection itself (though, admittedly, that may not do a child much good), but in the set of *ideas* that almost all of us learn in connection with this rejection. These ideas, ubiquitous in our fairy tales and other children's stories, include the notions that (1) your parents *must* show love and approval and that they behave *horribly* when they do not; (2) if your mother rejects you, you should feel worthless; (3) if you have no value, you have to keep failing important tasks; (4) if you do fail, you have committed a terrible crime, which proves again that you have no worth; and (5) if, out of fear of failing, you avoid certain tasks and never learn to do them well, this shows that you never had any ability and once again have no value as a person.

Ideas like these, most of them highly questionable but nonetheless widely promulgated in our society, put the real sting in maternal rejection and make an unpleasant event terribly traumatizing. Without the backing of these ideas, we doubt whether such rejection would prove as crippling as it frequently does.

By the same token, it would seem almost impossible for humans to feel severely hurt by anything but physical assault unless they have traumatizing *ideas* about what happens to them. For, aside from literally injuring you physically, what can external persons or things *do* to cause you extreme pain?

People can of course call you names, disagree with you, show that they do not love you, incite others against you. But, other than depriving you of food, clothing, shelter, or other physical comforts, all they can do to pain you severely involves their using negative words, attitudes, or ideas. And these work through *you*— through your *letting* their sallies affect you.

Suppose that some friend says unkind things about you behind your back; or snubs you to your face; or stirs up others against you; or writes an article labeling you as a blackguard. These all remain words or gestures, and *no* word or gesture can, in itself, hurt you unless you think it can—unless you let it or make it hurt. Do you serve your best interests, then, when you do not care *at all* when someone says unkind things to you? Or when you feel *totally* unconcerned when he or she writes nasty things about you?

Not at all! This kind of extreme lack of concern or involvement, at times wrongly recommended by Epictetus and other Stoics, stirs up our stout opposition. Why? Because concern and involvement have many distinct advantages which we hope that you do not overstoically (and insensitively) forgo.

Concern (along with caring and caution) helps you survive. If you had no concern about looking before you cross the street or arranging to get a meal when you felt hungry, how long would you remain alive?

Concern enables you to stave off obnoxious and happiness-destroying events. If you did not *care* when others acted nastily to you, how would you manage to get or keep a good job?

Concern contributes to your enjoyment. If you had no *caution* about some of the things you said or did, would you very likely establish satisfying friendships, find appropriate sex partners, or sustain good love relationships?

Concern aids the social welfare of the community in which you choose to live. If you had no social *involvement*, would you refrain from littering the streets, driving recklessly, or severely lambasting children?

So by all means *feel concerned* and *care* about your own behavior and its effects on others. But work against feeling *over*concerned, or anxious. They mean quite different things!

Stated differently: You can experience two basic kinds of pain: (1) physical pain, such as that felt when you have a headache, a stubbed toe, or a case of indigestion; and (2) psychological or mental pain, such as that experienced through rejection, frustration, or injustice. Over physical pain, you have relatively little control, since you may get hurt by an external force (someone punching you or something falling on you, for instance); and, once physically assaulted, you will normally feel pain and unhappiness for a certain period of time.

Even in the case of physical pain, however, you often have *some* degree of control over your discomfort. If you have a headache and keep telling yourself how terrible the pain feels and how horrible for you to unfairly have it, you will probably intensify and prolong your discomfort. But if you have the same headache and keep telling yourself that you can well bear the pain and that you have merely experienced one of those unfortunate events that frequently happen to humans, you may easily alleviate or conquer your pain.

Physical pain and unhappiness do not mean the same thing, though they significantly overlap. You can have fairly severe pain and not feel too unhappy about it; and can experience slight pain and feel exceptionally miserable. Not entirely the pain itself, then, but also your attitude toward it creates your unhappiness.

Over the second kind of pain, psychological or mental discomfort, you have considerably more control. For your attitude toward such pain largely causes your discomfort and your misery about your discomfort.

Thus, if people unfairly call you a liar or a knave, you have your choice, theoretically, of taking them or not taking them seriously. If you choose the former and tell yourself that you greatly value what they think of you, you will tend to feel sorry about their dislike. If you choose to take them overseriously and insist that you *must* have their approval, you will probably make yourself feel ashamed and depressed. If you do not take them at all seriously, and conclude that you don't lie or act knavishly, and don't care if they think you do, you may hardly even feel sad or peeved about their unfair name-calling.

When you feel hurt or psychological or mental assaults, you create this feeling by downing yourself about these assaults. Suppose people call you a liar and, because you would like them to favor you, you feel sorry about their falsely thinking you consistently lie. If you agree with them, however, and not only see yourself as having this trait, but condemn yourself for having it, you then feel hurt or self-deprecating. Moreover, once you down yourself, your totality, for lying, you make yourself overly prone to see other rotten traits, some of which you may not even have! You acquire such a lack of confidence or low self-esteem that you find non-existent faults or magnify real ones.

If, on the other hand, you fully accept yourself and refrain from any kind of self-damning, you will very likely think: "Now, how could they call me a liar when I rarely lie? They judge me mistakenly! Now let me see how I can prove to them that I seldom lie."

Or, in some cases, you might think: "You know, I believe they see me correctly. I have done some lying and I'd better admit it. And I'd better not behave that way if I want people to trust me. So I'd better stop this silly lying and prove that I can deal with people truthfully."

When you feel sorry or sad, then, you do not have the same experience as when you feel hurt. Although sorrow and regret constitute appropriate feelings, hurt does not. People may easily *deprive* or *harm* you by their words, gestures, or attitudes. But whenever you feel *hurt*, you give their words magical significance that they do not really possess. By sacredizing or deifying these words, you actually "hurt" yourself.

Suppose, by way of illustration, a close female friend, toward whom you have acted kindly over a period of years, unfairly accuses you of inconsiderateness and meanly chastises you. You say, "I feel terribly hurt by her behavior! Ah, woe!"

Balderdash! Much more accurately stated, she has deprived, frustrated, or harmed you. For, as a result of her meanness, you lose various advantages and reap several real disadvantages.

But your "hurt" really consists of your own self-downing. You create it by idiotically thinking, "What a dunce I feel for treating her so nicely! I can't stand her thinking badly of me! I must have no worth if she thinks that I have none! What will other people think of me, if they see how my former friend now treats me? I can't bear their seeing me in such a disgraceful position!"

What makes these thoughts idiotic? Several things: 1. You hardly turn into *a dunce* for *sometimes* acting foolishly. 2. You *can* stand your ex-friend's thinking badly of you, though you'll never *like* it. 3. Even if she now thinks you worthless, you do not have to *agree* with her. 4. If others do conclude that you have disgraced yourself because she now treats you meanly, you damned well can *bear* their thinking this. If you face, and vigorously contradict, your own silly hypothesizing here, you will almost certainly soon stop feeling "hurt." You will merely feel deprived and annoyed.

You can designate psychological pains (or negative feelings) therefore as appropriate and inappropriate. When something obnoxious happens to you, you'd better feel concerned and caring—meaning, appropriately sad, disappointed, sorry, regretful, frustrated, or annoyed. But you'd better not feel overconcerned and all-importantly caring—meaning, inappropriately panicked, self-downing, horror-stricken, depressed, or enraged.

The Freudian system and other kinds of psychotherapy which emphasize the enormous influence of the past tend to wrongly believe that children *have to* grandiosely demand and whine in their early years and consequently feel exceptionally hurt and self-hating when rejected and ignored by their parents. They don't *have to;* though they often *choose* to feel hurt, not because of their parents' injustices but because of their unrealistic insistence that these parents never act unjustly. And much evidence exists that some easily disturbable children act as arrant injustice collectors during their early years, while many others do not.

Even when young children do vehemently choose to upset themselves, and to feel exceptionally hurt and angry when deprived or frustrated, they have another important choice to make as they grow up: to remain or not remain childish in the future. For they not only learn, as they get older, that names and gestures feel painful (bring disadvantages) but that they also do not hurt (create self-downing). And they can choose to believe, mainly, the former truth or the latter falsehood. If they follow the teachings of the present book, they can almost always make this choice successfully.

No matter what your past history, or how your parents and teachers may have helped you feel disturbed, you remain so because you *still* believe some of the unrealistic and irrational thoughts which you originally held. To undisturb yourself, therefore, you need only observe your irrational self-indoctrinations and energetically and consistently work at deindoctrinating yourself. Your understanding of how you *first* made yourself neurotic may help somewhat, but you will hardly find it truly curative.

Emotional disturbance, in sum, originates in some irrational beliefs. Your job rests in uncovering the basic unrealistic ideas with which you disturb yourself; to see clearly the misinformation and illogic behind these ideas; and, on the basis of better information and clearer thinking, to *change* the notions which lie behind and keep creating your disturbance.

8 DOES REASON ALWAYS PROVE REASONABLE?

Let's face it, humans have trouble thinking straight and emoting well. No matter how bright and well educated they may seem, they find it easy, horribly easy, to act like dunces. And not merely once or twice in a lifetime. Continually, rather! Yes, almost continually.

Can we, then, call humans truly rational animals? Yes, we can. And no, we can't. They have the most incredibly mixed-up *combination* of common sense and uncommon senselessness you ever did see. They of course have done and will continue to do wonders with their mental processes, and remain so far removed from their closest animal neighbors (the higher apes) in this respect that human morons have distinctly more intelligence than these brightest of subhumans.

Yes, people grow up as highly reasonable, brain-using creatures. But they also have strong tendencies to act in the most ridiculous, prejudiced, amazingly asinine ways. They incline quite normally and naturally toward childish, suggestible, superstitious, bigoted, and downright idiotic behavior, particularly in their relations with other members of their own species. And even when they *know* they behave in a self-defeating, perfectly senseless manner, and *know* they would feel far happier and healthier if they acted otherwise, they have such difficulty achieving and sustaining a level of sound and sane behavior that they rarely do so for any length of time, but keep falling back to puerile ways.

Take a typical case in point. Marlo Long, when I (R.A.H.) first met her in my office, could be called an unusually attractive and intelligent woman of twenty three who functioned efficiently as secretary to the president of a large corporation. Although she had no more than a high school education, she started working for this firm at the age of nineteen and, because of her pleasant personality, intelligence, and industry, rose quickly from one of twenty women in a stenographic pool to the most responsible secretarial position in her company.

In her love life, however, Marlo had little effectiveness. At the age of twenty, she met an older man, began living with him after knowing him a few weeks, felt shocked to learn that he had no intention of divorcing his estranged wife, convinced herself that life was no longer worth living, and took a large dose of sleeping tablets. Discovered by a friend and rushed to the hospital in time to have her stomach pumped, she narrowly escaped dying.

Romantically enough, the young resident physician, Jake Golden, who pumped out Marlo's stomach, quickly fell in love with her and they began dating. She resisted his advances for many months, for she saw all men as "no good" after her experience with her first lover. This highly intelligent woman, in other words, found it surprisingly easy to make one of the most facile and ridiculous mistakes found in any primer of logic—that of absurd overgeneralization. Because *one* lover had turned out to act untruthful and unreliable, she categorized *all* potential lovers as acting equally irresponsible.

Her illogical thinking went further. By extreme patience and understanding, the young medic countered Marlo's overgeneralized fears and finally convinced her that he really did love her and wanted to marry her. She reluctantly agreed, but felt rather relieved that they had to postpone their wedding date for another year, until after he finished school and passed his medical boards. Even though she *knew* Jake as most loving and trustworthy, she also *felt*—meaning, strongly believed, in spite of complete lack of evidence—that maybe he did not really care for her.

In addition to telling herself that if her first lover seemed to care for her but really didn't, Jake's love seemed equally suspect, Marlo also convinced herself: "My first lover left me, not because of his own irresponsibility but because he finally discovered what I have known all my life, that I have no worth. And since I appear so worthless, and since Jake obviously has such good traits and great worth as an individual, he couldn't possibly care for me as he thinks he does. Just as soon as he finds me out—as my first lover did after a few months—he, too, will see no point in going on with me; and he, too, will then leave me. So it seems best that we wait a year before we marry, by which time he will have found me out, left me, and thereby avoided any drawn-out nightmare of marrying and divorcing."

So Marlo, this wonderfully bright and efficient woman,

"reasoned." And with this kind of magical thinking, she secretly awaited the breakup of her engagement to Jake, which she *knew* would come just as soon as he found her out.

Then the next logical step in this illogical chain of thinking occurred. Once Marlo decided that perhaps she could trust Jake a little and that she really did love him, she began to feel extremely jealous and possessive. If he met her ten minutes after his working day (or night) at the hospital ended, she would give him a third-degree grilling. If he smiled pleasantly at a patient, nurse, or hospital receptionist, she accused him of flirting.

Here again we have an extension of Marlo's irrational thinking. Since one man jilted her, this man might do the same. And since Jake really seemed to care for her, how could she certainly and absolutely know that she truly deserved his caring? Moreover, since she still felt somewhat indecisive (because of her general doubts about men, Jake, and herself), how did she know, how could she feel *sure*, of his decisiveness?

All kinds of thoughts such as these kept going through Marlo's mind, giving her deep-seated feelings of insecurity—which almost inevitably, in sexual relations, lead to intense jealousy.

Jake, recognizing Marlo's jealousy as evidence of her own insecurity, nicely put up with her compulsive inquiries and finally induced her to undertake psychoanalysis—which Marlo experienced three times a week for the next two years. Most of the analytic sessions reviewed Marlo's early life and the disclosure of the fact that although she loved her father and seemed his favorite child, she often feared that he would discover her badness and would reject her in favor of her older sister. Marlo's analyst thought this childhood pattern a percursor and a cause of most of her later behavior with her first lover and with Jake. Marlo didn't strongly disagree with him and did feel somewhat better as a result of her analytic sessions. But dredging up the facts of her childhood had no effect on her feelings of extreme jealousy and possessiveness. In considerable disgust and despair, she terminated her psychoanalysis.

By this time Jake kept getting discouraged himself and began to take an increasingly dim view of the prospect of his having a happy married life with Marlo. Knowing, however, her suicidal tendencies, he decided to place her under psychotherapeutic care before he broke with her; and he insisted that she try at least a few sessions with me. After she had seen me five times, and we had started working actively at her basic irrational thinking, Jake told Marlo that he had to break off his relationship with her and literally left her at my door.

Understandably, we had quite a session. Marlo, in spite of some sedation which Jake had given her during their talk that day, began acting hysterically as we started the interview. After fifteen minutes largely devoted to my helping her quiet down, she said: "Well, I know what I must do now. I must finish that job he delayed for three years."

You mean commit suicide?" I asked.

"Yes."

"That, of course, remains your privilege. And do you mind," I persisted in an almost jocular voice, "telling me why you plan to slit your throat when you could so nicely stick around and torture yourself for another half a century?"

I have found, through considerable experience with people intent on suicide, that often a good counterattack consists of discussing their intent openly, forthrightly, and with a certain degree of casual humor—as I discuss many all-too-serious matters in rational-emotive sessions. As a rational therapist I also hold a deep personal conviction that although life has many enjoyable aspects, others have the right to differ, and I believe that anyone, including one of my clients, has the privilege of deciding to stop living.

I do not get upset, therefore, when someone threatens suicide, but deal with this usually irrational thought in the same way that I (and other rational-emotive therapists) treat non-suicidal beliefs. My clients thus see that I know they seriously contemplate suicide, that I do not deny their right to commit it, but that I very much want them to reconsider some points about living and to see if they *really* want to die.

Back to Marlo. "I know I have the privilege," she said, "of taking my life. And since I do not find it worth going on with, I intend to do exactly that. Life seems a phony deal. I can't trust or depend upon anyone. Things always end up the same."

"How so? Just because two lovers in a row have left you? A hell of a big conclusion from a pitifully small bit of evidence!"

"Just the same—I find it always the same."

"Hogwash! How can a bright woman like you believe such twaddle? I see very little similarity between your first lover's leaving you because he didn't want to assume the responsibilities of divorcing his wife and taking on another, and Jake's leaving you because, to say the least, you've acted like the most godawful pain in the ass. And doesn't the solution—if you really want a solution to your problem of maintaining a secure relationship with a man of your choice—doesn't the solution lie in *you* not behaving like a pain in the ass, rather than demanding that the males of the world not do you in?"

"But how do I know that Jake didn't plan this, right from the start, just like Thorwald, my first lover, did three years ago? How do I know that he didn't deliberately take everything he could get from me and then leave me just before we could get married?"

"You don't know—for sure. But the situation certainly

64   *Does Reason Always Prove Reasonable?*

doesn't seem the way you keep setting it up. Not to me, it doesn't! Besides, let us suppose that you view the situation accurately, and that Jake really did, just like the first man in your life, plan to get what he could out of you sexually and then leave you waiting at the church. So? That would certainly show that he, just like Thorwald, behaved unethically. But why make that *your* problem? How does that emerge as a reason for *you* to splatter your brains over your lovely Persian rug?"

"But if I can't trust *anyone*," Marlo half wailed, "how can I see any prospect of my ever living happily?"

"Anyone?" I relentlessly persisted. "I can't see how two men in an entire lifetime, so far, equal *anyone.* Let's even say, for the sake of your argument, that both Thorwald and Jake proved entirely untrustworthy. Must you vastly overgeneralize? If you hired two girls in a row to assist you in your work at the office and both of them proved unreliable, would you necessarily conclude that you couldn't possibly ever get *anyone* more reliable?"

"No, I guess I wouldn't. I see what you mean."

"And even if we may grant—for the sake, again, of *your* argument—that you have had the unusual misfortune of meeting two individuals in succession who behaved abominably, does such an impressive record of adversity indicate that your whole life can include nothing but fraud and that you should forthrightly dispense with the entire process?"

"You seem to dismiss Jake and my losing him as nothing worth considering," Marlo (now quite unhysterically) said.

"Not at all. Could we not more appropriately say that you seem to consider *yourself* and your losing *you* as nothing worth considering?"

"You mean—I show, by getting this upset and by thinking of ending it all, that I don't consider *myself* sufficiently worth going on with?"

"Well, *do* you? You remind me somewhat of a woman on trial for speeding. Asked the judge, 'How come, madam, that you have five children, ranging in ages one to eight, when you just told me that the only husband you ever had died three years ago.' 'Well, Judge,' she replied, 'my husband died—but not me!' This woman, obviously, thought life worth living even with her husband irrevocably gone. She accepted herself. Do *you*?"

"But how *can* I accept myself when, as you can see, no one else seems to do so, when one man after another keeps rejecting me? Doesn't this indicate *something*?"

"Yes, it indicates something about you—that you believe it all-important to have others, particularly a man of your choice, accept you before you decide to accept yourself. It indicates that you continually rate yourself and make this self-rating dependent upon the approval of others, and that you illogically keep telling yourself, 'Because I have no value, and can only consider myself worthwhile if others approve me, and because two men in succession have not loved me sufficiently to take me to the altar, this proves what I knew in the first place: that I have no worth.' Don't you see the circularity of this reasoning?"

"Mmmm. Let me get that straight now. I keep saying and have always said to myself, 'I only have value and can consider life worth living if and when a man I choose truly cares for me.' And then, when I find one does not care as much as I thought he did, I immediately conclude that 'Yes, of course he doesn't care. Because, as I said in the first place, I have no worth, and how could he possibly really care for a worthless person like me?' Mmmm. That *does* make circular reasoning, if I actually say that to myself."

"Well, don't you?"

"Looks like it, doesn't it? I'll have to give this some more thought."

"Exactly what we want: for you to give this sort of thing more thought. And to have you think more about it outside these sessions. While you think about it, give a little thought to another aspect of it, too."

"Which aspect?" Marlo asked. She now, incidentally, kept looking at herself so intently in a problem-solving way that one would never have dreamed that, just a few minutes before, she had considered plunging out of my office window.

"Think, if you will," I said, "of the enormous *demands* you keep making on people, such as Jake, with whom you get involved. Precisely because you do consider yourself essentially worthless, and believe that you *need* their approval to make you 'worthwhile,' you don't merely, as you mistakenly think you do, ask them to act in a certain way toward you; rather, you demand that they do."

"I demand that Jake approve of me, no matter how I treat him or what I do?"

"Yes. To fulfill your own needs for great approval, you expect him to conform rigidly to your preconceived ideas of how a man intending to marry you *should* behave. And when he does not act precisely the way you think he *ought* to act—and Lord knows you try every possible test in the books to see if he *does* act this way!—you immediately raise hell with him and call *him* untrustworthy. Finally, by continuing to make your unreasonable demands, and forcing him—yes, actually forcing him—to turn away from you, you 'prove' to yourself that you cannot trust him. Actually, of course, you only 'prove' how dependent you remain on his and others' approval. Another round of circular thinking!"

"I think I need him to bolster me. Then I force him to conform to my so-called needs. Then he doesn't do so, because he finds me such a bother. Then I tell myself, 'Because he finds me such a bother, this proves that I have no worth and that I need him or someone else to bolster me and help poor unworthy me get along in this big bad world.' Golly, I really *do* have it in for myself—all along the line—don't I?"

"You do! And until we can help you to trust *yourself* most of the time, how can we expect you to trust people like Jake? Until we can help you to see that no catastrophe, but merely unpleasantness, occurs when you get rejected by a lover, how can we expect you to act well enough with such a lover that he will not find you too bothersome?"

So Marlo and I continued to talk. And by the end of this session she not only felt calm but perceptibly began to show a new kind of thinking about herself, which led to more self-acceptance than she had felt previously. I would like to report that as a result of many more sessions and hundreds of well-spent hours rethinking things with herself, she happily married Jake. That, alas, did not occur. In spite of her notable improvements in her attitudes, Jake felt he had already had it, and only occasionally saw Marlo again. But before another year had passed, Marlo found a new boyfriend, related to him with much more realistic expectations and with less jealousy, and consummated a good marriage.

To return to our main theme: Because of her humanness, Marlo found it very *easy* to mix herself up about her love life, even though in other respects she acted most intelligently and efficiently. She had no trouble overgeneralizing, retaining unchallenged premises about her own basic worthlessness, and believing she only wanted certain responses from her fiancé when she *demanded* unequivocal love from him. This exceptionally bright woman found these elementary logical errors the easiest thing in the world for her to make.

Why? Because Marlo behaved humanly. Because humans have ten or twelve years of childhood during which they act dependently and fail to discriminate very well between sensible and foolish behavior. Because, once having technically outgrown their childhood, they tend to remain affected by its experiences for the rest of their lives. Because, no matter how "mature" they may get, they find it difficult to objectively view their own behavior and their relations with others. Because they have strong biological tendencies to make themselves anxious and hostile, even when such feelings sabotage their desires. Because their families and their communities encourage them, from childhood onward, to remain gullible, suggestible, and conformist in many significant ways. Because, as humans, they have powerful tendencies (not instincts, but what Abe Maslow called instinctoid tendencies) toward habits, inertia, excitement-seeking, moodiness, and negativism that frequently interfere with productive thinking and planning and that help them, even when they "know" what they'd better do, to fall into self-defeating ways.

Particularly in regard to relating to others, people tend to act foolishly. For reasonably intelligent humans often find it almost impossible to discriminate between sensible and senseless modes of social behavior. If you lived alone on a desert island, you would probably have little trouble acting sanely most of the time.

But you don't live on a desert island. And, whether you like it or not, you feel forced to socially conform. Yet, at the same time, you'd better also, if you would fulfill your own destiny, achieve social independence and individualism—succeed in feeling *yourself.*

You will tend to find these two conflicting goals difficult to achieve to any near-perfect degree. In fact, you may find it impossible to achieve anything but a highly imperfect, temporary resolution of the goals of remaining yourself and simultaneously getting along well with others.

Take the relatively simple situation, for example, in which you sit around talking to a group of seven or eight friends. Suppose most of the other members of the group have good intelligence and sophistication. Suppose, also, that you don't have serious hangups.

Nonetheless, you remain in something of an individual-social pickle. If you cajole or force the members of the group to talk about the things that interest you most, some of them will soon feel bored and disgusted with your "hogging the floor." But if you completely go along with what the other members of the group spontaneously want to discuss, you will probably find yourself sitting in dead, somewhat pained silence for a good part of the evening.

If, when a subject about which you have strong views comes up for discussion, you honestly say what you feel about it, some members of the group will very likely feel hurt, insulted, or angry. If you carefully keep your mouth shut, or only very cautiously express some of your own most deeply felt views, you will feel frustrated and edgy yourself.

Though you try to considerately and politely allow other members of the group to have their say whenever they feel the urge to do so, some of them may not prove equally polite, will monopolize the conversation when you give them an opening, and will probably force you, by the end of the discussion, to remain silent about several things you think important and on which you very much would have liked to comment. If, however, you uninhibitedly break into the conversation when you have something pressing on your mind, some of the others will feel their toes stepped upon and resentfully think that *they* have not sufficiently expressed themselves in the course of the evening.

You really can't win—not completely. No matter what you do, no perfect solution presents itself. Even in this simple situation, if you behave as *you* really want to behave, some of the group members will feel their wants impinged upon and will tend to dislike you. And if you behave as you think the group members want you to do, you will find *your* basic desires frustrated and will tend to dislike the others. Unless, by sheer accident, your wants happen to coincide with those of all the other members of the group (a highly unlikely occurrence!), someone, you or they, gets frustrated. And distinct displeasure, not to mention anxiety or anger, on your part and theirs, tends to result.

Things get much more complicated, of course, if you unduly *care* about what other members of the group think of your behavior. For if you feel overconcerned about having the group members think well of you, you will lean over backward to do what they want you to do, instead of what you want to do yourself. Then you will tend to hate yourself for acting like a milksop and hate them for witnessing this act. Or else you will do what you mainly want to do—and then worry inordinately whether they still like you for doing it.

Such an inordinate degree of caring for the approval of others constitutes a form of neurosis. But even *without* such neurotic feelings and actions on your part, the careful discriminations you keep making between what you would *like* to do and what you'd *better* do in group situations prove difficult to make and lead to somewhat discouraging results. For you want what *you* desire. And you also want *others* to feel comfortable in your presence and to approve your behavior—quite apart from any neurotic needs for approval that you may have. You feel constantly torn, therefore, between two conflicting desires, and can hardly permanently resolve this conflict.

All this is the simplest kind of a social situation. In a more complicated kind of individual-group relationship, things get even hotter. Thus, in a highly competitive group—such as a school where most of the members of the class keep trying to get into favorite colleges, or in a business office where employees, at one and the same time, cooperate with each other to win out over rival businesses and compete with each other to make higher commissions or salaries—you will find it considerably more difficult to do what you want to do (1) for your own individual ends and (2) for gaining and keeping the favor of others.

In almost any social group, therefore, you will find it tough sledding to keep a sane, somewhat middle-of-the-road course and to avoid surrendering your personal tastes, preferences, and expressiveness while avoiding getting into real difficulties with other group members. You cannot fully calculate in advance your best *reasoned* or most *reason*able approaches in such groups, and you will shift, from time to time, with changing conditions. Thus, when you first enter a group, you may best keep your mouth shut for a period of time and let the other members have something of their say. Later, you may find it best to get in your own two cents' worth, even though those who previously held the floor would love to continue holding it. Finally, you may find it reasonable to give the others a chance to talk more again. But exactly when and where to draw the line between your own active participation and polite acceptance of others' participation you may never calculate in advance, since this depends on many different personal and group factors.

You may well acknowledge, then, that both self-expression *and* social acceptance seem desirable in virtually everyone's life. But while some form of hedonism, pleasure-seeking, or enlightened self-interest seems as good a plan of personal living as anyone has yet devised, enlightened self-interest includes, and cannot possibly sanely ignore, some degree of social interest as well. For if you *only* strive for your "own" good, and run roughshod over others in the process, you will most probably find that most people over whom you keep riding sooner or later thwart your "own" good. Therefore, to *some* extent in your concept of your "own" good you'd better include the good of others as well.

Similarly, if you mainly concentrate on striving for your *immediate* good—if you employ the general principle of short-range hedonism—you will almost inevitably sabotage many of your potential future enjoyments. "Live for today, for tomorrow you may die" seems a perfectly sane philosophy—*if* you have a good chance of dying tomorrow. Most of the time, however, you live to the ripe old age of seventy or eighty these days; and your tomorrows will probably turn out miserable if you live only for today. At the same time, if you only live for tomorrow, you will tend to make your todays overcautiously and drably lived; and again you will in the long run defeat your own ends.

Reason, then, proves a hard taskmaster. You won't find it *absolutely* good or certain as a standard of conduct, and you will find drawing the exact line between reasonable and unreasonable behavior quite difficult. When taken to extremes, moreover, you can make rationality highly irrational. For several reasons:

1. As we have previously pointed out, *some* degree of emotionality seems necessary to human survival and it would probably prove unreasonable, meaning self-defeating, for you never to have strong, rather prejudiced reactions—such as your wanting to hurt or even kill someone who deliberately attacks you.

2. Human tastes or preferences, though frequently quite "irrational" or "groundless," may add considerable pleasure and interest to life. You act, in a sense, "unreasonably" when you get obsessed with collecting stamps, devote yourself to making your

mate happy, or listen to music ten hours a day. But many people derive enormous, harmless enjoyment from these kinds of "irrational" or "emotional" pursuits. "Pure intellect," if this ever existed, would prove highly efficient but equally pleasureless. "Affects" (one of the older terms for emotions) receive that name because they *affect* you—influence you to go on living and to enjoy your existence. Without any kind of feeling or emotion, human life might persist but it would seem incredibly dull.

3. Reason, when carried to extremes, sometimes creates inefficiency and self-sabotaging. If every time you tied a shoelace or ate a piece of bread, you had to stop and reason whether this proved the "right" thing to do or the "best" way to do it, your reason would turn into more of a hindrance than a help and you would wind up, perhaps, highly rational—and unhappy. Extreme or obsessive-compulsive "reason" really proves irrational; because "true" rationality aids or increases human happiness.

4. A totally reasoned-out life would tend to lead to a mechanical existence—a life too cold, unfeeling, and machinelike. It would undermine the creation and expression of much that sensitive humans hold dear, particularly in the realm of art, literature, and music.

All these accusations against extreme rationality have some validity. But they also have a straw-man quality and keep getting taken to irrational extremes. When boiled down to their essences, they often arise from their promulgators' fear of the unknown. Even though the present, highly neurotic state of many "irrationalists" includes distinct discomfort and anxiety, they at least *know* the limits of the disturbances they have. Not knowing, of course, the degree of discomfort they might obtain if they lived rational lives, and (quite irrationally) fearing that it might even exceed their present discomfort, they dream up straw-men horrors about rationality in order to give themselves an excuse for not trying to attain it.

Or again: Knowing that their present irrational state produces unpleasant results, but also knowing that thinking and acting logically proves difficult and requires considerable expenditure of time and effort, disturbed people often lazily work harder at thinking up arguments against rationality than at experimentally trying to apply it to their lives.

One of my (R.A.H.'s) clients, for example, kept resisting my rational approach to his severe problem of anxiety and compulsive eating and frankly admitted his resistance.

"Do you fear," I asked, "that if you reconstruct your life along the ways we have discussed, you will turn into a kind of rational machine-monster?"

"Well, in a sense, yes," the client replied.

"All right. Now let's look at your fear of acting machinelike as a result of therapy just as we would examine any of your other anxieties. What evidence can you present to support this fear? Name a person you know who seems so rational that he doesn't appear to enjoy life and acts like a logical machine, as you have implied."

"Well, I don't know, exactly. But I must admit that at times you seem a bit, you know, that way yourself. You do seem awfully efficient. And you rarely get upset about things. Even when I break down and cry or rant, it doesn't seem to affect you. And that seems strange and, well, maybe a bit heartless to me."

"And this proves that I remain coldly and dreadfully incapable of enjoying life, or of feeling happy?"

"Not exactly. But I fear that *I* might lose my capacity for joy if I act so calmly and objectively as you do."

"Ah, quite a different thing! Here you feel almost as miserable as you can, with your extreme anxiety and compulsiveness; and as you just described me, I almost never upset myself about things. Obviously, if your description of me holds true, I don't feel very unhappy. And yet you fear that if you achieve calmness, like me, you will magically turn unhappy, or at least lose your capacity for joy. Right?"

"Yes. Somehow I feel that way."

"You mean, really, you *believe* that way. But I still ask: What evidence do you have for your belief? Have you experimentally tried, even for a few days or weeks, acting as calmly as I? Have you, in the course of such a trial, proven to your own satisfaction—or shall we say, your own dissatisfaction?—that you would then feel worse, more unhappy, than you feel now?"

"No, I can't say I have."

"Then why don't you, quite experimentally, try? After all, you can always return to your present depressed state, you know, if this kind of honest trial fails. If, somehow, you try behaving more rationally and start turning into an IBM-like zombie, you can always reintroduce whatever degree of nonrationality you care to get back into your life. You sign no contract to continue *ir*rationally behaving in a coldly 'rational' manner, if your experiment in logical thinking actually starts turning out that way. So far as I can see, however, since you haven't even *tried* rationality yet, and since you feel distinctly miserable living your present irrational way, you keep setting up a bogeyman as an excuse against the dangers, or what you consider dangerous, about changing yourself."

"You mean people like me actually so greatly fear changing their ways that they dream up exaggerated and false objections to doing so?"

"Precisely. Without even trying a new path, they set up so many theoretical and often highly fanciful objections to it that they never give themselves a chance to learn whether it would prove satisfying."

"So you think that my disturbance, right now, consists not so much of my acting irrationally, but of my refusing to even try rationality and then insisting that, if I did try it, it would make me into a mechanical-like unemotional zombie?"

"Exactly. Why don't you try it and see?"

And he did try working against his compulsive eating and seriously questioning the irrational beliefs causing his crippling anxieties. Several weeks later, after making considerable progress in these directions, he enthusiastically reported:

"Not only have I stopped eating when I don't feel hungry, as I did when I came to see you; but I've actually started a real diet for the first time in years and have already lost eight pounds. I feel sure I'll keep it up, too, now that I see that my eating mainly served to divert me from my central nutty idea; that I couldn't face the hazards of life myself, without the continual babying of my parents, my wife, and even my children.

"I really want to bring up another point. As my compulsive eating and some of my fears of standing on my own two feet kept going down, that mechanical-like feeling that I so feared getting a few weeks ago just hasn't materialized at all. Just the opposite! I feel so darned *more* emotional, in a good way, and so enthusiastic about my life, that I practically go to the office singing every morning. In fact, this very morning I *did* find myself singing, for the first time in years. And I stopped for a moment, as I listened to myself and said, 'Holy cats! That son-of-a-gun Harper—how right! If singing on the way to work illustrates how mechanical this rational-emotive therapy stuff will make me, I think I'd better get some heavier doses of that rational thinking and learn to warble like a nightingale!' Mechanical-schmechanical—I like acting like this kind of a robot!"

As this client began to see, a rational approach to life does not mean a one-sided, rigid kind of rationality. The definition of rational, as employed in today's social thinking, means: showing reason; not foolish or silly; sensible; leading to efficient results; producing desired effects with a minimum of expense, waste, unnecessary effort, or unpleasant side effects.

Human reason, therefore, includes appropriate emotionality, good habit performance, and whatever else helps create an effective, minimally anxious existence. Rational living does not amount to an end in itself. Life has rationality when you use your head to experience happier, more self-actualizing days and years. To act rationally, you act (and feel!) more joyously.

Rationality, as we use the term, shies away from perfectionism or absolutism. Although we consider ourselves pretty rational, we do not see ourselves as dedicated rational*ists*. Rational*ism* holds that reason or intellect, rather than the senses, provides the true source of knowledge. This we do not believe. Like most modern scientists and empiricists, we see knowledge as significantly influenced by and related to thinking. But we find it basically stemming from and validated by observation: by evidence involving our senses of touch, smell, sight, hearing, and taste.

Some devotees of rationality, such as Ayn Rand and Nathaniel Branden, think of reason as an absolute and find it necessary and sufficient for distinguishing between good and bad, healthy and unhealthy behavior. We do not agree; and I (A.E.) have written an entire book criticizing the failings of objectivism, the philosophy of Rand and Branden.

If we do not see rational thinking as an Absolute Good, or an end in itself, but more *reasonably* consider it a means toward the end of maximizing human happiness—and particularly of minimizing anxiety, depression, hostility, and other emotional blocks to happiness—we avoid the pitfall of getting *too* rational. Extreme, exaggerated, or dogmatic "rationality" displays a contradiction. As soon as we take reason to self-defeating extremes and make it into dogmatism, it no longer, of course, remains reason. It then turns into antireason.

Some followers of RET get accused of behaving "too rationally" and of helping their clients to act overly mechanical or unemotional. Such accusations may have some truth. But if so, these followers practice rational-emotive therapy badly. We find a helpful definition of rational thinking presented by Dr. Maxie C. Maultsby, Jr., a psychiatrist who uses and teaches RET (or Rational Behavior Training) and who founded the self-help group Associated Rational Thinkers (ART), which has various branches throughout the United States. As we previously noted, Dr. Maultsby indicates that rational thinking has five main characteristics. When you think rationally, (1) you derive your thought primarily from objective fact as opposed to subjective opinion; (2) your thinking, if acted upon, most likely will result in the preservation of your life and limb; (3) it will help you define your personal life goals most quickly; (4) it will produce in you a minimum of inner conflict and turmoil; and (5) if you act on it, it will prevent you from getting into undesirable conflict with those with whom you live and associate.

If you follow this kind of rational thinking, you will not embroil yourself in any amount of mechanized responding, overintellectualizing, or underemotionalizing. Various people mean various things by the term *rational*. We mean: sensible, efficient, *un*self-defeating. And we include human emotion, sensitivity, creativity, and art as quite rational pursuits—as long as you do not take them to such foolish extremes as to sabotage your living and other forms of enjoying.

As shown in the case cited a few pages back, when people fear rationality and clear thinking as methods of overcontrol and needless inhibition, they do not use the definition of *rational* employed in this book (and seem to us quite *ir*rational!). Or they may fear surrendering their present irrational ways and therefore rebel against "rationality." In which case their *rationalizing* may block their *rational thinking.*

Rationalizing means to devise *seemingly* rational or plausible explanations for your acts, beliefs, or desires, usually without your awareness that these explanations do not hold water. Rationalizing or excusing your behavior, therefore, amounts to the opposite of thinking rationally about it.

Similarly, although to intellectualize, in a philosophic sense, means to reason or to think, in a psychological sense it means to *over*emphasize intellectual pursuits such as mathematics and to consider them superior to other pursuits such as popular drama or music. To intellectualize also, psychologically, means to think about your emotional problems in such a detailed and compulsive manner as to deny their true existence and to avoid rather than to attempt solving them.

Although, therefore, the principles of rational behavior training and rational living, as their names imply, strongly favor a highly reasoned approach to human life, they do not favor a rationalizing or intellectualistic approach. To reason your way out of your emotional upsets makes you sane and sensible. But to rationalize or intellectualize about your self-defeating, neurotic behavior helps you perpetuate it endlessly. We will have no truck whatever with rationalization and intellectualization; and if our opponents, as they often do, falsely accuse us of advocating rationalized and intellectualized "solutions" to human ills, we see that as *their* problem.

9
REFUSING TO FEEL
DESPERATELY UNHAPPY

Anyone who tries to give you a rule by which you can always feel happy speaks foolishly or knavishly. And yet we brashly declare: We can teach you the art of (virtually) never feeling desperately unhappy.

Do we contradict ourselves? Seemingly so; actually not. Happiness, or a positive feeling of pleasure, joy, or elation, tends to arise as a by-product of what you do, and you cannot easily gain it by prescription. What you, as a unique human individual, do and how much pleasure you get from doing it largely depends on your personal preferences—which others cannot very well predict. You may adore a walk in the country; or you may hate it. You may feel ecstatic over going to bed with your spouse; or you may look upon doing so as an odious chore. How can we, then, tell you what will probably bring you joy?

We legitimately may, of course, tell you what makes *us* happy or what brings *someone else* joy, but we cannot predict, except by putting you through actual experiences or trials, what will make *you* highly satisfied. We can act cagily and tell you that something general, such as absorbing work or vital interest in a cause, will probably make you happy. But *what* work or *what* vital interest will do the trick for you we cannot honestly say. Only you, in the last analysis, by a process of your own trial and error, can sensibly answer that question.

If we can't tell you how to get happy, can we tell you how not to feel unduly miserable? Paradoxically, yes. Because while humans differ enormously in what brings them positive contentment, they have remarkable similarity in how they make themselves anxious and depressed. And we, as psychologists who have worked with many miserable people, can tell you almost to a T just what you do to make yourself desperately unhappy—and how to stop doing it.

Do we contend, you may ask, that you can have *no* legitimate unhappiness? No, not quite. Merely that you superfluously create an enormous amount of human emotional pain, suffering, misery, and horror. In fact, almost the only sustained and "unbearable" misery that we accept as legitimate or justifiable results from prolonged and undownable physical pain. You needlessly manufacture virtually all other prolonged agony.

"Oh, come now!" you may protest. "You don't mean to say, Drs. Ellis and Harper, that if my mother dies, my mate leaves me, or I lose a fine job—you don't mean to say that even *then* I don't need to feel terribly miserable or depressed?"

"But we do mean exactly that. No matter *what* happens to you, with the exception of continuous, intractable physical pain, we do not think it *necessary* for you to make yourself horrified or depressed. But we do believe that you will find it *desirable*, under certain conditions, to make yourself (or allow yourself to feel) distinctly sorrowful or annoyed."

"What kind of gobbledygook have we here? You find depression unnecessary but sorrow desirable? *Seriously*?"

"Yes, seriously! We'd better admit that feelings of unhappiness vary widely and that we consciously or unconsciously bring them on—or *choose* to experience them. And because we needlessly produce our feelings of depression and self-downing by telling ourselves silly, irrational beliefs, we can choose to bring *these* miserable feelings to a swift halt by disputing the philosophies by which we create them and replacing these views with intelligent, reality-founded, and joy-producing beliefs."

"Really? *Really!!?*"

Yes, really, but before you split a gut in your incredulity, perhaps we had better do a little defining of the terms "happy" and "unhappy." Then you may not think us so crazy as we may seem at first blush.

The dictionary loosely defines the term *unhappy* as: sad; miserable; wretched; sorrowful. This, however, tells only half the real story. Unhappiness actually seems to consist of at least two distinct elements: (1) a feeling of sadness, sorrow, irritation, annoyance, or regret at your not getting what you want or at your getting what you do not want; and (2) a second and quite different feeling of anxiety, depression, shame, or rage because (a) you see yourself as deprived or balked and (b) foolishly convince yourself that you *should* not, *must* not, suffer frustration and that things remain *horrible* and *awful* because you have suffered.

Misery, in other words, consists of two fairly distinct parts: (1) desiring, wishing, or preferring that you achieve some goal or purpose and feeling disappointed and irritated when you do not achieve it; and (2) demanding, insisting, commanding, and urgently necessitating that you achieve this goal or purpose and feeling bitter, enraged, anxious, despairing, and self-downing when you do not.

We distinguish, in consequence, between healthy feelings of sorrow or irritation when you lose something you clearly desire; and unhealthy feelings of depression or rage stemming from your childish refusal to *accept* a world with frustrations and losses, and from your *whining* that such things absolutely *must* not exist. If you choose to stay with these former feelings, you will feel appropriately (and sometimes keenly) disappointed or sorrowed at the loss of a person or thing you care for. But you need not also choose to feel utterly overwhelmed and depressed at the same loss. You may also sanely choose to feel strongly annoyed or irritated by a frustrating set of circumstances. But you need not insanely choose to feel inordinately angry, enraged, or upset about the same set of frustrations.

Whereas your feeling of loss or sorrow constitutes an appropriate response to a distinct loss you have experienced, your feeling of panic or depression does not. Why? For several important reasons:

1. When something obnoxious occurs to you at point A (your Activating Experience or Activating Event), you feel sorrowful or sad at point C (your emotional Consequence) because you tell yourself at point B (your Belief System), "I think it unfortunate [or disadvantageous or frustrating] that I have lost this person or thing." This represents a logical or empirically confirmable statement, a rational Belief (rB), since you can prove (in the light of your own value system, that you would like to remain alive and happy) that misfortune or disadvantage *does* follow from this loss. Thus, if you lose your mate or your job, you will suffer several disadvantages from this loss; and it seems asinine for you to conclude, "How fortunate!" and to feel happy about it.

2. Your feelings of anxiety or depression—which can range anywhere from mild to extreme upsettedness—constitute a radically different kind of emotional Consequence (point C). They stem from your irrational Belief (iB), "I find it *awful* or *horrible* that I have lost this person or thing." But the terms *awful* or *horrible*, when you use them in this context, virtually never really mean *unfortunate* or *disadvantageous*. They mean *more* than this. And (if you carefully think about it) you will see that something more than this cannot very well exist in the universe. No matter how very, very unfortunate you find it to have lost your mate or your job, it still emerges *only* as unfortunate. Even when you

deem it extremely, exceptionally, or outstandingly unfortunate, it still cannot rate as *more* than that. And the term *awful*, when it leads to panic or depression, really means—think about it now; do not merely take our word for it!—infinitely more than unfortunate. It has a magical, surplus meaning, which has no empirical referent (other, of course, than the reality already included in the terms *unfortunate, disadvantageous, frustrating,* or *inconvenient*). If you wisely follow the rules of Alfred Korzybski and the general semanticists and avoid using any higher-order abstractions of this kind which you can't accurately relate to reality, you will practically never feel pernicious emotional effects, such as depression and rage.

3. It may seem a quibble to keep terms like *unfortunate, disadvantageous,* and *inconvenient* in your vocabulary (and in your belief system), while eliminating terms like *awful, horrible,* and *terrible.* But it amounts to far more than a quibble! For if you convince yourself that you find it exceptionally *unfortunate* if your mate rejects you, you strongly imply that you would find it distinctly *fortunate* if you persuaded him or her to return to your relationship—and that you would deem it almost as *fortunate* if you could relate to someone else in a satisfying way. Consequently, you will feel motivated, by conceiving this event as unfortunate, to *do* something about it: for example, winning love again; getting into a good relationship with another mate; or enjoying as much as you can the advantages of *not* having a mate. But if you convince yourself of the *awfulness* of your mate's rejection, you will tend to do little or nothing about it, except: (a) mull endlessly about its *awfulness*; (b) put yourself down for having created that *awful* result; (c) convince yourself that you feel too upset to do *anything* about relating again to this mate or another one; (d) demand, magically, that somehow somebody or some supreme Power restore your mate to you; (e) foolishly predict that you can *never* relate successfully to a desirable mate again; (f) damn yourself totally and bigotedly "prove" to yourself that a worm like you *doesn't deserve* acceptance; and (g) otherwise convince yourself that the Demon of Awfulness has got you irrevocably in its grasp and that you have no power to help yourself or to cope with such a magical, undefinable, evil demon.

Your seeing any Activating Experience or Event as *awful, horrible, terrible,* gives you the illusion that you absolutely cannot control it and that you must remain too weak to cope with the *awful* essence of the universe that creates such horror and insists on plaguing you with it. No matter how *unfortunate* or *undesirable* an event seems, you still presumably have the capability of changing it or coping with it. But if you consider it truly *terrible,* you abdicate almost any control you may have over it (or over your reactions to it), and you make yourself completely subject to its imagined *horror.*

4. If you face yourself honestly, you can admit that whenever you conceive of some loss or frustration as *awful,* you really mean that because you find it exceptionally disadvantageous, it *should* not, *must* not, *ought* not, exist. You don't merely see its existence as undesirable but that therefore the powers that rule *shouldn't* foist it upon you. Nor do you mean that because of its disadvantages, this event or process *preferably* should not exist; you mean that it *absolutely* should not! This kind of *should*ing, *must*ing, and *ought*ing proves unrealistic and illogical for several reasons:

a. As far as we scientifically know, no absolute *shoulds, oughts,* and *musts* exist in the world. You can legitimately say that "*If* I want to survive, I *must* take reasonably good care of my health," because you do not make this *must* an absolute, but make it contingent on the goal you seek. But if you say, "I *must* survive, no matter how I take care of my health," or "I *must* take care of my health, whether or not I wish to survive," you make absolutistic statements and claim that a special law of the universe exists which says that *under all conditions* you must survive or must take care of your health. Such a law (as far as we know) doesn't exist. You dogmatically invent it.

b. When you devoutly believe in *shoulds, oughts,* or *musts,* you act incredibly grandiose and claim God-like powers that you do not possess. For your statement, "I *must* not get rejected by my mate, and therefore I find it *awful* that he or she has left me," actually means, "Because I *want* very much to have my mate love me, he or she *must.*" Well, what sense does that make? Do you—really—control your mate's (or anyone else's) feelings? Do you—truly!—rate as King of Kings or the Mother of the Universe? Lots of luck!

c. Whenever you say that something *must* exist, when it actually does not, you foolishly contradict yourself. If people truly *must* love you and remain related to you, then an incontrovertible law of the universe states that they have no other choice, and that they've *got to* act in your favor. But if you see that they no longer love you, and you find this *awful,* you apparently believe they really *must.* How could this contradictory state of affairs ever exist? If they *must* love you, then they obviously do (for the fates so ordain); and if they now don't, then that *must* can't exist. You can't at one and the same time, vehemently contend that people *must* love you and that they don't. Whatever *must* exist clearly does. Your original *allegation* of *mustness,* therefore, clearly has no validity. If it did, you'd never have any problems in this area!

d. If you think about it, you will see that *any* devout positing of a *must* will cause you to feel quite anxious, for it remains very

probable that what you say *must* exist actually (especially under
some conditions) won't exist—and then you'll tend to feel destroyed. If you say, "People *must* always love me sincerely," you
set things up so that you will not merely feel very sad and regretful if they don't, but you also arrange them so that you will feel
utterly destroyed and despairing if they lose affection for you. For
you really mean, by this statement, "If they ever stop loving me,
(i) I will emerge as a thoroughly slobbish person and (ii) I cannot
possibly, in any way, thereafter accept myself or lead an enjoyable
existence. Well! If you really believe this hogwash, you not only
place *some* of your happiness on the line in case people stop
having good feelings for you, but you place your entire existence
and virtually *all* your possibilities of feeling happy on the line, if
they happen to stop caring for you. You not only risk your relationship with them, you also (by your silly definitions, in your
head), risk *you*, your entire present and future happiness.
Knowing the great penalty involved—that you will insist on losing
yourself in case you lose *them*—you will almost always make yourself terribly anxious (rather than appropriately concerned) about
having a good relationship with them.

To make matters still worse, once you profoundly believe,
"People *must* always love me sincerely," not only do you prepare
for yourself an anxious bed of thorns in case they don't, but you
also keep lying in the same thorny bed when they do. For if you
say to yourself, "Oh! People really do love me now. How wonderful! What a great person that makes me!" you will almost
inevitably think, a short while later, "But suppose they no longer
love me tomorrow? How *awful*! What a worthless slob I would
then find myself!" So even when you do get what you think you
must get, you never truly cease feeling anxious over the possibility
that you will lose it in the future. For there always remains, in our
changeable world, the strong possibility that you *will* lose it.
People who now dote on you, for example, may die; move to a
distant part of the world; suffer severe physical or emotional
problems; naturally cease to care for you; or change their feelings
for a wide variety of reasons. How, then, can you unanxiously live
with any *musts* about their acceptance of you?

You can see, then, how you can appropriately feel deep loss
and sorrow when you lose a loved person or thing and how you
can inappropriately feel depressed, despairing, and self-downing
when you dearly care for the lost person or thing. Unhappiness, we
say, in the sense that it includes the former feelings, seems sane
and legitimate. But unhappiness in the sense that it involves *awfulizing, horribilizing,* and *catastrophizing* seems crazy and illegitimate. You create depression and despair not by the Activating
Events that happen in your life (at point A) but by your Belief
System (at point B). And since you invariably have some kind of a

choice of beliefs, and can *decide* to stick to reality, to evaluate something as unfortunate and unpleasant instead of going beyond reality and absolutistically defining it as awful and terrible, you really have an enormous amount of control over your feelings. *If* you clearly see exactly what you do to create them and *if* you will work at doing something more sensible to change them!

Having said this, let us immediately emphasize that we do not believe that any human can, for any length of time, feel *perfectly* or *completely* or *ecstatically* happy. The frenetic search for a perfect *anything*, in fact, almost inevitably dooms the searcher to severe frustration and unhappiness. And humans don't exist as the kind of animals that achieve perfection in virtually any ways—especially perfect happiness. Because of their ever-changing physical and psychological experiences, they remain subject to hundreds of irritations, pains, ills, diseases, states of ennui, conditions of tension, and other discomfort-producing situations. They can overcome many of their mental and emotional handicaps, as we endeavor to show in this book. But not all!

You can almost always tackle and conquer, for example, sustained depression. But you can effectively tackle it largely because you feel it steadily, and because you have sufficient time to think about it, track it back to its origins in your thinking, and contradict the thinking which you (consciously or unconsciously) employed to create and sustain it. Evanescent negative feelings, on the other hand, you cannot as easily tackle, because you feel them fleetingly and may not have a long enough chance to analyze and unravel them.

You rarely even completely win the battle against sustained psychological pain. When you feel unhappy because of some silly idea and you analyze and eradicate this idea, it rarely stays away forever, but often recurs from time to time. So you have to keep reanalyzing and subduing repeatedly. You may acquire the ridiculous notion, for instance, that you cannot live without some friend's approval and may keep making yourself immensely miserable because you believe this rot. Then, after much hard thinking, you may finally give up this notion and believe it quite possible for you to live satisfactorily without your friend's approbation. Eventually, however, you will probably discover that you, quite spontaneously, from time to time revive the groundless notion that your life has no value without the approval of this—or some other—friend. And once again you feel you'd better work at beating this self-defeating idea out of your skull.

Let us hasten to add that you will usually find the task of depropagandizing yourself from your own self-defeating beliefs easier and easier as you persist. If you consistently seek out and dispute your mistaken philosophies of life, you will find that their influence weakens. Eventually, some of them almost entirely lose their power to harass you. Almost. For the day may well come when, if only for a brief time, the same idiotic thought with which you once drove yourself crazy again returns, until you challenge it again and overcome it.

You tend to have several quite powerful ideas that cause emotional disturbance. Biologically, you, as a human, easily think in these ways. Socially, you live in the kinds of communities that encourage you to think irrationally.

Take, by way of illustration, the idea of your *having* to achieve outstanding success. Quite possibly, you have some innate tendencies like most humans, to try to perform very well: to strive to run the fastest, garden the best, or climb the highest. As Robert White has ably shown, you strongly prefer to master problems, relationships, and other things. And, considering what advantages such an urge may well have for human survival, we may well conceive of it as partly inherited.

To this possibly innate tendency, we can add the deliberately taught competitiveness that most (though not all) cultures inculcate, and we can understand the overwhelming achievement drive that we actually witness in the majority of people reared in these cultures. Consequently, if you have grown up in a competitive society and get depressed when you do not live up to your own demands for success, you may well have difficulty challenging your own (and your society's) standards. For you will then keep rationally challenging and fighting against characteristics or attitudes deeply ingrained in your "nature."

Difficult, however, does not mean impossible. Of course, you will find it hard to think and to act rationally in an irrational world. Of course you will have trouble reasoning your way out of circumstances which have unreasonably bogged you down for many years. All right, so you find it difficult. But it also proves difficult for a blind man to learn to read Braille, a victim of polio to use his muscles again, or a perfectly normal person to swing from a trapeze, learn ballet dancing, or play the piano well. Tough! But you still can do it.

Many critics of a rational approach to living also find it "unnatural" to expect a human to act consistently rationally. They deny that the nature of the beast works this way. And they state some truths. For people born and reared with many irrational tendencies do find it "unnatural" to use their reasoning powers to overcome these tendencies.

However, we can call it equally "unnatural" for people to wear shoes, employ contraceptives, study foreign languages, drive cars, and do hosts of other things that go opposite to their inborn tendencies and their early upbringing. We may also ask: How much sanity has the individual who rigidly sticks only to perfectly "natural" behavior?

I shall always remember the young and potentially attractive female who got referred to me (A.E.) by her male friend because she refused to take practically any care of her body or her physical appearance and, at the age of twenty-three, already showed serious signs of overweight, flabbiness, and aging. When I asked her why she didn't take better care of herself even though her friend (whom she said she cared for and wanted to marry) felt displeased with her appearance and kept threatening to leave her if she did not do something about it, she said:

"But would that really seem honest? Should I *pretend*, with lovely clothes and makeup and stuff like that, that I have more beauty than I really do? Would I have stayed true to myself—or to John? Wouldn't he know, actually, that I didn't look the way I looked on the surface, and wouldn't he resent me all the more? If he can't accept me this way, without the elegant clothes and makeup routine, if he can't accept me in my *true* state, what kind of love does he really have for me anyway?"

I did my best to show this woman that, quite apart from her friend and his opinion of her looks, she might well have several reasons why she herself would want to look neater and take care of her body. For her health, for instance; for her own aesthetic feelings when she looked in a mirror; and for the vocational advantages her good looks could offer her.

To no avail. She kept returning to the theme of how artificially, how unnaturally, she would behave if she tried to look beautiful. I came within a hair of irrationally angering myself and telling her what she could do with her goddamn feelings of "integrity"—such as get herself to a nunnery and have done with it!

Reason, however, prevailed. I reminded myself for the twentieth time that I could not label her a louse but merely a very mixed-up, defensive woman who, out of severe underlying fright, stubbornly held to her self-contradictory position because she desperately felt that she *could not* let go of it. I also told myself that even if I failed utterly to help her change her self-sabotaging philosophies, I would not have to hold *my* value as a person at stake: I would merely have one more good, if alas unsuccessful, try under my belt; and I might even learn something from my "defeat." So back I went to the therapeutic contest.

"Look," I said, "you have too much intelligence to believe the kind of hogwash you keep handing yourself and handing me."

"What do you mean, hogwash?" she asked rather belligerently.

"Just what I said, *h-o-g-w-a-s-h*. And you know, to some extent, what I mean already. I can see by the somewhat phony way in which you lift your eyebrows. But, more explicitly, you keep saying that you cannot do anything artificial and unnatural to make yourself look better, because that would make you dishonest. Right?"

"Yes, I keep saying just that—and, whether you think so or not, I mean just that."

"Perhaps so; but I don't feel so sure. Just let's take your argument, for a moment, to its logical extremes, to see whether it will hold up. You won't use makeup or attractive clothing because you call that unnatural. All right. How about drinking glasses, knives, forks, spoons, and other eating utensils. Do you find *them* unnatural?"

"Well, in a sense, yes. But not in the sense I mean."

"No, not in the *non*sense you mean. But what 'sense' *do* you mean?"

Of course, she couldn't tell me. She reverted to saying again, in a vague and evasive manner, that she just didn't think it *right* and *natural* to make herself look good, but that somehow she found it right and natural for her to use knives, forks, and spoons. I saw she kept getting nowhere, so I interrupted:

"Look: Why do you keep handing me this nonsense? Why don't we try, instead, to discover why you don't use the words *right* and *natural* consistently, and why you find helping yourself with one device, such as wearing glasses, OK, but helping yourself with another device, such as suitably tailored clothes, not OK. As I said before, you usually act intelligently. Now surely you have *some* reason why you remain so inconsistent. Why do you?"

She at first denied her inconsistency. But I wouldn't buy that and kept showing her how inconsistently she behaved. I took her inconsistency as a fact, not a debatable question, and said I would discuss with her *why* and not *whether* it existed. She finally seemed willing to discuss the ways of her self-contradictions; so I said:

"I don't want to try to convince you that you have only abnormal or pathological reasons for your inconsistency. Many therapists practically insist that *everything* a client does must have pathology behind it. In rational-emotive therapy, however, we look for some of the *normal* reasons why people may do things that defeat their own ends."

"So if I consistently refuse to use artificial aids to improve my looks, you think that I may have some healthy, as well as unhealthy, reasons for this?"

"Right. Let's take a fairly obvious normal reason. You said before that if your boyfriend cannot accept you the way you look, without artificial aids, what kind of love does he really have for you? Well, that view seems *partly* accurate. For if he *only* loves you because of the things you do to make yourself look beautiful, his love will prove superficial and probably unenduring; and you may well say to yourself: Who needs that kind of love?"

"Yes—who needs it?"

"Right. Therefore, you sanely question how far you may

wisely go to make yourself look beautiful, so that he may not love you only for your looks. And *that* reason for refusing to use artificial beauty aids, while at the same time using eyeglasses or forks and knives, seems healthy. But when you take this same reason and exaggerate it, so that you refuse to use beauty aids for your *own* aesthetic and health satisfactions, we'd better look for possible disturbed reasons for your self-inconsistency."

"Such as?"

"Such as your underlying fear that if you do try to keep yourself looking good, you may still fail, since you may believe that you really will remain ugly, no matter how you fix yourself up. Or the fear that you may succeed, look fine, and *still* fail to marry your friend; since he may dislike you in spite of your good looks."

"But *may* I not seem unattractive to him, no matter what I do? And *may* I not look fine to him and still ultimately get rejected by him?"

"Oh, certainly. Of course. We always remain in danger of trying to win someone's approval or to achieve some goal, and nonetheless falling on our faces and failing to get what we go after. So what?"

"But wouldn't that prove terrible if I dieted, wore the right clothes, and otherwise fixed myself up and *still* lost my friend?"

"It most certainly would not prove terrible—unless you insist on making it so. You would find it inconvenient, of course, or frustrating, or very sad to lose your friend. But why would you view it as *terrible*? Would you die of it? Would the ground open and swallow you up? Would you remain unable to get another boyfriend or to do other enjoyable things even if you did not have another suitable replacement?"

"I don't know. I don't know what I could do if I really lost John."

"You've now exactly pinpointed your disturbance. You believe, quite wrongheadedly but most definitely, that it *would* prove terrible to lose John, that you *wouldn't* know what to do if you lost him. And by having this belief, by *translating* a nuisance and a frustration into a horror, *you tend to bring about that very "horror."* By *believing* you can't live successfully without John, you practically make certain that you really *can't*."

"And because I believe it terrible to lose John, and know that I may lose him no matter what I do with myself physically, I deliberately shy away from doing much to keep him? I give up on getting him in advance, so that I will not suffer the torments of the damned later on?"

"Exactly. You quite sanely want John—because we'll assume that he has traits pretty well suited to you. Then you insanely tell yourself that because you want him you *must* have him, and would feel destroyed if you did not. Then you 'logically' give up trying for him in advance, so as not to feel hurt later. Or, more specifically, you set up exceptionally difficult rules of the game— such as your refusal to try any beauty aids. You assume that if he still loves you in spite of these almost impossible rules, he will later love you forever and never leave you."

"But does that seem so crazy?"

"Yes—because it practically never works. Like fearing that your maid will bring back the wrong groceries and therefore demanding that she have a Ph.D. degree in home economics before you hire her. How good a chance do you have of finding anyone with a Ph.D. in home economics who will want to work for a maid's salary?"

"I see what you mean. I'd have little chance of finding such a maid, however much I might desire to have one. And similarly I have practically no chance of winning my friend's love if I keep making these unreasonable demands on him?"

"Right. So instead of demanding that he change *his* characteristics, while retaining your own neurotic demand for absolute love from him, had you not better think carefully about and work hard to change your own nutty needs for total love security?"

"Hmmm. I never saw it that way before."

"But emotional disturbance largely consists of taking an initially healthy *wish* for approval (and a *desire* to get approval for less superficial characteristics than good clothes or a trim figure) and turning it into an unhealthy *demand* for approval and a refusal to do anything to win it. Think about this some more and I think you will see it more clearly."

And she did think about it some more; began to diet and take care of her appearance; and started to get along much better with her male friend. This case mainly shows that humans behave, simultaneously, reasonably and unreasonably. They frequently act intelligently *and* stupidly, thinkingly *and* suggestibly. Although they find it easy, almost automatic, to present themselves as rationally behaving animals, they just as easily present themselves as semi-idiots. Rational living, like all aspects of life, survives as a process, an ongoing attempt, an experiment. Hardly as a product or a final result!

Stated differently: Adults often tend to act in an immature, childish manner. That remains one of the essences of their humanity: fallibility. Because they behave so fallibly, they find it exceptionally easy to display careless thinking, devout religiosity, and other kinds of prejudice that make them have inappropriate affects.

But the fact that humans find it *easy* to behave childishly does not mean that they *must*. They *can* teach themselves to display mature, reflective thinking. If they do, they will hardly reach the state of complete happiness, or thorough lack of sorrow and disappointmont.

They can, nonetheless, with much work and effort, train themselves never—well, practically never—to feel desperately miserable or depressed for any sustained period of time. What more can one reasonably ask?

10 TACKLING DIRE NEEDS FOR APPROVAL

Several powerful, irrational, and illogical ideas stand in the way of your leading an anxiety-free, unhostile life. One of these, which we shall label Irrational Idea No. 1, comprises *the idea that you must*—yes, *must*—have love or approval from all the people you find significant.

"But," you may quickly interject, "do not most psychologists keep insisting that humans *need* approval and that they cannot live happily without it?"

Yes, they do. Wrongly! Humans strongly *desire* approval and would feel much *less* happy if they received *none* of it. In modern society, moreover, most people could hardly survive if they did not get *some* approval. For otherwise who would rent or sell them living quarters, provide them with food, or furnish them with clothing?

Nonetheless, adults do not *need* approval. In its strict definition, *need* derives from the Middle English word *nede*, the Anglo-Saxon *nead*, and the Indo-European term *nauto*—which mean to collapse with weariness (seen also in the Gothic term *naus*, or corpse). In English it mainly means: necessity; compulsion; obligation; something requisite for life and happiness.

Since humans *can* live in isolation without dying or even feeling terribly unhappy, and since they *can* live in a social group without disturbing themselves because the members of this group do not like them, obviously *some* persons do not *need* acceptance. Indeed, a few individuals do not even *want* love. But most men and women *do* want some kind of approval, when they defensively contend they do not. They prefer or desire acceptance and tend to feel happier when they obtain some measure of the approval they seek. But wants, preferences, and desires do not constitute needs or necessities. We would *like* our cravings fulfilled; but we do not really *need* this.

Considerable confusion in regard to human needs has arisen in psychological writings because the requirements of children and adults have got confounded. Children, for fairly obvious reasons, seem to need succoring, especially from their parents, to thrive healthfully and happily. Not that they will necessarily wither away when disapproved or unloved. For as Harold Orlansky, Lili Peller, William Sewell, Lawrence Casler, and other psychological and sociological writers have shown, they will not. But they *literally* depend on others and cannot find food, clothing, shelter, and health protection if no adult *cares* for them.

Children, again, cannot too easily protect themselves against the verbal criticism of others. If their companions and caretakers keep telling them they have no worth, they cannot easily say to themselves: "Who cares what *they* think? I know my life has value." Children suggestibly *accept* the negative views of others about themselves and often psychologically maim themselves by this acceptance.

Adults, however, *need* not act as children. If others around them do not care for them, they can usually manage somehow to shift for themselves and beg, borrow, or steal subsistence. And if others savagely criticize or reject them, they can stop and ask themselves, "*Why* did Jones say I have no worth? What motive does he or she have? How accurate do his or her observations prove?"

Even when adults agree that Jones correctly criticizes their behavior, they can still protect themselves against this attack by noting several things, including:

1. "Well, maybe Jones finds my traits pretty bad and therefore will not befriend me, but Smith and Rogers seem to like my ways well enough. So I can associate with them if Jones won't have me."

2. "Perhaps Jones and Smith do not like the way I do things; and perhaps they correctly assess my inefficiency. But I *still* think my way best and most enjoyable for me, and I would rather enjoy myself than do things the way they would like me to do."

3. "Maybe Jones and Smith correctly believe I speak badly, and maybe I would find it advantageous if I learned to talk better. In case I never talk well, however, I need not consider myself worthless—but merely a person who talks poorly."

4. "Perhaps Jones and Smith correctly see that I don't understand music. Why not admit to them, then, that I don't and see if they will help me understand it better. But if they see me as a

rotten person because of my musical (or other) deficiencies, they overgeneralize about me, and I do not have to take their over-generalizing seriously."

In many ways such as these, an adult may accept the dis-approval of others, make allowances for it, do something about it, and come off relatively unscathed. He may never learn to *like* disapprobation or negative criticism; but he may definitely learn to *tolerate* it and to *use* it for his own good.

Take Earl Thames, an unusually intelligent man of forty-five. He devoted a great deal of his energies, as he indicated when I (R.A.H.) saw him for psychotherapy, to gaining the love of others.

His widowed mother had praised him, indulged him, and led him to believe that he had such special and wonderful talents that he deserved the very best in life. Because he had considerable ability and charm, he found it easy to get the same kind of admir-ation from his classmates, teachers, and (later on) business asso-ciates. *At first!*

The trouble came later. After first winning their approval, Earl would find that people—of course—had other things to do in life than to continue telling him how lovely he behaved. Their initial enthusiasm for him would wane. Whereupon, feeling des-perately rejected, he would come around waving some new ac-complishment, witticism, or sacrifice to jog their tiring devo-tions. These sacrifices at the altar of love, when they worked at all, also had short-lived effects. In time, people felt too tired, busy, or (eventually) plain bored with Earl to give him the sort of effusive appreciation that his mother had endlessly be-stowed. When he noticed this, he would go into a rage, roundly condemn them for their stupidity and inhumanity, and run off to acquire a new and presumably more appreciative set of friends.

Between the ages of twenty-five and forty, Earl didn't do so badly with his field-running and managed to go through three wives and innumerable business and personal associates. Then Mama died, leaving him a considerable fortune, and he began to fail worse than ever in business and to drink heavily. He ran through most of his money in highly speculative deals and approval-seeking philanthropies. In the past, when other people withheld approval or things went wrong in any way, he always had Mama to help him and reassure him that he *had* great talents. Now he had nothing but the anesthetic provided by alcohol.

When a physician who specializes in the treatment of alco-holics referred Earl for therapy, he put on one of his typical charm dances for me. Even when desperately seeking help, he knew not how to relate in any other way. Believing fully and intensely that he *must* have, that he absolutely *needed*, approval, he applied the same standards to me as to the others and did his boyish handsprings in precisely the same manner that he had done them for almost forty years.

Some psychotherapists would doubtless have reacted to Earl's help-seeking dance just the way he wanted, and could have mightily striven to give this pitiful middle-aged man exactly the love he "needed." For the next five to ten years they might have coddled and suckled him to make him feel "really" wanted and approved, believing he would finally get over his desperate demands for approval and stand on his own two feet. I doubt whether they would ever have succeeded. For Earl seemed a bottomless pit who would accept all possible degrees of caring and keep demanding more.

My psychotherapeutic view and reaction radically differed. Feeling that to give Earl more approval would only serve to reinforce his silly notion that he direly *needed* it, I gave him nothing of the sort. Instead, I determinedly told him the facts of life, strongly insisted that he did *not* need approval and *could* live without it, and ruthlessly exposed to him the sad results of his campaign of the last two decades to con others into caring.

Earl fought hard. He quoted psychological scripture to indicate that he did need approval. He got the physician who referred him to pressure me for not treating him gently enough. He kept threatening to leave therapy and go back to the bottle. He pulled every stop on the organ to show me my heartlessness and how I would, doubtless, delight in exploiting helpless widows and orphans. No sale. I remained adamant. On one occasion I said:

"No use! It won't work. Maybe I act heartlessly. Maybe I beat my wife every night and take candy from little babies. If so, that constitutes my problem. *Your* problem remains that you still think you *need* love when, like most of us, you *want* it. And you think you need it because helpless you can't take care of yourself without it. Well, you *do* act the slob. Because you *believe* you must have love, *think* that it and it alone will save you from slobbery worse than death.

"Well, it won't. I wish I could really get someone in your own life—not me, but someone *you* live with—to love you the way you insist they must love you—just to show you that it *won't* work. For you'd still, under those conditions, feel slobbish. Not having done anything for *yourself* in life, you'd never prove that you *could* help yourself and you'd still feel helpless.

"But the hard and cold fact remains, whether you like it or not, that you'll probably never get anyone to love you the way you demand. And even if you did, you'd then feel afraid that he or she might later die, or leave you, or love you less than before—so you'd still feel terribly anxious and upset. No, you have one main solution to your problem—to give up the idea that you *must* have approval to deem yourself worthy of happiness. And if you refuse to give up this idea, you'll merely go on drinking, running your affairs into the ground, and doing other things that terribly anxious people do.

"So choose! Either keep thinking that you must have love—and defeat yourself royally. Or start believing that, however nice you find it to have others approve you, you do not *need* this. You'll then have a chance to rebuild your bollixed-up existence."

Earl remained a difficult client; and it took many more sessions to help him choose between his dire need for love and effective living. It took hard work, but we (he and I) made it. At last report, two years after I first saw him, he no longer drinks steadily, manages his business affairs well, and for the first time in his life has found a woman whom *he* loves rather than one who merely cares *for him*.

Didn't Earl Thomas constitute an extreme case of an individual who "needed" love and approval? Yes, somewhat extreme. He sharply and accurately illustrated the love-"need" theme that runs through the lives of millions of people. Even when these people experience this "need" in a less extreme form, it causes them considerable misery.

Why does anyone who insists that he or she must have approval act irrationally? For several reasons:

1. To demand that virtually everyone you consider important love you sets up a perfectionistic, unattainable goal. If you get ninety-nine people to love you, there will always remain the hundredth, the hundred and first, and so on.

2. Even if you demand love from a limited number of people, you cannot usually win the approval of all of them. Some of those whose love you seek will, because of their own limitations, have little ability to love anyone. Others will disapprove of you for reasons entirely beyond your control (such as the fact that you have brown eyes instead of blue). Still others will feel prejudiced against you forever because of some initial mistake you made, or for various other reasons.

3. Once you absolutely "need" love, you tend to worry about *how much* and *how long* desired individuals will approve you. Granted that your second cousin or your boss cares for you, does he really love you *enough?* And if he does, will he *continue* to love you tomorrow and the day or year after? With thoughts like these, your anxieties about love seem endless!

4. If you *always* need love, you must always appear distinctly lovable. But who fills this requirement? Even when you usually have lovable traits (such as a sweet disposition) how can you retain them at all times for all people?

5. If you could, theoretically, always win the approval of those whose love you "need," you would have to spend so much time and energy doing so that you would have no time for other

pursuits. Striving ceaselessly for approval means living your life for what *others* think and want you to do rather than for your *own* goals. It also usually means playing the patsy and buying others' approval at the expense of selling short your own desires and values.

6. Ironically enough, the greater your need for love, the less people will tend to respect and care for you. Even though they like your catering to them, they may despise your weakness and cease to find you admirable. Also, by desperately trying to win people's approval, you may tend to annoy and irritate them, to bore them to distraction, and again appear less desirable.

7. Feeling loved, once you achieve it, tends to seem boring and onerous, since the individual who loves you often makes inroads on your time and energy. Actively loving someone else constitutes a creative and absorbing act. But the dire need for love seriously blocks loving and minimizes its experiences. Perversely, it sabotages loving, since most individuals who demand intense and sustained love have little time and energy to devote to the growth and development of those on whom they make their demands.

8. The dire need for love almost always has as a concomitant or as a cover-up your own feelings of worthlessness. You keep telling yourself, when you have this dire need: "I must have love, because I remain a rotten, incompetent individual who cannot possibly get along in this world by fending for myself. Therefore, I *must* have, I *need*, succoring and caring from others." By desperately seeking love in this manner, you frequently cover up your own underlying feelings of worthlessness and thereby do nothing to tackle them and overcome them. The more you "succeed" in this seemingly benign but actually nefarious goal of having to feel greatly loved, the less you will tend to eliminate this goal. You will then continue to indoctrinate yourself with the nutty idea that you *cannot* regulate your own life and that you *cannot* get more of what *you* really want.

In view of the foregoing reasons, you can intelligently or rationally approach living by forgoing the goal of gaining complete or inordinate love from practically everyone you consider desirable. Instead, you'd better *accept yourself* (try to discover your *own* fundamental desires and values) and remain vitally absorbed in various people, things, and ideas *outside* yourself. For, paradoxically, you usually find yourself by losing yourself in outside pursuits and not by merely contemplating your own navel.

The Zen Buddhist and other meditational solutions to this problem encourage you to give up the dire need for others' approval (and for earthly satisfactions) and, instead, to concentrate on feeling at one with the universe. By meditating on merging with the universe (and not *needing* "yourself" or *needing* great love, you may temporarily feel very relaxed and peaceful. But this "solution" to life's problems has limitations because (1) it lasts temporarily; (2) it artificially involves the surrender of your selfhood and individuality (for do you ever really merge with the universe, or it with you?); (3) it encourages delusionary thinking, such as, "Now I understand the secret of it all," when no one really holds any "secret of it all"; (4) it discourages you from finding more elegant solutions to your problem, and especially from giving up all disturbance-creating awfulizing, demonizing, and from looking for magical panaceas.

So-called transpersonal psychology, in other words, seems a matter of throwing out the baby with the bathwater: an attempt to get rid of your problems by getting rid of yourself, your unique you-ness. We espouse, instead, a highly personal and to a large degree individualistic philosophy: to find out what *you* really want to do in life and to do your damnedest to do it. And you can largely do that by first minimizing the notions that you *need* others' approval or that others' goodwill has no importance *at all.*

Your accepting yourself and devoting yourself to outside activities may constitute reciprocal goals. For if you really follow your own basic bents and do not overly concern yourself about what others think of you, you will have so little time to spend in self-centered worrying that you will feel virtually forced to find absorbing interests on the outside. By the same token, if you throw your energies into outside activities and actively devote yourself to other people and things, you normally will tend to feel less concerned about what others think of you and, hence, to respect your own values.

Put somewhat differently, if you devote yourself enthusiastically to long-range hedonism—to activities that you consider desirable and enjoyable from a long-term perspective—you will clearly accept yourself because you do what you really want to do and do not falsely follow what someone else thinks you *should* do.

Our clients and associates frequently ask: "I can see that accepting myself rather than desperately needing the love of others constitutes a more realistic orientation. But how will this help me love other people? As I less and less concern myself about whether others approve of me, won't I find it more and more troublesome and unnecessary to give a damn about them—to relate lovingly to them?"

No, for several reasons. First of all, if you direly *need* love, you will feel so preoccupied with obtaining it that you have as much chance to honor your own choices or to love others as a dope addict has to relate freely and self-confidently to the person who supplies him with drugs.

Secondly, if you surrender your dire need for love, you will still retain, in most instances, a strong *desire* for acceptance by others. People often wrongly assume that your not direly needing love means the same thing as your feeling love has no value. Not at all. You can easily enjoy well-written stories and plays even though you have no *need* to do so. Why can you not, then, *enjoy* and *seek* intimate relationships without believing that your life depends on them?

Thirdly, when you free yourself from your *demands* that you receive love, you can better love. You can see more clearly the lovable traits of others; stop hating them when they do not immediately respond to you; learn what you really enjoy in a relationship; risk committing yourself to loving, even when you know that a given affair may not work out well; and feel unanxiously free to experience and experiment with loving because you realize that although you may lose your beloved you can never lose *yourself.*

Another frequently asked question: "Granted that loving has more rewards than desperately needing love, should I therefore give up all my desires for approval and recognition?"

Answer: Certainly not. Complete self-sacrifice or the total surrender of your own desires for approval can prove just as foolish as your obsession with winning the esteem of others. Again for several reasons:

1. You act quite normally when you *want* to express your own unique conceptions of the world to others and *want* them to take pleasure in some of your expressions. You would hardly seem *human* if you did not derive some satisfaction from relating to others.

2. Wanting acceptance from others constitutes one of the main essences of desire; and men and women entirely free from desire again do not appear entirely human. According to the Hindu classic the Bhagavad-Gita, the strongest individual "has indifference to honor and insult, heat and cold, pleasure and pain. He feels free from attachment." A few select individuals may find this a worthy ideal. But we doubt whether many humans could ever attain it. To lean so far over backwards to get rid of psychological pain that you also eradicate all pleasure does not seem too rational to us. By all means try, if you will, to eliminate your extreme, unrealistic, self-defeating desire; but not desire itself!

3. From a practical view, if you ardently want various things—such as material goods or more leisure—you had better win the approval or respect of *certain* people such as your parents, teachers, or bosses. Though you may wisely eliminate your inordinate demands that others love you, you'd better sanely retain, in any social group, *some* wishes for acceptance by other group members.

Granted that having an inordinate need for others' love will serve to defeat your own ends, and that having *some* wish for acceptance seems eminently sane, the question arises: How can you somehow manage to attain a middle-of-the-road policy in this respect?

First and foremost, by admitting that you do have a dire need for love in many instances; by making a continual effort to *observe* this need in operation; and by then continually *challenging, questioning,* and *disputing* it.

A good illustration of combating one's own inordinate love needs came up recently in a group therapy session. Three young women in the group brought up their woeful unhappiness because their husbands did not continually love them. Whenever they noted lack of love, one of them habitually felt depressed; the second got angry at her husband and the whole world; and the third woman started looking around for possible lovers.

All these women, after talking over their problems with the other group members, admitted that they had a tremendous love need. One of them asked the group: "All right. Now what can I do to get over my love needs and keep myself from feeling depressed when they do not always get met?"

One of the males chimed in: "Oh, easily! You merely have to see what you do to keep annoying your husband and stop doing these things. Then he will appreciate you and care for you much more than he does—especially if you act nicely to him when he acts badly to you."

"Oh, no," chimed in the one who got angry whenever her husband didn't show great love for her, "that won't solve the problem at all. If you only act nicer to those who do not love you, even if you succeed in winning more love, you don't do anything for *yourself.* You still go on *needing,* or thinking you need, their love. And just as soon as they don't give it again, you land right back in the soup, just where you started. So that plan won't work at all."

"Right," said the one who had asked the question. "I've tried that many times, and often have succeeded in getting Johnny to show more love by acting very nice to him. But it doesn't last. He still doesn't love me *all* the time. And then I go right back into my dive. I agree with Phyllis that that plan won't work at all."

"I can see what you mean," said the male who had answered the first woman. "I guess I said the wrong thing. Getting a better technique to induce people to love you won't do the trick. You've got to not need them."

"What do you mean?" another male member of the group asked. "How can you not need others?"

The first male smiled. "A good question! I don't think I can answer it."

"Well, let me try," said the second woman. "You stop telling yourself that you *do* need others—right?"

"Can you put that more specifically?" asked still another group member.

"I think I can," she replied. "Let's see. I told you before that whenever my husband looks at me cross-eyed, I tend to shrivel up and die—and then I get very angry at him. And sometimes, as Mabel said in regard to her husband, I even start looking around for other men, though I know I won't really do anything about them. But strike out that 'whenever.' I *used* to feel 'whenever.' I'd *always* die at first, and then feel terribly angry when Jim gave me a dirty look or otherwise indicated he didn't love me at the exact second I wanted his love. But now it only happens once in a while. I find it much better now."

"And what did you do to make it better?" asked the first woman.

"Oh, yes. I nearly got lost there. I started out to say that I used to go through hell every time Jim didn't come through with the ever-lovin' spouse bit. But then, when he obviously didn't give much of a damn for me at certain times, and I began to feel my gorge rise, I started saying to myself: 'All right. So he doesn't love me dearly right at this minute. So what? Will the world come to an end? Do I really *need* his adoration and devotion every second of the day? Of course I don't! Sure, I would find it *nice* if he always cared, whenever I really wanted him. But why can't I live happily when he doesn't care? Goddamn it, I can!' And I found that I could. Not always, unfortunately. As I said before, I still at times get angry as hell when he doesn't immediately pat me on the head when I think I need it. But much less often than I used to get. And, by God, I intend to make it still much less in the future!"

"In other words," said the first male, "you now keep disputing and challenging your dire need for love, not all of the time, but at least often enough. Do you keep reducing it that way?"

"Yes," she replied. "I find it one heck of a hassle. But I keep challenging and questioning."

And so you can, too. If you do have a dire need for love; if you accept the fact that you have it; and if you keep challenging, questioning, and disputing it, it will ultimately, and often quite quickly, start decreasing. For remember: It remains *your* need; and *you* keep sustaining it.

Other methods you can use to combat and minimize your inordinate love needs include the following:

1. Ask yourself what *you* really want to do, rather than what *others* would like you to do. And keep asking yourself, from time to time: "Do I keep doing this or refusing to do that because *I* really want it that way? Or do I, once again, unthinkingly keep trying to please others?"

2. In going after what you really want, take risks, commit yourself, don't desperately avoid making mistakes. Don't act needlessly foolhardy; but convince yourself that if you fail to get something you want and people laugh at or criticize you for your

failure, *they* may have a problem. As long as *you* learn by your errors, does it make that much difference what *they* think?

3. Focus on loving rather than on getting love. Try to realize that vital living hardly consists of passive receiving but of doing, acting, reaching out. And just as you can force yourself to play the piano, do yoga exercises, or go to work every day, you can also often forcibly commit yourself to loving other humans. In so doing, your dire needs for love will probably decrease.

4. Above all, don't confuse getting love with having personal worth. If you must see yourself as having any intrinsic worth or value as a human (which we would not advise, since we think that *any* kind of self-rating, positive or negative, tends to bring pernicious results), you'd better claim to have it by virtue of your mere existence, your aliveness, your essence—and not because of anything you do to "earn" it. No matter how much others approve you, or how much they may value you for their own benefit, they thereby can only give you, as Robert S. Hartman explains, extrinsic value, or worth to them. They cannot, by loving you, give you intrinsic value—or the worth you have to yourself. If intrinsic value exists at all (which we seriously doubt, since it seems a well-nigh undefinable Kantian thing-in-itself), you get it because you *choose*, you *decide* to have it. It exists purely because of your own *definition.* You emerge as "good" or "deserving" because you *think* you do and not because anyone in any way gives you this kind of intrinsic value.

If you can really believe this highly important truth—that you need not rate yourself, your essence at all (and that you can choose to *call yourself* intrinsically worthwhile just because you decide to do so)—you will tend to lose your desperate need for others' approval. For you need—or *think* you need—their acceptance not because of the practical advantages it may bring, but because you foolishly *define* your worth as a human in terms of receiving or not receiving it. Once you stop this kind of silly defining, the dire need for their approval generally evaporates (though the strong desire to have them like you may well remain). Similarly, if you rid yourself of your dire need for approval, you will find it relatively easy to stop rating yourself as a person, even though you continue to rate many of your traits, and to *accept* yourself merely because you remain alive and kicking—and for that reason alone "deserve" to continue to exist and to have a maximally enjoyable life.

To underscore this last point about human worth, consider the case of Herbert Flisch, a forty-year-old successful businessman who recognized, after eight sessions of rational-emotive therapy, that almost every single one of his actions for the past four decades had stemmed from his dire need to win the approval of his parents, wife, children, friends, and even employees. At his ninth session he asked:

"Do I understand you correctly to mean that if I stop trying to win everyone's approval and do what *I* think I would like to do (and what would not at the same time defeat my own ultimate ends) that I'll then love myself because I'll consider myself more worthwhile?"

"No," the therapist replied. "Those of us who have worked to develop this system of rational-emotive psychotherapy have come to realize that *worthwhileness* proves just as illegitimate a concept as its counterpart, *worthlessness;* and that, in fact, just as soon as you tend to think in terms of personal 'worth' you must almost automatically tend to think, at the same time, in terms of personal 'worthlessness.'

"Thus, if you consider yourself 'worthwhile' today because you function effectively, make wise decisions, or think bright thoughts, you'll tend to consider yourself 'worthless' tomorrow because you then function less effectively, make some unwise decisions, or think dull thoughts."

"But *wouldn't* I have no worth if I never functioned effectively?" asked the client.

"No, definitely not. Even if you had mental deficiency and never functioned well, you would then have no extrensic 'worth'— meaning that *others* might not find you a suitable companion or employee—but you could have, intrinsically, as much 'worth' to yourself as any other more efficient individual. You would have 'worth,' in other words, if you believed you had. But if you believed, as you obviously do, that inefficiency makes you 'worthless,' you would then feel exactly that."

"So I remain worthwhile if I think I do—no matter how inefficiently I may actually perform in life?"

"Yes—except that, as I said before, the very concept of 'worth' has dangers, since it implies the concept of 'worthlessness.' Just like the concept of heaven implies the concept of hell. In fact, the way we usually employ the terms, to have 'worth' really means pretty much the same thing as to behave angelically or heaven-directed; and to have 'worthlessness' means to behave demonically or hell-directed. Doesn't it?"

"In a way, I guess it does. I can see what you mean," said the client.

"Moreover, if you have the concepts of 'worth' and 'worthlessness,' even if you avoid extreme self-designations in using these concepts, you will tend to remain preoccupied with varying degrees of 'worth.' Thus, you will tend to say to yourself: "Today I have *great* worth; yesterday I had *less;* I hope and pray tomorrow I can have *more.'*

"This kind of concept of 'worth' (and, hence, of lack of worth or less worth) carries with it irrational and undesirable aspects of guilt, self-disrespect, self-blame, shame, anger, hostility, and other self-sabotaging emotions. The counter-concept, that you have neither 'worth' because of your effectiveness nor 'worthlessness' because of your ineffectiveness, but that you merely *exist*, this concept, difficult as it seems for almost all people to see and accept, safely eliminates the notion of intrinsic 'worthlessness' and self-damnation."

"I'll have to give this some more thought," said the client. "But it does seem to have something to it. However, how does it tie in with self-acceptance?"

"It has a most important tie-in with self-acceptance. For self-acceptance means fully accepting yourself, your existence, and your right to live and to devise as happy a life as you can for yourself—no matter *what* traits you have or performances you do. It does not mean self-esteem, self-confidence, self-respect, or self-regard. For all these terms imply that you can accept yourself *because* you do something well or because other people like you. Self-acceptance, however, merely means that you accept yourself because you remain alive and have *decided* to accept yourself. Only a relatively limited number of talented, intelligent, competent, or well-loved people can gain self-esteem or self-confidence. But anyone, merely because he chooses to have it, can gain self-acceptance."

"Does self-acceptance mean that I consider myself worthy or deserving of living and enjoying no matter *what* I do?"

"Yes, though we don't like the words *worthy* or *deserving*, since they imply a rating—that you have to *do* (or refrain from *doing*) something in order to feel 'worthy' or 'deserving.' When you have what we call self-acceptance, you make *minimal* assumptions about your (and other people's) intrinsic worth or value."

"What minimal assumptions?"

"Several: One, you exist. Two, you can probably, by continuing to exist, achieve more pleasure than pain, thus making it desirable for you to keep living. Three, to a considerable degree, you can help minimize your pain and maximize your pleasure. Four, you decide—and this constitutes the essence of self-acceptance—that you will try to live and make your existence as pleasurable and as unpainful as you can make it. Or, putting it another way, you choose as the main purpose of your existence short-range (here and now) *and* long-range (future) enjoyment. Not achieving for the sake of achieving. Not receiving adoration from others. Not proving your greatness as a person. Not getting into heaven. Just plain damned enjoyment!"

"So instead of my continuing to ask myself, 'What worth have I?' 'How do I keep proving myself?' 'How can I outstandingly impress others?' or 'What do I have to do to ennoble myself?' I'd better, instead, ask, 'How the devil can I avoid needless pain and find out what I truly enjoy in life and do it?' Right?"

"Exactly right! You *make* the purpose of your existence having a present and future ball—in whatever idiosyncratic and harmless ways *you* experimentally discover."

"You mean that I may then enjoy myself and accept myself and my existence as more enjoyable. But that I still will not really exist as more 'worthwhile'—only more alive, happier?"

"Right. And you will not, we hope, blame yourself or punish yourself whenever—as an imperfect human—you do something wrong or unwise. You will accept yourself with your foolish thoughts, feelings, perceptions, or actions, and use the experience that you get as a result of these unwise acts to help you enjoy yourself and behave more rationally in the future. What greater acceptance of self (and through that, potential acceptance of and tolerance for other humans) could you then have?"

11 ERADICATING DIRE
FEARS OF FAILURE

If you only overwhelm yourself with dire love needs, you will create sufficient woe to last you a lifetime. If you wish to feel even sorrier, you can easily add one more idiotic notion—namely, Irrational Idea No. 2: *The idea that you must prove thoroughly competent, adequate, and achieving,* or a saner but still foolish variation: *The idea that you at least must have competence or talent in some important area.*

Several of our clients beautifully—and tragically—have exemplified the extreme fear of failure and of incompetence that commonly assails people who believe these ideas. Client No. 1, a brilliant and talented woman, very proficient in solo activities, such as writing and composing music, refused to take part in any group experiences, for fear she would not come off as well as the other group members. In her writing and composing, moreover, she rarely put anything down on paper, but restricted herself to composing in her head: so that she need not take the risk of committing herself fully.

Client No. 2, an exceptionally bright woman, feared she could not hold a suitable conversation with the guests at her own house parties, and usually clammed up and said virtually nothing during the whole evening. At other people's gatherings, however, where she did not have the responsibility of a hostess, she conversed very well.

Client No. 3, a twenty-five-year-old physicist, never realized satisfaction when he had sex relations, since he concentrated only on how to prove his capability to his partner. If he had a second orgasm on the same evening, he could enjoy that immensely—because he then felt his adequacy proven.

Client No. 4, a thirty-year-old teacher, felt anxious that if she went out on a date someone might insult her and her date would not defend her adequately from such an insult. If this happened (which, of course, never did) she felt she would suffer horrible humiliation and would sink through the floor.

Client No. 5 felt afraid to think for himself during the therapeutic sessions: because *that*, like so many other things he had tried, might end in failure and he might not think too well. Therefore, he did not work at his therapy.

These examples, typical of hundreds of individuals we have seen, represent people fearful of failing at some task or goal, who usually manage to avoid trying for what they want because they construe failure as the worst of all possible crimes. And we see so many of these people not only because they come to us for help, but because so many of them exist in every walk of life. Just glance around you and you will soon see!

The notion that humans have value proportional to their accomplishments, and that if they lack competence or adequacy, they might as well curl up and die, includes several irrationalities:

1. Obviously, *virtually nobody* can prove competent and masterful in most respects and almost *no one* can display perfect adequacy and achievement. Even Leonardo da Vinci had many weak points, and certainly the rest of us mortals, including the authors of this book, do! Trying to achieve outstandingness in *one* field of endeavor remains difficult, since millions of individuals compete with you in the same area. And your goal of behaving *generally* successfully has perfectionistic elements that doom you to serious disappointment.

2. Achievement does not, except by arbitrary definition, relate to your intrinsic worth. If you *think* yourself "better" or "greater" because you succeed at something, you may temporarily feel "worthier." But you actually do not change your intrinsic value one iota by your successes; nor do you lower your I-ness by your failures. You may achieve greater happiness or more efficiency by achieving this or that goal. But feeling "better off" does not make you a "better person." You emerge as "good," "worthwhile," or "deserving," if you want to use these poor terms, simply because you exist, because you have aliveness. To raise your "ego" by material or other achievements really means *falsely* to think yourself "better" than you previously proved. Most of what we call "pride" in accomplishment actually amounts to false pride: the silly belief that you have no worth unless you have accomplished, and the equally silly belief that because you have accomplished you have value as a person.

3. Technically, you "are" not any particular thing. D. David

Bourland, Jr., a student of general semantics, points out that whenever you use any form of the verb "to be," you speak incorrectly. You "are" not a butcher, baker, or candlestick maker. You "are" only, if anything, a human individual who *practices* these various kinds of occupations—but who also practices many other things. I, Albert Ellis, "am" not a psychologist—since, although I spend a good deal of my time *doing* psychological work, I also spend a considerable part of it writing, speaking, traveling around the country giving workshops, seminars, and marathons. I, Robert A. Harper, also "am" not a psychologist—since I, in addition to practicing psychology, garden, run in the woods with my dog, spend a considerable part of my most enjoyable time with my wife, Mimi, read, write, travel, give public talks, and do various other things.

To identify, much less to rate your*self* according to your performance of some particular human activity, tends to create the illusion that you, a person, have only as much worth as that activity. And how much sense does that make?

4. Although accomplishment may bring you considerable advantages, fanatic devotion to the bitch-goddess success usually involves discomfort as well. Those hell-bent on achievement commonly push themselves beyond their limits of physical endurance; tolerate or invite painful conditions that they might avoid if not so determined to succeed; and rarely give themselves sufficient time to relax and enjoy what they do, nor time to lead better-rounded existences. They also may literally kill themselves with overwork. If they really *enjoy* working more than most other people do, fine; let them create sixteen hours a day—as I, Albert Ellis, prefer to do but as I, Robert A. Harper, rarely prefer.

5. The frantic struggle for achievement usually reflects a dire need to excel *others*, to show that you act as well as or better than they do. But you remain you, and you will not exist as "yourself" (do what *you* largely like to do) if you *must* excel others. What have the others really got to do with you? If they have inferior traits, does that make you by one whit a better *person*? And if they excel you in this or that performance, does that make you a louse or a nogoodnick? Only by magical notions in your head do others relate to your you-ness. If you think, shamanistically, that your "worth" as a human depends on how well your traits shape up and compare to those of others, you will practically always feel insecure and "worthless." You will act other-directedly and divorced from what *you* might want to do with your one earthly existence. You will believe self-flagellating statements, such as: "I accept and enjoy myself only *if* I do as well as or better than others do."

6. If you inordinately strive for success and feel anxious about failing, you will fear taking chances, making mistakes, doing

the wrong thing, or doing many things you would really like to do. By insisting on outstanding achievement, you will leave yourself the pitifully narrow choices of (a) making mistakes and feeling depressed about them, or (b) refusing to try to do things for fear of making mistakes and feeling self-hating about them. Having an unrealistically high level of aspiration foredooms you not only to failure but to fear of failing—which often has more pernicious effects than failure itself.

One of the most common and most gruesome illustrations of the fear of failure proving worse than failure itself shows up in clients with impotency and frigidity problems. As we have noted in other books (including *The Art and Science of Love*, *Creative Marriage*, and *The Sensuous Person*), you can first fail sexually for a number of reasons, including fatigue, illness, worry about some unrelated problem, lack of attraction to the sexual partner, or fear of pregnancy. Frequently, however, you may develop a deep-seated feeling of inadequacy and tell yourself, once you first fail, "I shall probably keep failing because I have such basic inadequacy that I cannot possibly succeed."

Whatever the original cause of your sex failure, you may well have many subsequent failures because you *fear* failing. Thus, you may keep saying to yourself: "Oh, my God! I failed the last time and may fail again. How awful, embarrassing, and calamitous if my mate sees me repeatedly ineffective!"

If you approach sex with such an awfulizing and catastrophizing philosophy, you may frequently find yourself impotent or frigid. First of all, you focus on your fears about your inadequacy rather than on sexually satisfying stimuli. Secondly, and worse still, you specifically indoctrinate yourself with the idea that you probably will *not* respond. You thereby fill yourself with dread about the very situation to which you want to respond in a relaxed, erotic, enjoyable way. This seems like sending ice water instead of warm blood to your genitals!

More generally, you can make yourself impotent or incompetent in almost *any* respect if you keep *demanding* that you succeed. One of my (A.E.'s) clients seemed to have a natural ability for athletics when a child, and played ball better than any of the other kids on his block. But when he began to compare himself to older and even more talented athletes, he got so worried about hitting and pitching that he lost all interest in the game of baseball and stopped playing it entirely. As he did the same thing in other areas, he eventually felt afraid to try almost anything new, and by the time he came to see me (in his early thirties), he had no real interest in anything and believed he could never get absorbed in any physical or mental pursuit.

For more details of an extreme example of fear of failure, let me (R.A.H.) cite a case from my files, that of a thirty-four-year-old office manager who kept losing his erection. He said:

"I know that my fear of failure causes impotence, but how can I *help* feeling afraid? I *don't* want to fail. And I *do* think failure awful. I do feel inadequate when I try to have intercourse with Janie and can't even make an entry. I do think it *terrible*, so how can I tell myself otherwise?"

"But let's look at why you call it *terrible*," I replied. "You have already told me that you can satisfy Janie by clitoral manipulation and that she seems relaxed and happy after achieving orgasm by this means. Right?"

"Yes. But what about *me*? Where do I get *my* satisfaction?"

"Just a moment; we'll get to you soon enough. Anyway, the 'dreadfulness' of your impotency, as you can see, relates to your failure to have complete satisfaction through intercourse. Correct?"

"Well, not quite. I don't like to have Janie think of me as impotent. And, damn it, I don't like to think of *myself* that way."

"Ah, so we have more than your merely regretting the loss of your own satisfaction. You seem to tell yourself: 'Here I keep missing out on all the fun and satisfaction of sex and what a damned pain in the neck!' And your statement seems true or empirically validatable, since you *do* miss out on a good thing. But you also add the highly false sentences: 'Janie will doubtless think me a pansy or something. And maybe I do have latent homosexuality! And wouldn't that prove terrible! What an awful mess I remain.' Do you keep telling yourself something along those lines?"

"Just about that."

"Well, then don't you have a fairly obvious solution to your problem?"

"Uh—well, I guess so. Stop saying the false sentences and keep telling myself only the true ones. Correct?"

"Exactly. Stop telling yourself how *awful*, how *horrible* you would find it if you failed sexually, and how that would make you into a homosexual—which again you'd call *terrible*. And go back to the true sentence—that you keep missing much of the joy of sex—and work on correcting this sentence by focusing on your wife and how much pleasure you can find with her."

"But what will I tell Janie, while I work on this? Shall I discuss it with her, too?"

"By all means. The next time you and Janie decide to get together sexually, tell her something like this: 'Look, dear. My therapist told me the trouble lies strictly in my head. It consists of nonsense that I keep feeding myself. He says that you and I can take a more indirect approach to this sex business at first, forget coitus as the ultimate end and largely concentrate on having *fun* with each other. We can have a pleasurable experience and not focus upon whether I do or don't have an erection. You caress me in any way that seems fun to you and me, and I'll fondle you in any way that seems enjoyable to both of us. And, as we do already, I'll make sure that you get satisfied in one way or another. Then, he says, if we stop worrying about whether or not I get a good erection, my body will amost certainly take care of itself and soon I'll prove more potent than probably ever before. But the main point: Whether or not I do achieve anything in coitus, we can still enjoy sex immensely. And if we concentrate on that, we can solve most of our problems.'

"Well, I hear what you say and it sounds good. But it also sounds just a little bit crazy. Won't we just kid ourselves, Janie and I, if we say that we don't give a damn whether or not I get an erection?"

"Yes, if you fool yourself into believing that it doesn't matter at all. It does matter somewhat. But it doesn't prove *all-important*, as you keep imagining. As Janie has already demonstrated, she, like practically all women, can have an orgasm even when you do *not* show great prowess sexually. And I feel sure that you, too, can get a great deal of enjoyment when you do not fully realize your potential. Many of my clients, in fact, keep having enjoyable relations even when they don't have actual coitus. Granted that both you and Janie may well enjoy yourself *more* if you have full potency. But you can still greatly satisfy each other when you do not.

"If you stop focusing on the *necessity* of copulating well and look upon doing it as a highly *desirable* thing instead, you will probably soon have satisfactory intercourse. But remember: Don't take this approach insincerely and try to fool yourself that you believe it. It won't work if you falsely say to yourself, 'I will pretend to have fun in other ways since it will help me to get an erection with which I can then have coitus.' Really *convince yourself*, really believe no horror exists if you never have coitus—merely disadvantage and inconvenience."

"So I can show myself that even though I *want* coitus, I don't *need* it. I can convince myself that having *fun*, not copulating, means most in my sex relations with Janie."

"Right. If you focus on trying to have fun, you will almost certainly succeed at copulating. But if you focus on copulating, you may well not have any fun."

After this talk the client had sex with his wife that very night, had a long talk with her along the lines suggested by me, and simply tried to enjoy himself rather than achieve potency. For the first time in years, he not only did enjoy himself, but maintained an erection for twenty minutes and had the most enjoyable copulatory experience of his life.

The method of dealing with sex inadequacy outlined here (and originally developed by us in the 1950's) differs from but also overlaps with the methods pioneered by Masters and Johnson. For Masters and Johnson, as a result of many years of experimental and clinical work with individuals suffering with sex problems, recognize clearly that people mainly develop such problems not because of early childhood training, or guilt about incestuous wishes toward a parent, but because of their fears of failing. An impotent man, for example, usually vests his ego or self-rating in his sexual competency; he continually spies on himself (before, during, and after intercourse) to see how well he performs; and he consequently diverts himself from the real activity at hand—having a sexual ball.

Noting that overfocusing on the horror of failing leads to sexual inadequacy, Masters and Johnson have devised various techniques, particularly what they call the sensate focus, to induce sex partners to concentrate on other things: especially on their own and their partner's physical enjoyment. This works exceptionally well in large numbers of cases; and, trained by a Masters and Johnson-type sex therapist, previously inadequate individuals stop worrying about and start enjoying foreplay, intercourse, and afterplay.

Rational-emotive therapists frequently use the sensate focus approach—especially as detailed in *The American Sexual Tragedy*, which I (A.E.) originally published in 1954, before Masters and Johnson began their researches. But in RET two other approaches, which they and their disciples largely ignore, also come into play. First, the therapist teaches people to deliberately focus on sexually exciting stimuli, if they have difficulty getting aroused or coming to orgasm. Secondly, and more importantly, they learn the usual kind of RET anti-awfulizing: how to fully accept themselves whether or not failure ensues. If, as often happens, they accept this radically different philosophic viewpoint, and learn how to refrain from downing their *selves*, while still fully accepting the fact that their *performance* lacks efficiency, most of their *need* for succeeding disappears, and sex turns much more experimental and enjoyable. At the same time, the therapist helps produce a *general* uprooting of the self-castigation process, so that nonsexual fears of failure also wane, and success in other areas comes about.

The idea that you must have competency and adequacy in all important respects boils down to the notion that you should see yourself as superhuman rather than human; and that if not, you turn into a subhuman—a sort of devil incarnate. We remorselessly propagate this inane idea in our homes, schools, books, newspapers, movies, advertisements, songs, TV shows, and other media. Other cultures, too, have taught their people that they must excel in various ways; but none, perhaps, to the enormous degree to which we teach this nonsense to *our* people.

Although RET often gets falsely accused of having too rational—meaning, too mechanistic or unfeeling—approaches, it remains one of the most humanistic therapies ever invented. For it has as its core philosophy the antidote to the view mentioned in the previous paragraph: it persistently propounds the view that humans exist merely as human. They have no superhuman characteristics; nor do they ever degenerate into subhumans. If you fully—and we mean *fully*—accept your humanity and your fallibility, and if you give up all aspirations to holier-than-thouness, to sit on some God's right hand while the rest of us poor slobs sit on His left hand (or eternally burn in hell), you will have one heck of a time making yourself emotionally disturbed about anything. Only your pigheaded insistence on grandiosity, on demanding that you develop into a better (or more godly) *person* than the rest of us, makes you *have to* succeed at various tasks. And with that *have to* you remain emotionally cooked!

What, instead of believing this kind of balderdash, can you as a thinking and reality-accepting individual believe, and how can you act in regard to competence and achievement?

First of all, you can stress your *doing* rather than your having to do things *perfectly well.* Not that you'll never find it *desirable* to perform well. Often, you will: since by doing so you gain more goods, services, and favors. Fine! But not *necessary.*

Seek enjoyment, then, rather than accomplishment. Often, the two go together: the better you play tennis, the more you may enjoy the game. But if you enjoy *only* what you do well, then you fairly obviously keep saying to yourself (1) "I like this activity because I find it my natural cup of tea," and (2) "I like it because I keep proving how much better I rate than others who perform it."

While (1) emerges as a perfectly legitimate sentence, (2) does not. The "ego-raising" that you obtain from proving superior to others at any activity comes from *false* pride, which stems from the notion that you prove no damned good *unless* you better others' performances. This kind of "ego-raising" will last only as long as you succeed in what you do, and in the last analysis demands perfect performance and absolute superiority over others.

If you would act truly rationally and self-fulfillingly, try to enjoy the *playing* of the game and only incidentally your success at it. Artistically, try to better your *own* performance and don't obsess about outperforming *others.* Accept the fact that you may do well under *some,* but hardly *all* conditions and that even when you accomplish what you set out to do, you won't achieve *perfectly.* Maintain high but not unrealistic levels of aspiration. And if you fail to achieve what you would like, try to feel disappointed but not desolate; regret your failure but do not rate yourself in regard to it.

If you approach the problem of achievement in a rational manner, you will more probably do well than if you desperately *need* to succeed. For you will learn to welcome your mistakes and errors, instead of feeling petrified about them, and to *use* them to improve future trials. You will realize that *practice* more than anything else reduces errors and betters performance. You will also, not fearing error, take more risks and will consequently *try* many tasks that otherwise you would avoid.

If, then, you would like to achieve competence at some project, profession, or activity, and will unblamefully accept yourself in case you make an honest attempt and fail, you will try to do *your* best rather than *the* best, and you will not falsely invest your "ego" in your endeavor. You will honestly strive to win mastery over your material, and perhaps over yourself. But you will not try to prove yourself a better *person*, even though a better *performer*, than others.

A twenty-five-year-old physicist came to see me (R.A.H.) because he felt that he kept failing. Objectively, he kept doing very well and appeared not only normal but supernormal. Not only had he obtained his Ph.D. at an early age but in addition he had played on the college football, baseball, and basketball teams. People considered him tall, muscular, and good-looking. At the age of twenty-five, his colleagues recognized him as one of the country's leading physicists. Here we see an individual who had almost everything—but who felt, nonetheless, terribly unhappy.

"The whole trouble," said the client at one of his early sessions, "lies in my phoniness. I live under false pretenses. And the longer it goes on, the more people praise me and make a fuss over my accomplishments, the worse I feel."

"What do you mean your phoniness?" I asked. "I thought you told me, during our last session, that your work got examined at another laboratory and that some of the people there think your ideas revolutionary. Can these scientists easily fool themselves about you?"

"Oh, that data and my interpretations probably seem sound enough. But I have wasted so much time. I could do so much better! Just this morning I sat in my office, stared into space, and accomplished nothing at all. I do this often. Also, when I actually work on my problems I do not think with the clarity and the precision I should. Just the other day I caught myself making a mistake that a college junior wouldn't have made. And in trying to write my paper for the next meeting of my regional professional organization, I keep taking many hours to do what I should knock out in an hour or two at most."

"Don't you come off too hard on yourself?"

"No, I don't think so. Remember that book I told you I want to write for popular consumption? Why, for three weeks now I've spent no time on it. And this kind of simple stuff I should do with my left hand while I write a technical paper with my right. I have heard that people like Albert Einstein and Robert Oppenheimer could reel off material to newspaper reporters twice as good as what I keep mightily laboring on in this damned book!"

"Perhaps so. And perhaps you don't do quite as well—yet—as a few other outstanding people in your field. But you have the most perfectionistic standards for judging yourself that I've heard in, well, the last few months. And I hear about perfectionism practically every day in the week! But here, at just twenty-five, you have a Ph.D. in a difficult field, an excellent job, much good work in process, and probably a fine professional paper and a good popular book also in progress. And just because you haven't yet reached the level of an Oppenheimer or an Einstein you savagely berate yourself."

"Well, shouldn't I do much better?"

"No, why the devil *should* you? As far as I can see, you already do well. But your major difficulty—the main cause of your present unhappiness—seems your perfectionistic criteria for judging your performance. You pick the *one* physicist, such as Einstein or Oppenheimer, known for truly outstanding communication, and you lament that you don't do as well as he. And you compare yourself, at one relatively uncreative time in your life, with your most furiously creative periods. Studies made of the creative process—of creators such as Oppenheimer, Einstein, Newton, and Rutherford—showed their uneven activity. Nobody, and I mean *nobody*, just steadily creates. In fact, during those periods in which the creator putters, stares out of the window, and apparently just wastes time, he may dredge up and recombine ideas which may develop into his best creations."

"Perhaps. But that does not prove that *my* periods of staring out the window produce masterpieces."

"Right; it doesn't prove that. But let us suppose that you do waste a fair amount of time staring out of the window. What makes that horrible? Why must you act so perfectly, so productively?"

"Well, I need to produce. I need to utilize my genius fully—to stop feeling like a phony."

"Why? Why the hurry? What makes you so compulsive? Suppose you do have great talent—like a potential Newton or Einstein. Must you work perfectly, like some unimaginably wonderful brain machine that turns out the maximum number of brilliant ideas before it stops running? It would seem nice, perhaps, if you did, and might well advance human knowledge. But why *must* you? If you *enjoy* fulfilling your creative potential to the hilt, fine. But this self-berating, this constantly pushing yourself to your absolute utmost limits—do you call *that* enjoyable?"

"So you don't think I owe it to myself or to mankind to make use of my potential productivity?"

"No, I don't. You owe to yourself, if anything, full enjoyment, not just for the moment but for most of your life. And if perfect, maximum productiveness does prove the best manner of long-range enjoyment, fine. But *does* it? Or would you act far wiser—and perhaps in the long run more productively—if you worked *somewhat near* your potential capacity, instead of your striving for *perfect* achievement? And would it not seem better, for both you and society, if you strove for *your* fulfillment as a scientist, rather than, as you fairly obviously strive, for outdoing *others*?"

We had a hard, tough therapeutic battle. But ultimately the client agreed that he strove compulsively for achievement and that he could less desperately try to master his chosen field. As he reported at one of the closing sessions:

"I used to try to do the best I could, as if my life depended on it. Now I still try to finish each of my projects in the best way I know how—but *not* as if I turn into a criminal if I fail. If my *best* doesn't quite measure up, too bad; but I *accept* it as my best. I work more efficiently and enjoy my work more since I stopped giving myself hell. If I can accomplish what I want to do today, I'll do it. If somehow I can't finish, I remember I shall have a to-morrow. And if some of the things I want to do *never* get finished, too bad. As you once said to me, I rate as no goddamn God or angel; and I now really accept my mortal limitations."

Did, through this kind of therapy, potential genius get lost to mankind? Not at all. Since he has begun enjoying himself at his work, this young physicist has made even more outstanding contributions than before. Instead of working less productively, he has done more. What has he lost? His perfectionism and misery.

We most definitely do not oppose mastery and achievement drives. People with excellent brain cells feel impelled to use their heads to create new, original, superior artistic, scientific, indus-trial, and other products. Long may they so feel! Maximum happi-ness, in their cases, accompanies creative striving. As long as they do not insist on a perfectionistic never-a-single-wasted-moment philosophy.

As we sometimes say to our clients: You may choose to climb the highest available mountain for several good reasons. You may, for example, enjoy climbing; delight in the challenge this difficult peak presents; or want to thrill to the view from the top. But you also may have bad reasons for climbing the same moun-tain: to look down on and spit at the people below.

12 HOW TO STOP BLAMING AND START LIVING

We can designate the essence of emotional disturbance in a single word: blaming—or damning. If you would stop, really stop, damning yourself, others, or unkind fate, you would find it virtually impossible to feel emotionally upset about anything. And you can probably omit "virtually" from the preceding sentence.

But you probably do, frequently, condemn yourselves and others. And tend to hold tenaciously to Irrational Idea No. 3: *The idea that when people act obnoxiously and unfairly, you should blame and damn them, and see them as bad, wicked, or rotten individuals.* This idea, the working hypothesis for a considerable portion of human behavior and interpersonal relations, stands as invalid and irrational for several important reasons:

1. The idea that we can label some people wicked or villainous springs from the ancient theological doctrine of free will. Although we cannot accurately say that humans have *no* free choice whatever, modern findings have shown that they have relatively little free will in the sense that this term usually gets employed in theological discussion. As Freud thought, and as many studies have shown, humans have genetic or inborn tendencies to behave in certain ways—including tendencies to learn or develop conditioned responses. Then, as a result of both innate and conditioned tendencies, once they get oriented in a "good" or "bad" direction, and hold philosophies that drive them to follow certain behavioral pathways, they find it most difficult (although not impossible) to change. In these circumstances, blaming or condemning them for their wrongdoings

unfairly attributes to them a perfect freedom of choice of behavior which they simply do not have.

2. The idea that people emerge as "bad" or "wicked" as a result of their wrongdoings stems from a second erroneous notion: namely, the concept that we can easily define "good" and "bad" or "ethical" and "unethical" behavior and that reasonable people can readily see when they act "right" or "wrong." The last century of philosophic and psychological discussion has again shown morality as a relative concept that differs widely according to places and circumstances. People in a *given* locality rarely reach a unanimous decision as to true "goodness" or "badness." As Joseph Fletcher and various other theologians have shown, we can see ethics as more situational than absolutistic. Most people, when even they theoretically "know" or accept certain standards of "good" conduct, easily and unconsciously rationalize their own behavior and find "good" reasons for doing the "wrong" things. If we excoriate humans for their difficulties in defining and accepting "good" behavior, we act unrealistically and unjustly.

3. Even when we agree upon standards of "wrongdoing," we cannot accurately blame people for not following these standards. We'd better induce wrongdoers to say to themselves: (a) "I have done a wrong or immoral act" and (b) "Therefore, how shall I correct myself and avoid this kind of act in the future?" But blaming and damning humans for their mistaken behavior induces them to say quite a different set of sentences: (a) "I have done a wrong or immoral act" and (b) "What a louse I remain for doing this act!"

Once people accept the concept of blame and devalue themselves as humans for having done a wrong act, they will tend either to consider themselves worthless and inadequate (instead of merely mistaken or unethical) or will (rather than devalue themselves) refuse to admit that they committed errors in this act; or they may even refuse to admit that they committed the act at all. Otherwise stated: By believing in blame and punishment for sin, people tend to feel worthless, obsessed with their wrongdoing, deny the wrongness of their acts, or repress knowledge of their wrong deeds. They don't get around to the relatively simple act of correcting their behavior, because (due to self-blame) they feel preoccupied either with punishing themselves or with refusing to admit that they did wrong in the first place. Blame or guilt, then, instead of alleviating wrongdoing, often leads to further immorality, hypocrisy, and evasion of responsibility.

4. People who accept the philosophy of damning themselves for their errors will tend to feel so afraid of making further errors that they will forgo experimentation, risk-taking, and commitment to life.

5. Blaming yourself or others for your "sins" leads to an

evasion of sane morality. Normally, you act morally and do not needlessly harm your fellows, not because you see yourself as a louse or a "sinner" if immoral, but because in the last analysis you will harm yourself and your loved ones. If you gratuitously interfere with the rights of others, they or their friends or relatives will tend to retaliate against you. And even if you personally escape scot-free, you will thereby help set up an anarchistic, unjust system under which you would normally not want to live. Out of enlightened self-interest, therefore, you behave morally in accordance with the rules of your community; and you do not act ethically because some arbitrary or definitional God or convention says that you *should*.

6. Blaming people confuses their wrong *acts* with their sinful *essence*. But no matter how many evil acts they perform, *they* cannot remain intrinsically evil because they could, today or tomorrow, change their behavior and commit no additional wrong deeds. Just as people who fail don't emerge as *failures* (but simply people who so far have frequently failed), those who have often done wrong or acted immorally never turn into *sinners*. People's (good or bad) acts *result* from their existence but don't constitute that *existence* itself. Their intrinsic value arises definitionally. Or, if it does exist, it has nothing essentially to do with their extrinsic value, or worth to others. To call a man a criminal, a blackguard, or a villain implies that because he has in the past committed wrong acts, he *must*, by his very nature, continue to do so in the future; and no one can prove this. Once we label people as *sinners*, we help give them the conviction of their hopelessness—that they cannot stop committing wrongs in the future.

7. To blame others means you get angry or hostile toward them. Feelings of anger reflect your grandiosity. You essentially say, by feeling angry (a) I do not like Joe's behavior and (b) because I do not like it, he *shouldn't* have acted that way. The second sentence here represents a grandiose non sequitur: because why *shouldn't* Joe have acted the way he did, merely because you do not *like* the way he acted? You act unrealistically and God-like when you believe that your *preference* regarding Joe's behavior *should* make him act differently.

8. Blaming yourself or others not only leads to anger, as just noted, but to many unpleasant consequences of hostility. Even if you rightly see Joe's acts as wrong or immoral, your belief that he *shouldn't* act wrongly and your subsequent anger will hardly serve to stop him from acting badly again (in fact, it may give him an incentive to continue acting wrongly just *because* you hate him and he hates you back). It will almost always stir up your guts, lead to possible ulcers or high blood pressure, and deflect you from the real problem: how can you determinedly and effectively induce Joe not to act badly again? Fistfights, duels, capital

punishment, international wars—in fact, virtually every violent aspect of man's inhumanity to man that you can think of—have frequently resulted from people's grandiosely and unhelpfully blaming others whose actions they (perhaps rightly) consider wrong. And just as two wrongs don't make a right, anger against them probably constitutes the worst way of trying to correct wrongdoers.

9. As pointed out in our books, *Sex Without Guilt* and *Growth Through Reason*, if you roundly condemn others for what you (often arbitrarily) consider their wrong behavior you will tend to turn your blaming standards on yourself and end up with considerable self-loathing. Lack of forgiveness toward others breeds lack of self-forgiveness, with consequent perfectionistic attitudes toward your own failings and incompetencies. To devalue others because they have made some serious mistakes helps you devalue the whole human race, including your own humanity.

10. In view of the reasons just given, it would appear that a designation like 'I've turned into a rotten person [or bum, knave, or slob] in doing that immoral act" constitutes an unscientific and unverifiable conclusion. Although you may prove your *behavior* "rotten," "bummy," "knavish," "slobbish," or "immoral"— because you can concretely observe such behavior and demonstrate that it leads to disadvantageous results—you can't prove *yourself* rotten. For the proposition "I've turned into a rotten person!" does not merely hypothesize that *some* or *much* of your behavior lacks desirability. It really means, in its overtones and undertones, (a) you have behaved badly, (b) you will always and can only act badly, and (c) you deserve utter damnation for allowing yourself to perform that way. While the first of these statements may have truth, the second appears unprovable, and the third quite definitional, unprovable, and harm-creating.

As an illustration of blaming and self-blaming tendencies, witness the case of Mr. and Mrs. James Smart, who came to therapy largely because of their mutual hostility, and who I (A.E.) saw together during most of the therapeutic and marriage counseling sessions. Mr. Smart, a newspaperman, had gained a national reputation by his accurate and objective reporting of interracial tensions and struggles in his hometown, in the South. A large metropolitan daily offered him an important job, with a considerable advancement in both prestige and pay. After talking over the offer with Mrs. Smart (who expressed fears and misgivings, but no definite objections), he accepted.

Mr. Smart came to the big city ahead of his family to find a house; and here the trouble began. For twice the amount they had invested in their home in the small Southern town from which they came, he found that they would only obtain inferior quarters in the North. Not having any considerable savings, he rented a large apartment "to give us a place to live while we hunted for a home."

The rest of the story will probably sound familiar enough to those who make good salaries but reside in cities with high living costs. The high rent, higher costs of food, clothing, and other expenses soon consumed Smart's increase in income; and the recreational activities and meals away from home which seemed necessary to give Mrs. Smart and the children a relief from their close living quarters in their new apartment added to the family's financial woes.

On top of these living problems, Mr. Smart felt increasingly disappointed with his new job. He had administrative responsibilities for which he had poor preparation and in which he lacked interest. His superior on the new newspaper put up the front of a liberal newspaperman of the old-time tradition, but in practice whenever his employees tried to report the news fearlessly, he began to jump and tremble that some large advertiser would feel alarm and would withdraw his support.

By the time Mr. and Mrs. Smart came for psychotherapy, they felt despair. Family and professional happiness seemed lost forever. Mrs. Smart blamed her husband for acting stupidly about his profession and for not caring about her and the children. Mr. Smart damned himself for misjudging his new job and for managing living conditions so poorly. He also saw his wife as highly uncooperative, sexually frigid, and a poor mother.

One of the early sessions with this couple ran as follows:

Mrs. S.: And just to make things worse, Doctor, as if they didn't seem enough already, he's even taken to staying out after work and drinking. He doesn't make a *good* newspaper man anymore, so he has to *act* like one by sitting around at the bar and telling the boys how well he could have covered the Battle of Bull Run.

Mr. S.: I find more bull running around home these days than anywhere else. Why should I come home to hear you read that same old speech about what a louse I've turned into.

Therapist: I think you've both made it quite clear what kind of complaints you have against each other. Now, just for the sake of discussion let's assume for a moment that you, Mr. Smart, have been making some really, stupid, selfish, and malicious mistakes.

Mrs. S.: I didn't say "malicious." I don't think he thought about it enough to have any malice. But I'll go along with the other adjectives.

Mr. S.: I'll say she will! And a few other choice invectives, if she can think of any. She has no difficulty at all in dreaming them up by the thousands.

Therapist: OK. Let's grant that your husband, Mrs. Smart, has made some real bad mistakes. We *could* make a number of excuses for him. We could point out, for example, that he couldn't possibly have known, with his past experiences, what bad things would happen in this new city, and that therefore his mistakes appear legitimate. But let's waive all these extenuating circumstances and just plainly state that he made a series of stupid errors—and that he still keeps making them, including the drinking with the boys. All right: so what? So he's made mistakes. Now what good does it do for you to savagely denounce him for his errors? How helpful do your denunciations seem?

Mrs. S.: Well—but—! Do you expect me to give him a medal or something for acting like such an idiot? And then for making things worse with this weak-livered running away from the problem into alcohol? Do you expect me to comfort him, like a good wife, and to cheer him on to *more* mistakes along the same order?

Therapist: No, not exactly. Though it might surprise you, if you really tried it, how well your satirically made suggestion might work. But let's not ask you to go to *that* extreme. Granted that your husband has made serious mistakes, what good will *blaming* him do? Has your blame made him commit fewer mistakes? Has it made him feel more kindly toward you? Has it made *you* feel happier in your own right?

Mrs. S.: Well, no. I can't say that it has.

Therapist: Nor will it ever, in all probability. For the more you damn your husband—or anyone else, for that matter—the more defensive he will usually get, and the less *likely* to admit his errors, especially to you. As we saw a minute ago: when you criticized him, his main line of defense consisted of sarcasm, a very common human tendency: to protect yourself against blame by blaming back the one who attacks you.

Mrs. S.: Oh, he does pretty well at that, I must admit!

Therapist: Yes, but who doesn't? And the more he blames you back, after you keep jumping on him, the less he will tend to face the real problem at hand: "Now, let's see. I did badly this time; how can I change my ways and do better next time?" Moreover, the more he *accepts* your blame, and beats himself down the way *you* try to beat him down, the less he will think himself *able* to cope with the real problem, even if he faces it. For he will keep saying to himself: "My wife sees me correctly. How could I have acted so stupidly? What a perfect fool! Absolutely right! And how can an idiot like me get out of this mess that I've gotten myself into? Right: I seem just about hopeless. No use trying to do the thing over again, I'll just mess it up even worse. I might as well drink myself into a stupor and forget about the whole horrible business since I have no ability to resolve it, anyhow."

Mr. S.: You hit it right on the head! Exactly what I said to myself! And who wouldn't—when his own wife keeps telling him, over and over, what a hopeless fool and an incompetent louse she lives with?

Therapist: Right. Who wouldn't? Almost everyone in this society would. And they'd all, every one of them, prove one hundred percent wrong.

Mr. S.: Wrong? But you just said that I'd naturally feel that way when my wife kept beating me down like that.

Therapist: Yes—*statistically* natural, in that the great majority of husbands would do exactly what you have done. But that still doesn't mean that they would prove *right* in doing so, or that they'd *have* to do so.

Mr. S.: But what else could I have done? What would you expect me to do?

Therapist: I would *expect* you to do nothing other than you did. But I would *hope*, once I induced you to acquire a new idea or two, that you would not do what you did, accept your wife's blame and use it to belabor *yourself* with, even though the majority of husbands *would* do exactly that.

Mr. S.: What new idea do you mean?

Therapist: Mainly the idea that you don't *have* to accept anyone's negative views of you and use them against yourself—even when these views contain some amount of truth.

Mrs. S.: But how can you help accepting them in those circumstances—when you know you did wrong?

Therapist: Very simply. By following what we call the A-B-C-theory of rational-emotive therapy. A (or what we call an Activating Event or Activating Experience), in this case, represents the fact that you've done badly and that your wife castigates you for your mistakes. And C (an emotional Consequence) stands for the fact that you feel like a fool and keep drinking yourself into a stupor. You look at A, what seems her justifiable blame, and you look at C, what seems your own justifiable feeling of shame, and you say to yourself: "Well, A naturally leads to C. She rightly sees my behaving badly and blames me for this crummy behavior."

Mr. S.: Well, *doesn't* A lead to C in this case? Shouldn't I admit my mistakes and blame myself for them? How else will I ever change?

Therapist: No, A does not automatically lead to C, as you think it does. Rather, between A and C comes B—your Belief System about A. And B stems from your general philosophy of life, which you (as well as your wife) easily tend to construct and which you have also learned in this silly society—the philosophy that you *should* blame yourself (down or damn yourself as a total human) for doing the wrong thing, for making serious mistakes. Therefore, when your wife verbally rips you up at A, you *interpret* her criticism (at B) as accurate and you *agree* with her hypothesis that not only does your *behavior* stink but that *you* turn into a thorough stinker for behaving in that stinking way. You *then*, as a direct result of your Belief System (at B) bring about the emotional Consequences you get (at C): including considering yourself hopeless, taking to drink, and experiencing other self-defeating results.

Mr. S.: But I still say: Doesn't she rightly criticize me at A?

Therapist: No. She would rightly criticize if she objectively, determinedly called to your attention, at A, that you make wrong moves, commit errors. But her criticism does *not* do that. She *first* calls your wrongdoing to your attention and *then* says: "But you *shouldn't* do wrong, you louse! You have no *right* to act so stupidly." But humans do have the right to do wrong. And even though it may prove *undesirable* for you to make mistakes, your humanity makes you do so, and you do *not* turn into a rotten *person.*

Mrs. S.: So I'd better determinedly call my husband's errors to his attention and try to help him do better in the future?

Therapist: Right. His mistakes belong in the past. *Now*: What can you do about improving the present? What realities can both of you face to make the future different from the past? What can both of you learn from your errors? What can you do now that will make life more enjoyable for you and your children?

Mr. S.: I begin to see what you mean. And I guess, for one thing, I can stop acting like an ostrich by sticking my head in the corner bar.

Mrs. S.: If you make that promise, I'll match it with one of my own. I'll stop blaming you for your past mistakes—including the mistake, I thought, of dragging us in here to confess all our woes to the doctor. I feel glad I came. I *do* understand, now that I look at it more rationally, how you could have made this move, and got the wrong apartment, and made those other mistakes. I guess I haven't exactly acted angelically myself!

Mr. S.: Wow! I wish I had brought along a tape recorder to get down that historic statement! That admission has made more history than Bull Run ever did. But I, too, can see now how I could have made those idiotic moves. And how you could have reacted so unangelically, too! Hell, if we'd only spend some of this self-blaming and blaming-the-other time in looking at our real problems, we'd get much further with them!

Therapist: You see. Turn off the heat of blaming and damning and you already begin feeling better about yourselves and each other. Now let's see if we can't get both of you to do less blaming and more problem-solving in the future. In which case you'll still have some real hassles, but none of them will seem insoluble.

Which proved quite true. Months later, after Mr. Smart had managed to secure another job in a middle-sized city, purchased (with his wife's full consent) a small house, and cut his drinking almost to zero, I received this letter from Mrs. Smart: "James the First keeps reigning benignly and supremely in his new job. If you didn't see his syndicated series on Jim Crowism in the North, let me know and I'll modestly mail copies of the articles to you. Home seems wonderful—just like home. All the kids and Jim and I have made a lot of fine friends. The children like their school. I like the house and the neighborhood. And, though we probably remain prejudiced, we all seem to like each other. What did you say about blame? Never heard of the word. Thanks and love."

Now let us not give the impression that all or even most cases of marriage counseling get quickly solved as a result of therapeutic intervention and the teaching of both partners the A-B-C's of emotional disturbance and getting them to change their B's or Belief Systems. That would prove nice!—but, alas, it does not ring true. Many couples will simply never admit that they upset themselves but continue to insist that their mates *make* them disturbed. Others admit to their own culpability, but find considerable difficulty changing their B's. Naturally, in books like this one, we tend to present as models those cases where the counselees quickly saw the A-B-C's of RET and worked hard at changing themselves. Don't feel amazed in your own case, however, if you have trouble zeroing in on and changing your irrational Belief System. Almost all humans *easily* think crookedly about themselves and their intimate associates, and it may require some considerable amount of therapeutic intervention and self-practice before you really start thinking more straightly and acting more rationally when you, by yourself or with a loved partner, get deeply involved in self-sabotaging behaviors.

What can you do to catch your damning yourself and others and to tackle and challenge the irrational assumptions behind your blaming? Several things:

1. Whenever you feel depressed or guilty you can recognize that you probably, on some level, condemn yourself, and can immediately try to track down the specific sentences you keep telling yourself to create this self-damnation. Generally, you say to yourself: (a) "I did this wrongly" and (b) "I therefore emerge as no good or worthless for doing wrong." And you can change these sentences to: (a) "Perhaps I definitely did wrong," (b) "Humans frequently do wrong," (c) "Now how do I find out exactly what I did wrongly and determinedly try to correct it *next* time?"

2. Resolving to correct your misdeeds in the future will frequently not suffice, any more than resolving to make yourself a good pianist will do the trick. You can only play the piano, diet, or correct your past errors by *work* and *practice*—by literally *forcing* yourself to follow a new path. Thus, if you want to act morally you'd better literally force yourself to behave honestly, responsibly, and noninjuriously to others. And convince yourself that

although you may more easily *in the short run* act dishonestly and irresponsibly, you will most probably achieve long-range self-interest and happiness by moral behavior.

Rational morality stems from self-interest. You do not practice it by saying to yourself: "I have done wrong; I have turned into a blackguard; therefore I must stop my misdeeds in the future." You achieve it by saying: "I have done wrong; I will keep defeating my *own* ends and helping create the kind of a world in which *I* do not want to live if I continue to do wrong; therefore I had better change my ways." And to surrender self-blame you require not only Insight No. 1—"I feel like a louse because I often heard my parents call me one and I foolishly agreed with them—but also Insight No. 2—"I still believe this drivel because *I* now choose to believe it." You follow this with Insight No. 3: "To stop viewing myself as a damnable, rotten person, I'd better *work* at disputing my assumptions and keep *acting* against my self-castigating beliefs."

3. You can learn to distinguish between *responsibility* and *blame*. You often have responsibility for your behavior, in the sense that you actually *did* it and theoretically *could have* not done it. But because you irresponsibly performed certain acts does not mean that you must view yourself as a worthless person for performing them—that you can legitimately damn yourself.

4. You can try to distinguish between *actually* and *seemingly* wrong behavior. Having premarital sex experience, for example, gets *called* wrong by many religious and community groups. But do *you* think it wrong? Do *you* believe you needlessly, definitely harm anyone, including yourself, when you have such relations?

Do not unthinkingly *accept* a given act as wrong or immoral; but *determine*, as best you can, its wrongness. If it seems wise to conform to certain laws, even though you do not believe in their value, then (in order to avoid bringing down certain penalities on your head) do your best to conform. But if you disagree with certain customs, and you can get away with disagreement, by all means stand up against them or quietly flout them—as long as you do not too badly defeat your own ends by your rebellion.

5. When you find that you feel angry or hostile admit your own grandiosity and perfectionism. If you merely dislike or feel annoyed at others' actions, you may have appropriate feelings. You then *prefer* that people act differently and you feel frustrated or disappointed when they don't. But anger arises from telling yourself: "I don't like what Dick does; and therefore he *shouldn't* do it," instead of: "I don't like what Dick does; now let me see how I can persuade or help him act differently." In these circumstances, tackle your *own* grandiosity and force yourself—yes, force yourself—to accept Dick *with* his unlikable actions, and thereby undo the blame and anger that *you* create.

If, by employing the foregoing techniques, you keep challenging and contradicting your self-blaming and other-blaming tendencies, you will not end up as a saint or a Pollyanna. You will still, on many occasions, thoroughly *dislike* your own and others' behaviors. But you will have a much better chance of changing what you dislike instead of boiling in your own juices. To err proves human, to forgive leaves you sane and realistic.

13 HOW TO FEEL
UNDEPRESSED
THOUGH FRUSTRATED

Ninety-nine and nine-tenths percent of the people in this world seem inextricably wedded to a thoroughly false notion: that they must feel miserable or depressed when they get frustrated. Even most contemporary psychologists believe the famous Dollard-Miller hypothesis: that frustration necessarily leads to aggression. And they all, these billions of laymen and thousands of psychologists, remain almost 100 percent wrong.

The frustration-aggression hypothesis stems from Irrational Idea No. 4: *The idea that you have to view things as awful, terrible, horrible, and catastrophic when you get seriously frustrated, treated unfairly, or rejected.* This idea proves false for several reasons:

1. Although you may find it indubitably unpleasant or unfortunate when you do not get what you want out of life, you do not feel it as catastrophic or horrible unless you *think* it that way. When things go badly, you have the choice of saying: (a) "I don't like this situation. Now let me see what I can do to change it. And if I can't change it, life remains tough but not necessarily catastrophic." Or you can say: (b) "I don't like this situation. I can't stand it. It drives me crazy. It shouldn't exist this way. It simply has to change, otherwise I can't possibly feel happy." The second of these chains of sentences will turn you miserable, self-pitying, depressed, or hostile. The first set of sentences will lead you to feel undelighted and regretful but not necessarily dejected or angry.

2. Although children frequently won't tolerate any amount

of frustration, adults can determinedly do so. Children largely develop at the mercy of their environments. They cannot easily look ahead to the future to see that if they now suffer frustration they may not do so *perpetually*. We cannot expect them to think *philosophically* about their frustrations. Not so adults. Adults, if not mentally deficient, *can* see an end to their present frustrations; *can* change their own environments; *can* philosophically *accept* their existing life handicaps when these will not, for the nonce, change.

3. If you make yourself—yes, *make* yourself—terribly upset and depressed about your frustrations, you will almost invariably block yourself from effectively removing them. The more time and energy you expend in lamenting your sorry fate, ranting against your frustrators, and gnashing your teeth in despair, the less effective action you will tend to take to counteract your handicaps and deal with those who may frustrate you. Even if you correctly surmise that others unfairly block your wishes—what makes that so terrible? So it proves unfair, and unethical. Who said that people *shouldn't* act unfairly and unethically—however nice if they didn't?

4. In the case of inevitable and unchangeable frustrations—when your parent or mate dies, for instance, and you cannot possibly bring him or her back to life—you senselessly upset yourself because of your deprivation. So life deprives you! Will your wailing and moaning bring back your loved one? Will your ranting at unkind fate really make you feel better? Why not, instead, maturely accept the inevitable, however unpleasant you may find it? It does, let us assume, amount to a very bad, very sad state of affairs. But how (except by your own God-like fiat) does it prove *awful*?

5. Whether you like it or not, you'd simply better accept reality when you cannot change it. Reality *exists;* if it has misfortunes and frustrations, you can view that as bad. But not as catastrophic. As long as *you* still live and have reasonably good health, you remain the master of your fate, the captain of your soul. Reality may block and defeat your ends. Sometimes it can even kill you. But it cannot fully defeat *you*. Only *you* can defeat yourself—if you believe that what exists *shouldn't* exist, or that because things oppress, you *must* feel depressed.

Let us look at a few illustrative cases. Mary Manahan kept coming to see me (A.E.) for session after session, always complaining that her husband didn't love her, that he never gave her the things she wanted, and that he therefore amounted to a no-good son of a gun. Her complaints, from what I could see, had at least some justification. For Tim Manahan hardly acted as the best husband in the world and most wives he might have had would have complained about his inconsideration and neglect. But even after admitting this to Mary, I still refused to buy her whining. Then she turned her anger on me.

"But look here," she exclaimed, "you've seen Tim for yourself and you admit that he often treats me unkindly and inconsiderately—especially during my pregnancy, when I need additional help. How can you say that I've got no right to complain?"

"Oh, I didn't say that at all," I calmly replied. "You have every right in the world to complain, if you want to—just as you have every right in the world to commit suicide, if you want that. But if you *do* keep complaining, as you have done for the last several weeks, you might just as well cut your own throat. For what you keep doing amounts to that. You just raise your own blood pressure all the time. And what good will *that* do you and your unborn child?"

"But you don't seem to understand. *He* makes me unhappy. *He* keeps acting badly, not me."

"True: he acts badly. But you act even worse—to yourself. All the more reason, since he does you little good by his behavior, that you'd better stop doing yourself in. And, compared to the harm *you* keep doing to you, he acts almost like an angel. So who *really* does the killing? You!"

"But how can I stop him from acting the way he does? That seems the real problem, as I see it."

"Yes—as you see it. But the problem as I see it involves, first: How can you stop *you* from acting the way *you* do? Then maybe you'll have a chance to help change him."

"What do you mean? How will my acting differently change him?"

"Very simply. You say that your husband loves you much less than you want him to and acts much worse than you would want him to act. And with these statements I agree: since I can see for myself, by talking to him, that he doesn't love you too much or treat you too well."

"See! Even you agree that he treats me badly."

"Yes, even I agree. But the worse you treat *him*, because he treats you so badly, the worse he will tend to treat you in return. And the more you beat him over the head for *not* loving you, the less he will tend to love you. If you really want him to treat you better—which you say you do, but make no efforts to arrange—then you could obviously love him more and treat him less critically—especially when he acts nastily and inconsiderately. For if you give a human love and kindness when he does not, by his actions, merit it, he will see that you probably *really* love him. And if, in those circumstances, he does not love you more and act better toward you, nothing, I fear, will do the trick of winning him to your side."

"But he *started* treating me badly, didn't he?"

"No matter. If he treats you badly, and you then criticize him for treating you badly, he will, as he has done, end up by treating you still worse. In fact, he'll probably forget that he *did* treat you badly in the first place, and claim that he treats you that way now *because* you keep criticizing him."

"Exactly what he does contend!"

"See! So you won't win, the way you play the game. But if you play it differently, and return his lack of love with *increased* kindness, then at least you've got a chance to win some real love from him."

"But does that seem fair? Should I *have* to do it that way, after how he's acted."

"No, that doesn't seem fair. So it doesn't! Still: What will you do, other than berate your husband, to win more love from him? When will you stop all this it-must-prove-fair nonsense and do something to make your life *fairer*?"

As usual, I had a tough go with this client, and several times she almost quit therapy in disgust. But by sheer power of persuasive logic, I finally won, and she did try several weeks of giving her husband more love and less criticism even though he kept acting inconsiderately, as usual. A near-miracle then ensued; and just four sessions later Mrs. Manahan had quite a different story to tell:

"I don't know how you figured out Tim so well," she said, "but you hit it right on the nose. For ten days he acted like the biggest louse in the world, refused to help me with any of the heavy work around the house, stayed out late at the office almost every night, and even hinted about taking up with one of his old woman friends again. But even though it at first killed me, I gritted my teeth, said (just as I've heard you say to me so many times) 'All right, so he remains his usual crummy self. It won't kill me. I don't like it, but I don't have to cry in my beer all night about it.' And I didn't say a word to him, went out of my way to make things nice, and instead of withdrawing sexually decided to extend myself more than usual. Well, you should have seen the quick change! He now comes home early every night, sometimes actually brings me flowers, acts so solicitous of my condition that I can hardly believe it, and has turned into practically a different person. Quite a change from just a couple of weeks ago! I really have to hand it to you, Doctor. Just as soon I began to *work* for the love I wanted from Tim, I began to get it. Much better than crying all the time over my horrible frustration!"

Myra Benson was another good example of how a changed philosophy of living helped a disturbed human get over a deep-seated feeling of frustration and pain. Myra came to see me (R.A.H.) after her male companion of the last two years had broken off their relationship and got engaged to a much wealthier woman. She felt desolate, insisted that life didn't seem worth living anymore, and that she could never possibly replace her lover. I felt duly sympathetic, but more than a bit adamant and held that she kept telling herself rot, that within a few months or a year or two she would doubtless love some other man just as intensely as she loved this one.

"But you don't seem to *understand*," Myra wailed. "He has *left* me. I not only loved him, but had my whole future planned in and around him. *Nothing* has meaning anymore. Everything I try to do, everywhere I go, everything I even try to think about feels just plain empty without him." And she dived, for the twelfth time that session, for her wad of Kleenex tissues.

"Too bad," I said. "But it has clearly happened. Your relationship with him has ended. No doubt about it. Ended; finished; over with. What good does it do to depress yourself about it? That certainly won't bring him back."

"I know. But you don't—"

"Yes, I don't seem to understand. But I *do* understand; and you, in all probability, don't. You don't—or, rather, I'd say you *won't*—understand that it *has* ended and you can't do a damned thing to start it up again. You especially don't or won't understand that the sane thing to do, at the moment, lies in thinking about what else and *who else* can interest and delight you. No use repeating over and over that 'life remains empty without Robert'—thereby *making* it as empty as you say. If I began telling myself that life feels empty without old Lyndon Johnson and repeated this often and grimly enough, I surely could feel sad as hell about old Lyndon and about old worthless me, who just couldn't get along without him."

"You keep making fun of me!"

"Yes, I guess I do make fun of you a bit—a darned sight better than what you keep doing: making mincemeat of you. And don't you think that I just make up this stuff about feeling depressed years later. Why, just the other day I had a fifty-four-year-old man in here who literally began to cry when he talked about his mother. Know how long ago his dear old mother had died? Twenty-five years. Only yesterday to him. Genuine emotion? Deep love for dear old mother? Absolutely. But the poor guy had kept it alive for twenty-five years by regularly saying to himself: 'Mother has died. How awful, how dreadful! What a fine, wonderful, self-sacrificing woman! And now dead—gone forever. Poor Mother! And poor motherless me! How awful!' "

"Well, you'll have to admit," and Myra smiled a little through her tears, "that I don't do quite as badly as that yet."

"No—not yet. But you probably will if you keep feeding yourself this hogwash about indispensable Robert, and about how your life can't go on without him. If you want to follow the noble example of my fifty-four-year-old client, and his dear departed mother (and me, of course, with my dear departed Lyndon Johnson), I feel sure, in fact I have every confidence, that you can go on telling yourself for the next twenty-five years what a stinking, horrible, catastrophic shame that Robert has left you and rendered your poor, poor life infinitely barren. You can do it, all right, if you just keep telling yourself such nonsense. On the other hand, if you decide that instead of sitting around in feebleminded grief you'd like to develop an interesting and enjoyable life—this you can do by saying different kinds of sentences to yourself and learning to believe and act on them."

"You certainly seem a hard-boiled and hardhearted person. You make fun of my genuine bereavement by comparing it with a sick old man's sentiment for his mother and your cynical fiction about grieving for Lyndon Johnson."

"Yes, I make fun because I have found from long experience in helping people that they find it exceedingly difficult to leave my office and start catastrophizing with the same consistency and intensity if I have ridiculed their dire needs. For you to feel sad and bereaved for a while about Robert's desertion makes sense. And it especially makes sense if you want to examine as critically and objectively as possible—with my help—what things you did or didn't do to contribute to Robert's leaving you. But for you to sit around and tell yourself how hornswoggled horrible, how devastatingly catastrophic it remains because you no longer have your dear Robert—that makes no more sense than my two examples. So Robert deserted you. Now: what can *you* do to enjoy your life *without* him? Stop crying over unfair reality. It exists the way it exists. Let's see what you can *do* to make it *better*."

As I proceeded to hammer away at Myra Benson's irrational preoccupation with her loss, she began to substitute other self-verbalizations for the ones with which she had kept herself depressed. She soon began to develop new interests, activities, associations. Life ceased to seem empty. Not that *it* had intrinsically changed; but *she* began to interpret it differently. And that made all the difference in the world.

What paths, more specifically, can you take when faced with real-life frustrations, including possible injustices and more than your share of accidental misfortune? Some major ways to cope with actual difficulties and unpleasantries:

1. When faced with a frustrating set of circumstances, you can first determine whether it includes true handicaps in its own right or whether you essentially *define* it so. Does your less than perfect appearance *really* prevent you from going with desirable members of othe other sex—or do *you*, because of your silly *need* to appear the best looking person in town, sabotage your own dates? Has your parents' opposition to your having a certain career

truly prevented you from following this career—or have you given up too easily, failing to plunge ahead despite their opposition, and perhaps using them as an alibi to cover up your own possible fear of failure? What, when you cancel out your own negativistic definitions, actually *makes* this or that frustration get you to cop out? Challenge, question—*see*.

2. If you face truly considerable frustration and there seems no way to change or control it, then you had better gracefully and realistically *accept* it. Yes: not with bitterness and despair, but with dignity and grace. As Epictetus noted two thousand years ago: "Who, then, remains unconquerable? He whom the inevitable cannot overcome." Schopenhauer, many centuries later, similarly stated: "A good supply of resignation seems of the first importance in providing for the journey of life." Sydney Smith put it this way, "If [I must] crawl, I will crawl contentedly; if [I may] fly, I will fly with alacrity; but as long as I can avoid it, I will never [feel] unhappy." You can take a philosophy of resignation to irrational extremes. But, within sensible limits, you can benefit from it.

3. Determine to overcome serious frustrations that you can ameliorate or eliminate. Rational thinking does not overstoically or fatalistically surrender to any difficult or obnoxious condition. It does not include a philosophy of submission or resignation. It largely counsels that you accept the inevitable only when it really *has* inevitability—and not when you can change things. In this respect, it follows the rule of St. Francis, of Reinhold, Niebuhr, of Alcoholics Anonymous, and of several Oriental philosophers. In the RET formulation: "Let me have the determination to change what I can change, the serenity to accept what I cannot, and the wisdom to know the difference between the two."

4. Ask yourself, whenever frustrations and annoyances beset you, "Who says that they *should* not beset me? *It would surely prove nice* if they didn't. But they do. Tough! Will it kill me to know frustration? Hardly! Will it hinder and bother me? It may! All the more reason, therefore, why I'd better not hinder and bother myself—make myself upset at feeling upset. Then I'll just have two self-botherings for the price of one!" Convince yourself, in other words, that frustrations and irritations remain the *normal* human lot; that virtually no one lives without many of them; that they do not ordinarily create catastrophe; and that you have the thinking power to survive quite well in spite of their existence.

5. The greater your loss or frustration, the *more* philosophic you can make yourself about it. Almost all modern people (unlike, among other peoples, the ancient Spartans) seem to believe that the greater their loss, the more miserable or depressed they have to feel. Hogwash! The greater your loss or frustration, the more you will tend to *regret* or *dislike* it. But regret and dislike need not

equal dire depression. The latter arises from your thinking: (a) "I cannot have my dearly loved person or my ardently desired object. How regretful!" and (b) "Because I cannot have what I dearly want, life turns terrible, horrible, catastrophic, and totally unfair; and it shouldn't!" While the first of these beliefs seems sensible, the second constitutes arrant nonsense. You can philosophically challenge and uproot it.

6. When conditions include real-life handicaps, such as physical pains that you cannot ease, you will do well to practice sensation-neglect or distraction. Thus, either you can try to ignore and forget about the painful or annoying sensations; or you can deliberately think about or do something else. If, for example, you have a headache, you can try to forget about it instead of continually telling yourself: "My, what a terrible headache! How can I stand it if it continues?" Or you can deliberately try to think about something pleasant (such as the good time you had the day before or the picnic you plan for next Sunday). Or you can participate in some distracting activity, such as chess, reading, or painting. Since you may not easily put a painful stimulus out of mind, the second plan, that of deliberately trying to distract yourself with other, more pleasant stimuli, usually proves more effective.

Although the use of distraction remains palliative, and does not solve basic problems permanently, it sometimes produces beneficial results where other anti-unhappiness techniques fail. Years ago, I (A.E.) felt impressed with its possibilities when I discovered that I could eliminate most of the pain of drilling or other dental work by deliberately focusing, when my dentist was hacking away at my teeth or gums, on recent pleasant experiences (especially sexual experiences) that I had undergone or by composing songs in my head while sitting in the dental chair. I taught this technique to several of my clients who dreaded visiting the dentist and who used it with good results.

Many years later, when I went to the hospital for a month after falling down a dimly lit flight of stairs in an Oklahoma City hotel, I again used this principle of distraction to relieve some of my physical pain. I focused on pleasant fantasies; I planned things to do when released from the hospital; I wrote much of this revised edition of *A New Guide to Rational Living;* and I kept myself busy, mentally and externally. I can't say that these diversions completely eliminated my bodily suffering, for they didn't. But they certainly decreased it measurably; and for the large part of my hospitalized days, I hardly felt it at all.

The use of distraction to alleviate psychological problems may have undesirable side effects: since people thereby may merely temporarily soothe themselves rather than permanently eradicate disturbances. Acts of aggression against others, sex diversions, alcohol, marijuana, heroin, and even tranquilizers overeffectively help them "feel good" for the moment, and thereby believe that they do not have to do anything else to eliminate basic anxiety and hostility. Abreactive and cathartic techniques employed in some types of psychotherapy (such as those used by some psychoanalytic, Reichian, Gestalt, and experimental therapists) may also nicely divert clients from underlying problems and thereby bring about considerable immediate gratification. Various kinds of indulgence therapies may do the same thing and may help the individual *feel better* rather than truly *get better*.

In the course of these indulgences, clients may also see things much differently from the way they did before—see having pleasure or releasing feelings, for example, as unshameful—so that they may significantly restructure self-defeating ideas, and may actually think more rationally. Since, however, they may use distraction merely for its own sake, may throw themselves into it *instead of* attacking major irrationalities, and may derive from it some additional foolish ideas, it has its dangers as a therapeutic method. But used judiciously, especially to combat physical pains and annoyances that one cannot for the moment undermine at their source, it has real advantages.

In the main, however, you will discover no easy means of dealing maturely with frustration. The hardest paths of all, the extreme renunciation of life philosophies of the Christian martyrs, of certain Oriental sects, and of various other religious fanatics, prove too difficult for most humans and suspiciously redolent of masochism and crackpotism. A more moderate degree of accepting the inevitable frustrations and unpleasantness of life, however, seems desirable for unanxious and unhostile living.

Ted Byrd may serve as an apt illustration of the desirability of acquiring a self-disciplined philosophy in regard to frustration. When I (R.A.H.) first saw Ted I found him one of the worst injustice collectors I had ever met. With apparently good reason, since his wealthy family had sent him off to camps and boarding schools from the age of eight. There seems little room to doubt that they had not wanted him from birth onward. His four older brothers and sisters, much more welcome than he, had gone on to considerable success (at least as far as I could tell from his story); but he had drifted, lost jobs, taken to alcohol, and bitterly resented the world and its treatment of him.

Ted, who had done a great deal of reading about psychotherapy, particularly in some of the highly fictionalized and dramatized case histories which masquerade as nonfiction, expected me to place him on the sofa, sympathetically listen to his tale of woe for the next few years, and encourage him to express and act out his deep-seated hostility for his parents and other family members. I fooled him, however, by immediately plunging into a counterattack on his injustice gathering.

"So your parents didn't love you," I said. "They rejected you and treated you shabbily. All right: granted. But what the devil makes you so angry *now*? As a child, yes, you had a real tough time of it. But now you've grown up—remember? So why *go on* feeling sorry for yourself about what you didn't get during your childhood? Why not do something constructive, interesting, and enjoyable with your *present* life? What fun do you get out of sitting around and telling yourself what a dirty shame that your parents rejected you at the age of eight? Since you now—chronologically at least—have acquired maturity, let's see if we can't get you to think some grown-up thoughts."

Ted seemed visibly taken aback. "But surely you know—" he started. "Surely you, as a psychologist, realize that it doesn't come that easy. I think, even with my limited understanding of your field, I can say that psychologists generally agree that—well, with rejection in the formative years and that sort of thing, a person never does get over his need for love. Unless, perhaps, by long-term analysis. I think I need that. The kind of stuff I've read about in Robert Lindner and Theodor Reik, for example, where the client, over a long period of time, lives out and works through his past hatreds and frustrations, and really sees what keeps bothering him. Don't you do that, that kind of psychoanalysis?"

"No, not anymore. I used to do something of the sort years ago, when I, too, felt impressed by the kind of books you cite. But the more people I saw and the more I put them through active relivings of their past experiences, and violent rehatings of their parental figures, the more I saw that it just didn't work. They loved it, all right, and had great times reenacting their early frustrations and hostilities. But they just didn't get better. So for a good many years, in association with Dr. Albert Ellis of New York, I've used a radically different approach to psychotherapy. And though it doesn't seem as dramatic or as gratifying to some clients as what I used to do, it certainly works a hell of a lot better. My clients used to love me like crazy under the old therapeutic system. Now, believe it or not, I actually help them to accept *themselves.*"

"Well—uh, I can see what you mean. But don't you really think that in special cases like mine, since I have suffered so much rejection by my parents and have stored up so much negative emotion about it in the past, that I have to work this through, on a long-term analytic basis, before I can possibly come to the more rational kind of approach that you and Dr. Ellis—and quite rightly, no doubt—emphasize?"

"No, I don't think anything of the sort. Orthodox psychoanalysis might *possibly* help you, over a long period of time, to work through your feelings of rejection. But, more likely it would not. For, after years of dredging up the minute details of just what your parents said and did to you at the age of two and three, and just how you reacted to their words and deeds, you would *still* have to reconstruct your *present* philosophy of rejection and frustration and stop telling yourself the nonsense that, after thirty years, you keep continually repeating to yourself."

"What kind of nonsense do you mean?"

"The kind you have told me about for the first twenty minutes of this session and what you still obviously uphold; namely, that rejection, especially by your parents, makes for horror, and that unless you can express yourself angrily against it, and somehow induce the world to give you the living which you still think it owes you, life doesn't seem worth living and you might as well drink yourself to death."

"But *doesn't* rejection turn into a very bad thing, *doesn't* it feel excruciatingly painful when you know frustration?"

"Yes—to a child. A child who does not think straight and fend for himself. But you *can* think straight and fend for yourself—though you don't try to do so. You've brilliantly avoided, all your life, changing your own attitudes toward frustrating circumstances, and have only tried to change the circumstances themselves—or else run away from them. You leave an unpleasant job (instead of trying to make it pleasanter) or drift from one place to another (instead of trying to make the best of the place where you reside). And *still*, right this minute, you keep trying to avoid facing frustration by inducing me to put you lazily through several years of abreactive psychoanalysis, which will give you more time to wallow in your bitterness instead of doing something to change it and will allow you the continued luxury of hating others instead of looking them in the eye and surrendering your own needless feelings of hatred."

"So you think I still avoid instead of face the basic issues of my life."

"Well, don't you? So you want to look closely (oh, so closely!) at what your parents did to you thirty years ago and how *that*, what they did *then*, makes you act the way you do today. But you don't want to, not for a minute, look even moderately closely at what *you* do, day after day, to make yourself feel so blocked and deprived."

"What do I do, if I may ask?"

"Why don't you look and see? You'd better come here for that. And together we'll look at the silly sentences you keep telling yourself that *now* make you and keep you upset—instead of trying to look at the sentences your poor, disturbed parents said to you years ago."

"Sentences that I keep telling myself?"

"Yes, sentences like: 'Oh, how awful for me to have gotten rejected by my parents and to have suffered their discrimination in favor of my brothers and sisters! How can I possibly amount to anything when those lousy parents of mine treated me in that despicable fashion?' Can't you see what a ridiculous nonsequitur you set up in those internalized sentences—making *their*, your parents', past actions magically influence *your* present behavior? And sentences like: 'Lord, how difficult I find it to stand on my own two feet and battle the frustrations of the world. Life shouldn't treat me this way!' Can't you see how that kind of self-repeated nonsense adds to instead of eases the real annoyances life often has to offer you?"

"Hmm. You take quite a different tack from those psycho-analytic books I've read. According to them, you and your lec-turing won't go deeply enough into my problems to help me solve what basically ails me."

"OK—If you want to live by those books, take that prerog-ative. And if you want to go for a long-term, 'deep' psycho-analysis, I'll be glad to send you to one of my associates who still believes in this sort of thing and will feel delighted to put you through the paces for the next seven or eight years. But, in the final analysis, you'll still have to do things the hard way, if you really want to change your ways, and revamp *your* (and not your sainted parents'!) philosophy of living."

"So if I really buckle down and work *now* and forget for the most part what happened to me in the past, and what dirty dogs my parents seemed for treating me the way they did, you think that I can work through my problems relatively quickly and still deeply understand myself?"

"Correct. You won't go deeper in life than facing your own fundamental philosophy—however or whenever you originally acquired it—and challenging the basic assumptions by which you live. Your philosophy, in a nutshell, remains: 'I had it hard in the past and suffered more than the average lot. Why, therefore, should I have to suffer any more deprivations and annoyances today? Why can't I merely revel in my justified hatred for my parents for the rest of my life and thereby feel better and magi-cally change the world so it goes more my way?' A very lovely philosophy—but totally ineffective. When will you start growing up and building a more realistic, less self-defeating way of looking at life?"

"You seem a hard man, Dr. Harper. But I begin to think I can use your kind of hardness. You know, now that you make me think of it, it all did seem just a little too easy, a little too good, when I kept reading how John Smith or Joe Blow, after years of lying on the sofa, suddenly saw the light, admitted that all his life he had really wanted to replace his father in his mother's bed, and then quickly lost his neurotic symptoms. Yes, I guess I have, as you say, looked for magic. I wanted you or some other therapist, with esoteric mumbo jumbo, to cure passive, little old me, while I did not a damn thing to lift a finger in my own behalf. You judge correctly: A psychoanalytic process like that would nicely *keep* me from changing, give me a great excuse not to change myself, for years and years.

"I have a friend, Jim Abramsky, who's kept using it that way for hell knows how many years. He goes religiously to his analyst, four or five times a week, and keeps calling him up on the phone whenever he gets into the slightest bit of trouble. But he still drinks like a fish. And whenever I ask him how he does in his analysis, he says: 'Fine; really fine. We keep going deeper and deeper all the time. Real deep. One of these days we'll hit rock bottom and then I'll know what lies at the base of it all and I'll no longer feel blocked up like this.' But I can see now, from what you've just said, that no bottom exists for someone like Jim. He really doesn't *want* to get better—for that would require real work and change on his part."

"Right. As long as he keeps going religiously for his analysis, he has the best excuse in the world *not* to get better—not to look at his own nonsensical self-sentences and work his tail off at changing them. But *he* has that problem. What will *you* do about *your* self-reiterated balderdash, about your crummy philosophy of life?"

"I don't want to promise you anything, Dr. Harper, for I've made many promises to myself and others before, and damned if I haven't goofed on all of them. But I can tell you this and mean it: For once, I'll try, really try. I'll try to look much more deeply at myself—or, as you keep putting it, at my own sentences. I guess I've had enough of this self-pitying, this look-what-a-horribly-neglected-child-they-made-me sort of jazz, to last me for the rest of my life. I think I'll try it your way for a while and see what happens."

And Ted Byrd did try, for the next six months, looking at his own beliefs and seeing what his own (rather than his parents') nonsense consisted of. His drinking decreased considerably. For the first time in his life he thought in terms of staying in one place. At the age of thirty-six, he went back to school and started to prepare himself for the one profession, electronic engineering, that he had toyed around with for many years but never seriously pursued. He hasn't got, at this present writing, entirely out of the woods. But though an average amount of frustrations and annoyances remain his daily and yearly lot, his attitude toward them has changed enormously and his bitter rantings against the injustices of his past and present world have almost entirely ceased.

The foregoing case, recorded many years ago, remains typical of individuals who would rather look at the past than at their present thinking and acting, so that they can thereby gain magical "insight" that will make them spontaneously better. Throughout the years, these historical and insight approaches have remained popular, partly because people who believe devoutly in them can thereby avoid taking full responsibility for their present behavior and for working actively to change it. They think, wishfully, that when they spontaneously begin to feel like doing things, those frustrating things will get done easily and enjoyably. Actually, the opposite often proves true: The more people *uneasily* force themselves to do many annoying but valuable pursuits (such as studying), the more they *then* find these pursuits easy and enjoyable.

When historical-oriented, Freudian type approaches to therapy get combined with physically abreactive, Reichian-type approaches, the clients experience a highly powerful set of cop-outs. Arthur Janov's primal therapy, and various other kinds of screaming or feeling-venting therapies, provide somewhat gruesome examples in this regard. Disturbed individuals first have offered to them the excuse that their parents "hurt" them, "enraged" them, or "upset" them during their early childhood; and that they still bear the terrible scars of these "hurts" and must fully acknowledge them and get them out of their system. Actually, of course, they *chose* to feel hurt or enraged when young; and they still *choose* to carry on their original whinyness and demandingness and to *command* that the world turn into an utterly kind, loving place.

Secondly, the devotees of screaming therapies now divert themselves from growing up and adopting adult views of reality by childishly insisting that deprivation *remains* awful and horrible. And they continue to have two-year-old temper tantrums and pat themselves on the back for having them. Their chances of reducing their low frustration tolerance decrease, and they remain babyish all their lives. Maybe their practicing whining helps them assert themselves, but it also may do real harm.

This does not mean that abreactive therapies have no value; since they sometimes do help. Because they contain powerful cognitive elements (e.g., "I *can* change myself by screaming my guts out"), assertive elements ("I feel determined to say how *I* feel and get what *I* want"), shame-attacking exercises ("I can see that wailing at the top of my lungs may *look* foolish but doesn't *make me* a total fool"), and other philosophic aspects which its proponents often ignore. Expressing and revealing your feelings may constitute an important part of therapy—if accompanied by a more mature outlook that helps you change some of those very feelings you acknowledge and express.

14 CONTROLLING YOUR OWN DESTINY

Most people consume so much time and energy trying to do the impossible—namely, to change and control the actions of *others*—that they wrongly believe that they cannot do a normally possible thing—change or control their own thoughts and acts. They firmly hold and rarely challenge what we call Irrational Idea No. 5: *The idea that emotional misery comes from external pressures and that you have little ability to control or change your feelings.*

This idea makes no sense for several reasons. First of all, outside people and events can do nothing, at worst, but harm you physically or cause you various kinds of discomfort or deprivation. Most of the pain they "cause" you (especially feelings of horror, panic, shame, guilt, and hostility) actually stems from your taking their criticisms or rejections too seriously: by your falsely telling yourself that you cannot *stand* their disapproval or cannot enjoy life without their acceptance.

Even physical injury that comes to you from without—as when a flowerpot accidentally falls and breaks your toe—will often cause you relatively little trouble if you philosophically *accept* the inconveniences of your injury and stop telling yourself, over and over again, "Oh, how awful! Oh, how terrible to have this pain!" Not that you have complete control in this regard: for you don't. Some externally caused events almost inevitably cause you considerable annoyance and discomfort, no matter how philosophic about them you may remain. As Bertrand Russell once remarked: "Any man who maintains that happiness comes wholly from within should [get] compelled to spend thirty-six hours in rags in a blizzard, without food."

Nonetheless, you *do* have considerable ability to minimize, though not entirely eliminate, the physical pain. And you have virtually complete ability, if only you would use it, to eradicate your inappropriate emotional and mental pain.

Not that controlling your self-created upsets happens easily. On the contrary, as we keep emphasizing, hurting yourself, giving yourself a terribly rough time, taking others' words and actions and insisting on depressing or overexciting yourself about them—you find these exceptionally easy things to do once you have gotten born and raised in a social community. But—as we keep bringing to the attention of our clients—however effortless you may find it to hurt yourself emotionally, you can make it easier in the long run, and more rewarding even in the short run, to force yourself *not* to do so.

Take, for example, the common statement: "Jerry called me stupid and he hurt me very much by saying that."

"No!" we immediately interrupt. "*Jerry* couldn't possibly hurt you by calling you stupid. Nor could Jerry's *words* hurt you either. You actually mean that you hurt yourself, once you heard Jerry's words, by saying to yourself something like: 'Oh, how terrible for Jerry to call me stupid! I don't come off as stupid and he *shouldn't* say that!' Or: 'Oh, how awful! Maybe I really do look stupid and he sees that I do. How terrible if I exude stupidity!' And, of course, not Jerry's words but *your* beliefs about them make you feel 'hurt.' For you could easily say to yourself: 'Jerry thinks I consistently behave in a stupid fashion. Either he views me wrongly, in which case he seems quite undiscriminating or prejudiced. Or he views me correctly, in which case I'd better try to act less stupidly or accept myself when I act less intelligently. In any event, Jerry overgeneralizes, if he labels me as stupid, for if so I would *always* have to act stupidly. And he wrongly states or implies that I exist as a *bad person* for behaving stupidly. I may well engage in persistent stupidities—but I remain *I*; I never turn into a worm!' "

Our clients, again, frequently remark: "I can't stand it when things go wrong."

And, once more, we quickly interrupt: "What do you mean you can't stand it? Of course you can! Maybe you'll *refuse* to stand it—by withdrawing from the scene precipitously, when you could probably stay and make things better. Or maybe you'll pigheadedly escalate your misery while you *do* stand it—by whining about how terrible it seems and how it *shouldn't* exist that way. But obviously you won't disintegrate because this obnoxious set of circumstances exist. Clearly, you can stand, however much you may *dislike*, their existence. Now, why don't you look at this nonsense you keep telling yourself, decide that you can gracefully lump these poor conditions, while they last, but also work hard at changing them?"

Still again: When humans say that they can't control their feelings, they usually mean that *right now*, at this very moment, they have upset themselves so greatly that their autonomic nervous system (as shown by the overactivity of their sweat glands, visceral reactions, and heartbeat) has temporarily gone out of kilter and that they cannot *immediately* control it. True. But if they expended some *time and energy*, and forced themselves to look at the internalized sentences with which they upset themselves, and by means of which they temporarily drove their autonomic nervous reactions out of control, they would discover that they can *eventually* bring their feelings under control again—and sometimes in a surprisingly short length of time.

Ironically, people can give themselves contradictory messages in this respect and thereby think better and help themselves. In primal therapy, for example, Joe Jones tells himself (1) "If I let out my feelings I *can* stand it" and (2) "My mother hurt me severely years ago and I can't stand this hurt." But if he believes (1) more strongly than he believes (2), he will vote in favor of his controlling himself and may benefit therapeutically. The expression of his feeling of hurt (his abreaction) affects him less than his changing his *idea* about his ability to stand this hurt and control his feelings about it.

I (R.A.H.) found interesting the case of Rick Schule, who spent the first several weeks of therapy insisting that he could not possibly control his frequent and deep-ranging feelings of depression because, before he knew it, they overwhelmed him; and then he felt so severely depressed that he did not feel like doing anything to combat this low state.

"I understand all that you say about looking at the sentences that I say to create these feelings of depression," Rick said on one occasion. "But I don't see how this occurs in my case. For one thing, you must realize that I *unconsciously* bring on my depressed feelings. So how can I possibly consciously see them, before they arise, and thereby stop them from occurring?"

"You can't," said the therapist. "At least not at first. You can initially observe your depressed states after they have already risen, and then see that you have brought them on by telling yourself some nonsense. If you look for this nonsense, you will almost certainly find it—because it does not consist of one of ten thousand diverse unconscious ideas you told yourself but of a few basic irrationalities, which you can easily find if you know the principles of RET or emotional education."

"So if I get depressed, for whatever unconscious reason, I can stop myself, right in the midst of the depression, and tell myself that I keep bringing on my depressed mood. And I can then look for the concrete sentences with which I am bringing it on."

"Exactly. You'll find it difficult to do this, especially at first; but nonetheless you can. Take a recent instance, as an example. When did you last feel depressed?"

"Mmm. Let me see. Well, how about yesterday. I got up late on Sunday, read the newspaper, listened to the radio awhile, and then suddenly felt myself getting very listless and depressed."

"Hadn't anything happened other than your reading the newspaper and listening to the radio up to this time?"

"No, not that I can recall. Let's see if anything else happened. No—oh, yes. Nothing really. But I thought about calling my woman friend and I decided against it."

"Why did you decide against it?"

"Well, I usually see her every Saturday night. But this time she had another date. I didn't like it, of course; but since I definitely don't want to marry her myself, I couldn't very well tell her not to. Anyway, I thought of calling her on Sunday, to see if I could see her later that day. But—" Rick hesitated.

"But—?"

"Well—. Well, you see, I wondered if her date of the night before had stayed over, and whether she would feel embarrassed if I called just then and—"

"Oh! It seems obvious what you told yourself to bring on your depression—doesn't it?"

"Mmmm. I see what you mean. I told myself, 'Well, what if she still has her date there? And what if she's spent such a pleasant time with him all night that she just doesn't want to see me anymore? What if he performed much better in bed with her than I? Jesus, what an awful thing!' "

"Yes: quite obviously. What an *awful* thing if he proved a better lover than you, and she gave you up as her steady boyfriend for him. What a stupid jerk that would make you! Didn't you tell yourself that?"

"I guess you've got it, right on the nose. Exactly what I told myself. And I felt afraid to call her—afraid I'd find out the score. Afraid she'd no longer think me any good—and that that would prove me really worthless. No wonder I got depressed!"

"Yes—no wonder. Can you see how, even though you 'unconsciously' gave yourself such a hard time and depressed yourself, can you see how you can bring those 'unconscious' thoughts to consciousness, how you can quickly ferret them out and see exactly what you say to yourself?"

"By just asking myself like this, like we've just done. By seeing what sentences I say to myself, just as you keep showing me. By 'unconscious,' then, I really mean those things that I don't look at too closely, but that I nonetheless tell myself. Right?"

"Exactly right. We usually mean that by *unconscious*. Occasionally, perhaps, we have truly unconscious thoughts—or thoughts we repress because we feel ashamed to look them in the face, and that we therefore sort of deliberately forget, and cannot easily bring to consciousness anymore. That rates as one of Freud's great discoveries: the existence of repressed thoughts and feelings. Unfortunately, however, he went much too far, and started believing, after a while, that virtually all unconscious thoughts stem from repression and remain inaccessible to conscious review again. A mistake! You will find most of your so-called unconscious thoughts quite available to consciousness—if you dig for them a bit."

"So if I unconsciously depress myself, I can usually find out pretty quickly what I told myself to bring on this depression—and can then undepress myself again?"

"Yes—though, as I said before, this will often prove difficult. For once your depression sets in, as you noted a while ago, you don't *feel* like undepressing yourself again; you almost *want* to stay depressed. And unless you combat this feeling, and actively go after your underlying sentences with which you created your depression, you will stay quite miserable. So you have, in a sense, a choice of evils: remain depressed indefinitely; or forcing yourself, against your own feeling, to combat the depression by seeing what you did to create it. A tough choice, I'll admit. But if you keep taking the lesser of these two evils—combating your negative feelings—eventually the time comes when your basic philosophy of life matures, and you rarely depress yourself, and you have an easier time getting yourself out of your vile mood when you *do* unconsciously put yourself in one."

Rick listened thoughtfully. The next session he came in highly enthused. "Well, Doc," he said, "looks like I made it this time. I got myself into one of those old unconscious depressions again, but I also got myself out of it."

"Good. Tell me about it."

"Well, like this. I told you about my woman friend last week, and her going out with another fellow. I saw her again this week and before I knew it, I heard her saying: 'Rick, get that frown off your face. What makes you so gloomy? You look like a corpse!'"

"Jesus Christ! That hit me right in the solar plexus. I realized, right away, that I still brooded over what had happened the previous week and that my glum mood showed. Which suddenly depressed me all the more. Within the next five minutes, I felt like taking the rope.

"Fortunately, however, I heard your words ringing in my ears: 'When you start to get depressed, ask yourself what you've said to yourself to make yourself depressed.' 'OK,' I said to myself, 'what the hell do I keep saying to make me depressed?' And I got it, as you might expect, right away. I said, first of all,

'Here she sees me again, but how do I know she really wants to? Maybe she'd rather go out with that other guy that she saw last week. Boy, what a terrible thing, if she wanted him instead of me?' And then, once she commented on my frowning, I started saying to myself: 'Well, that finishes it. Not only does she like this other guy better than me, but she thinks I act like a killjoy. After this sort of thing, she'll never want to see me again, for sure. And that will prove, once and for all, what a jerk I turned into!' "

"You certainly gave it to yourself good, didn't you? A fine double dose!"

"You can say that again, Doc. I did myself in beautifully. But for once I caught it—yes, I really caught it! 'Look what you've said to yourself!' I thought. 'Just as the doc pointed out. Boy, what malarkey! Suppose she does like this other guy better than me— what does that really prove about me? And suppose she doesn't like my gloomy face. Does that confirm me as a hopeless idiot who will never make it again with her? Now, why don't I stop telling myself this junk and do my best to act my old pleasanter self again. Then I can see if she really wants me rather than this other guy. And if she wants him rather than me, tough! But not fatal. I'll live.'

"Well, would you believe it, Doc? Within no more than five minutes—maybe even less—I actually stopped that depression *cold*. Every other time I've gotten like that I've gone into a real doozy of a miserable period, with sick headache and all. But not this time! Within a few minutes, I returned to actually smiling and joshing the pants off my friend. And we finally had just about the best day we ever had and she told me that she just didn't want to see the other fellow at all again, since she had such fun with me. You know, Doc, I even think of marrying her now. But the main thing remains me. You said I could control my darned depressions, and blast it if I can't. I find that the best thing that ever happened to me!"

Thus did one person learn to observe his own thinking and, at times, control his depressed feelings. Other techniques that you can use to this same end include:

1. When faced with actual physical injury, deprivation, pain, or disease, you can attempt either to eliminate or to rectify your painful circumstances; or, if not rectifiable to accept them philosophically and try, as best you can, to ignore or distract yourself from them. Instead of telling yourself: "Oh, what a frightful thing keeps happening to me," you can instead say to yourself (and others), "Too bad that I find myself in this unfortunate situation. So it remains too bad!"

2. When faced with emotional assaults from without, you can first question the motives of your attackers and the truth of their statements; and if you honestly think their attacks warranted, you

can try to change your behavior to meet their criticisms or accept your own limitations and others' displeasure that accompanies such limitations.

3. When you feel, for any reason, overwhelmed with anxiety, anger, depression, or guilt, you can realize that outward people and events *don't*, but your own irrational internalized sentences *do*, create these feelings. Even in the midst of these feelings, you can still generally look objectively at your own ideas and images, ferret out their irrationalities (the *shoulds*, *oughts*, and *musts* which you have illegitimately woven into them), and vigorously dispute and challenge these irrationalities.

You rest in your own saddle. You cannot expect complete happiness at all times. Freedom from all physical pain and real deprivation won't remain your lot. But you *can* have an extraordinary lack of mental and emotional woe—if you *think* you can and work for that result.

4. You can also control feelings of compulsion, as when you think you *have* to smoke or overeat, by vigorously disputing that *have to* and making it a strong *desire* that you can still inhibit. Joseph Danysh, in his fine book *Stop Without Quitting*, shows how you can even change your desire, let alone compulsion, to smoke by forcing yourself, many times, to bring to your mind *all* the major meanings of "smoking" and "quitting." Thus, you normally make "smoking" mean to you *only* ease, sophistication, relaxation, and enjoyment—and fail to keep thinking about the pain, expense, sickness, and death which it *also* really means. If you constantly bring to mind the *whole range* of meanings of the term, you will look at smoking and *feel* about smoking much differently. In RET we use Danysh's technique of referenting words like "smoking" and "quitting" (which you, as a hardened smoker, only tend to give gruesome meanings to) to apply to many other emotional problems: so that you can by this referenting see what terms like these *really* mean, and thereby change your semantic concepts and emotional feelings about them.

15
CONQUERING ANXIETY

Our clients and associates often try to confound us on one special point, where they feel that our technique of rational-emotive therapy comes a cropper and sadly begins to bog down. "You may rightly insist," they say, "that most difficulties arise from irrational beliefs we feed ourselves and that we can overcome our difficulties by changing these beliefs. But what about anxiety? How can we possibly control or change that by challenging and disputing our own assumptions? You'll never change that trait very much, no matter how rationally you approach it."

Rot! We can approach and control anxiety by straight thinking. For anxiety, basically, consists of Irrational Idea No. 6: *The idea that if something seems dangerous or fearsome, you must preoccupy yourself with and make yourself anxious about it.*

We don't claim that real or rational fears do not exist. They certainly do. When you prepare to cross a busy intersection, you'd better fear the possibility of getting hit by a moving vehicle and therefore feel *concerned* about your safety. Fear of this sort not only seems a natural human tendency, but also a necessity for self-preservation. Without your having appropriate fear or concern about your safety, your days on this earth would not continue very long!

Nonetheless, fear and anxiety differ. Anxiety, (as we employ the term in this book) consists of *over*concern, of *exaggerated* or *needless* fear. And it most frequently doesn't relate to physical injury or illness but to mental "injury" or "harm." In fact, probably 98 percent of what we call anxiety crops up as *overconcern for what someone thinks about you.* And this kind of anxiety, as well as exaggerated fear of bodily injury, appears needlessly self-defeating on several counts:

1. If something truly seems dangerous or fearsome, you may take two intelligent approaches: (a) determine whether this thing *actually* involves danger and (b) if so, either do something practical to alleviate the existing danger; or (if you can do nothing) resign yourself to the fact of its existence. Bellyaching about it or continually reiterating to yourself the holy horror of a potentially or actually fearsome situation will not change it or better prepare you to cope with it. On the contrary, the more you upset yourself, the less able you will prove, in almost all instances, to accurately assess and cope with this danger.

2. Although certain accidents and illnesses (such as airplane accidents or the onset of cancer) *may* befall you one day, and it will prove unfortunate if one of these misfortunes *does* occur, once you have taken reasonable precautions to ward off such a possible mishap you can usually do nothing else about it. Worry, believe it or not, has no magical quality of staving off bad luck. On the contrary, it frequently increases the probability of disease or accident by unnerving the vulnerable individual. Thus, the more you worry about getting into an automobile crack-up, the more likelihood exists that you will get yourself into just such a crack-up.

3. You exaggerate the assumed catastrophic quality of many potentially unpleasant events. Death emerges as the worst thing that can happen to you—and sooner or later you will die anyway. If you suffer from dire physical pain for a long period of time (as when you have an incurable cancerous condition and cannot find relief in drugs), you can always commit suicide. Virtually all misfortunes which might occur—such as loss of a loved one or loneliness—turn out, when they actually occur, far less dreadful than you might have worriedly fantasized. The worst thing about almost any "disaster" proceeds from your exaggerated *belief* about its horror rather than its intrinsic terribleness.

Life holds innumerable pains in the neck for all of us; but true catastrophies (such as experiencing torture or witnessing a major disaster in which scores of people suffer or perish) rarely happen. And "terrors," "horrors," and "awfulnesses" arise from fictional demons—which we foolishly make up in our heads and cannot really define or validate. A "horror" doesn't mean something *very* unfortunate or *exceptionally* disadvantageous. It means (if you look honestly at your feelings) something that you think *more* than unfortunate and *beyond the realm* of human disadvantage. Clearly, nothing of this kind exists; and your most devout belief in its existence will still not make it true.

Something "horrible" or "awful," moreover, really means

something that you see as (a) unusually obnoxious and (b) absolutely should or must not exist *because* you find it obnoxious. Although you can fairly easily prove the first part of this belief—that you find the thing or act uncommonly obnoxious—you cannot prove the second part: that it *therefore* must not exist. Indeed, if a law of the universe held that Activating Events (at point A) that you find extremely unpleasant (at point B) *must not* exist (at point C), A and C could not possibly coexist. So when you dogmatically contend (a) that such events must not prevail and (b) that they distinctly (and horribly!) *do*, you patently believe in the impossible. If you accept reality—and stop making up immutable laws of the universe in your silly head—you can accept the obvious fact that whatever exists exists—no matter how unpleasant and inconvenient you find its existence. Consequently, nothing truly winds up as "awful," "horrible," or "terrible."

4. Worry itself develops into one of the most painful conditions. And most of us would remain better off dead than "living" in its continual throes. If you unavoidably encounter the real dangers of blackmail, injury, or death, you'd better frankly face such problems and accept whatever penalties may accrue from them, rather than continue to live in panic. You may well prefer a life in jail or even no life whatever to spending the rest of your days running, hiding, and panting with intense anxiety.

5. Aside from the possibility of physical harm, or acute deprivation, what can you *really* ever fear? So people may disapprove or dislike you. So some of them may boycott you or say nasty things about you. So they may besmirch your reputation. Tough, disadvantageous; rough! As long as you do not *literally* starve, go to jail, or suffer bodily harm as a result of their censure, why give yourself a super-hard time about the wheels that turn in their heads? If you stop worrying and *do* something about their possible disapproval, you will probably counteract it. If you can do nothing to help yourself; tough again. So the cards fall that way! Why make the game of life more difficult by fretting and whining about its inequities? Do—don't stew!

6. Although many things seem terribly fearful to a young child, who has little or no control over his destiny, as an adult, you usually *have* more control and can change truly fearful circumstances or, if you cannot, can philosophically learn to live without making yourself panicky about them. Adults do not *have* to keep reactivating fears that may once have had but no longer have validity.

Mrs. Jane Borengrad provides us with an illustration of the foolish perpetuation of childhood fears. As a child, she unprotestingly accepted her sadistic father, who would severely punish her for the slightest questioning of his authority. Then (because she believed she deserved no better treatment) she married an equally sadistic man and remained with him for ten years until he turned openly psychotic and got committed to a mental hospital.

During both her childhood and her first marriage, then, she lived under truly fearful circumstances. But not during her second marriage to Mr. Borengrad. For she could scarcely have found a meeker, nicer partner. Nonetheless, she felt exceptionally disturbed and came to therapy in a veritable state of panic. Having majored in psychology in college, she stated her symptoms to me (A.E.) in somewhat sophisticated terms:

"It looks like I keep behaving exactly like Pavlov's dogs. I apparently conditioned myself to react to anyone close to me with fear and trembling, with submission and underlying resentment, and I keep going through the old conditioned-response business over and over. Even though my husband acts like the kindest man in the world, and my teen-age daughters behave like lovely dolls, I live in constant, generalized fear. Ring the bell just before presenting the steak, and pretty soon the dog slobbers for the food he knows he will get. Well, ring the bell with me, and I immediately cringe with terror—even though the sadistic treatment I used to receive from my father and my first husband no longer follows its ringing. When simply in the presence of any member of my family, bell or no bell, I quickly start cringing."

"Maybe it looks like conditioning to you," I said, "but I feel that the very word 'conditioning' seems so vague and general that it actually masks the detailed processes that go on. Now let's look much more closely at these so-called conditioning processes. First, let's see what used to go on with your father and your first husband."

"They would get so angry at some little thing that I did or didn't do that I noticed their anger, and also saw how they followed it up—by punishing me severely in some manner. Then, naturally, whenever I began to see them growing angry, I immediately felt very fearful of the punishment that would follow. And I either ran away, went into a panic state, or asked them to beat me quickly and get the horrible thing over with."

"All right; that sounds like a good description. But you left out a very important part of the process."

"What?"

"Well, you said that they got angry? and you knew they would punish you; and then you went into a panic state. But the second part of the process—the part where you knew that they would punish you—you gloss over that too easily. You probably mean, don't you, that you perceived their anger and then, in a split second, you told yourself something like: 'Oh, my heavens! There he goes again, getting angry at me for practically nothing. Oh, how terrible! Oh, how unfair! What a poor miserable, helpless creature I remain, having an unfair father (or husband) who takes advantage of me like this and against whom I feel too weak to protect myself!' Didn't you say this, or something like this, to yourself once you perceived your father's or your first husband's anger?"

"Yes, I think I did. Particularly with my father, I would tell myself how awful that I had a father like that, while Minerva Scanlan, my best girl friend, had such a nice, easygoing father who never yelled at her and never hit her or punished her. I felt so *ashamed* to have a father like mine. And I thought I came from such a terrible family—so bad, in fact, that I wouldn't even want Minerva or anyone else to know just *how* badly they treated me."

"And with your first husband?"

"There, too. Only this time I didn't feel so ashamed of *him* but of my *having married* him. I kept saying, whenever he got angry and I knew he would pounce on me, 'Oh, how could I ever prove so stupid as to marry anyone like him? After I saw so much of this kind of thing at home, too! And then I went right out and repeated this horrible mistake, voluntarily. And now I keep staying with him, when I should have the guts to leave, even if I have to work my hands to the bone to take care of the children myself. How could I act so stupidly!' "

"All right, then. Note how we not only have the stimulus, the anger of your father and your first husband, and the conditioned response, your great fear of punishment, but we also and more importantly have your self-blaming *interpretations* of the horror of the stimulus. You theoretically could have told yourself, 'There goes crazy old Dad getting angry again, and about to punish me unjustly. Well, too bad; but I can survive his punishment and eventually, as I grow up, get away from him and live in a nonpunishing environment.' You actually largely said to yourself, however, 'I feel blameworthy for coming from such a crazy family and for having such weakness as to let the old buzzard take advantage of me.' And, with your first husband, you could have said to yourself, 'Too bad: I made a mistake in marrying this individual who acts sadistically, but I feel strong enough to get away from him and leave him to his own crazy ways.' But you again said: 'I see myself as no good for making the terrible mistake of marrying this bastard; and now I remain too weak and idiotic to get away from him.' "

"You seem to say then, that neither my father's nor my husband's actions—their anger followed by their punishment—actually conditioned me to down myself, but my own unjustified interpretations of their actions really did the job."

"Yes, your own *partly* unjustified interpretations. For you existed, of course, especially when you lived with your father, as a little girl who appropriately could have suffered from your father's physical assaults; and no matter what you might have told yourself philosophically, you experienced some *real* danger, and you would have emoted inappropriately if you did not feel frightened at all."

"But things proceeded differently when I married my first husband."

"Yes. Again, with him, you might have had some reason for fear, since he behaved psychotically and could literally have killed you when he got angry. But as you yourself pointed out before, you also could have left him—which you couldn't do when you lived as a girl in your father's home. So most of the so-called conditioned fear with your husband you taught yourself: By falsely telling yourself that you couldn't cope with the situation, shouldn't have married him in the first place, and turned into a slob for staying with him. If you had told yourself other and more sensible things, you would soon have left him—or might even have stayed and felt unterrified of him."

" 'Conditioning,' then, represents something of a cover-up word for what we largely do to ourselves?"

"Yes, very often. In Pavlov's case, don't forget that *he*, Pavlov, conditioned the dogs from the outside: he completely controlled whether they would or would not get their piece of steak when the bell rang. And in the case of your father, a much bigger and stronger person than you, he also largely controlled whether or not you would get beaten once he got angry. But not entirely! For had you had a better and different philosophical outlook when you lived with your father—which not very many young girls manage to acquire—you could have (unlike Pavlov's dogs) changed the situation considerably. Thus, you could have somehow influenced your father and induced him to punish one of your brothers or sisters, rather than you. Or you could have managed literally to run out of the house most of the time you knew he might punish you. Or you could have accepted your punishment more stoically and not bothered yourself too much about it. Or you could have tried many other gambits to change or ameliorate the effects of your father's behavior. But because of your poor philosophy of life at the time—which, admittedly, your father helped you acquire—you passively submitted to his blows, and also blamed yourself for having such a father and for having to submit. Although your situation had fear-inspiring elements, you helped make it positively *terrifying.*"

"I can see what you mean. And with my first husband, I guess, I did even worse. There, I didn't have to submit at all; but I just about forced myself—with what you again would call my poor philosophy of life—to do so, and again made myself terrified."

"Exactly. Although you brought about only some of your so-called conditioning in your relations with your father, you probably created the far greater part of it with your first husband. Where you could have nicely *un*conditioned yourself—by telling yourself how ridiculous it proved to suffer the punishments of such a palpably disturbed man—you did the reverse and worked very hard to condition yourself still more."

"And what about my present state, with my second husband?"

"Your present state proves, even more solidly, the thesis we have discussed. For you will remember, again, that in the case of Pavlov's dogs, when he kept presenting the bell without steak, the dogs soon got unconditioned and stopped salivating, since they soon realized, or somehow signaled themselves, that the steak and the bell did not go together any longer. Accordingly, therefore, if you had gotten classically conditioned by the experiences with your father and first husband, both tyrants, you would have gradually got unconditioned by your several years of experience with your second husband, who acts practically angelically when compared with the first two."

"He does. Unbelievably nice and unpunishing."

"But your merely staying in his or your daughters' presence, you say, causes you to go into a state of panic?"

"Yes, I can't understand it. But it just happens."

"I think you really *can* understand it, if you look a little more closely, and stop convincing yourself that you got 'automatically' conditioned by your past experiences. For if your husband's behavior obviously did not reinforce your previously learned fear, and this fear still actively persists, then *you* keep doing something to reinforce it, to keep it alive, yourself."

"You really think so?"

"Yes—unless we believe in some kind of magic. If you, as we just noted, at least partly set up the original terrible fear of your father and your husband, even though they certainly also contributed to the context of the fear, and if your present husband doesn't contribute to that context to any serious degree, who else but you *does* keep the fear alive?"

"Hmmm. I see what you mean. And what do you think I keep telling myself to keep my fear alive?"

"What do *you* think? If you start asking yourself, you will soon start to see."

"I probably tell myself what you pointed out before: that I always exuded weakness and inadequacy and that I still do. And that therefore I *do* have something to remain afraid of—my own weakness."

"A good point. These things usually develop circularly, just as you indicated. First, your father abuses you, then you tell yourself you can't do anything to stop his abuse, then you get terribly anxious. But, once you get anxious, and you only half-heartedly try to overcome anxiety, you start telling yourself that you can't do anything about *that*. So you get anxious of getting, and of not feeling able to do anything about getting, anxious. Quite a pickle!"

"Precisely. I used to fear my father and my first husband— though, really, myself, my weakness. And now I fear *remaining* anxious—remaining weak. And even though my present husband and daughters do *not* abuse me, I feel afraid that I couldn't handle the situation if they *did*. I stay afraid of inadequacy—and so afraid of feeling afraid—that I make myself panicky most of the time."

"Precisely. Then, to take it one step further, you actually do get so frightened, and act so badly because of your fright, that you then get convinced of your original hypothesis—that because you have such weakness and inadequacy, no one could ever possibly love you, including, especially, your own present husband and daughters."

"So I really start with a great need for love and a fear that, because I remain so worthless, I won't get this need fulfilled. Then because of my fear I behave badly. Then I note that I behave badly and say to myself: 'That proves my worthlessness! Then, because I have doubly proved this 'worthlessness,' I get even more afraid that I won't deserve love the next time. And so on, and on."

"Right. And then, going one step further, you hate yourself for staying so weak and for having such a dire need for love; and you resent your present husband and daughters for not fulfilling your dire need to the exact extent you demand that they fill it—and for not making up for all the anger and punishment that your father and your first husband foisted on you. So that amounts to a goodly degree of resentment—which only tends to make you still more upset."

"As you said before: Quite a pickle! But what do I do now to get out of it?"

"What do you think you do? If you tell yourself sentences One, Two, Three, and Four to get result Number Five, and result Number Five seems highly undesirable, how do you manage not to get it again?"

"By untelling yourself sentences One, Two, Three, and Four!"

"Yes. And also, 'Why, if I do happen to get anxious because I remind myself of some past threat that really doesn't exist anymore, can't I then *see* what I've done and calm myself down pretty quickly?"

"And if I try this kind of disputing and challenging and persist at it, I can see no reason why I have to continue to live in this kind of panic state I've forced myself into for such a long time?"

"No, no reason at all. Try it and see. And if it works, as I think it will, that will prove great. And if it doesn't then we'll quickly discover what *other* nonsense you tell yourself to stop it from working."

"I mainly better believe that no matter what seems upsetting or frightening, I now do it myself. I may not have done it in the past. But now I do!"

"In the main, yes. Occasionally, you may have a truly fearful circumstance in your life—as when you navigate a sinking boat or a defective car. But these kinds of realistic fears occur rarely in modern life; and the great majority of the things we now get panicked about constitute self-created 'dangers' that exist almost entirely in our own imaginations. *These* we do ourselves. And these we can undo by looking at our crooked thinking and straightening it out."

"OK. What you say sounds reasonable. Let me do a little trying."

Mrs. Borengrad did try. Within the next several weeks she not only ceased feeling terrified when in the presence of her daughters and her present husband, but felt able to do several other things, including making a public speech at her community center, a thing which she had never felt capable of doing before. She learned, and as the years go by she still continues to learn, that unlike Pavlov's dogs she can recondition or uncondition her feelings and her responses *from the inside* and that she does not *have* to respond to actual or possible anger with woeful feelings of fright.

Pavlov, as not generally realized by many of those who quote him, thought that although rats and dogs and guinea pigs largely get conditioned by mere contiguity of stimuli (for example, a bell) and unconditioned responses (for example, salivation when smelling and tasting food), humans respond more complicatedly and get symbolically conditioned by what he called their secondary signaling system, their thinking. B. F. Skinner also talks about verbal as well as nonverbal behavior and states and implies that humans get conditioned—or self-conditioned—by things that they tell themselves about their environment, as well as by purely external changes in their contingencies of reinforcement. Skinner, in *Beyond Freedom and Dignity*, states:

> *Methodological behaviorism limits itself to what [we can observe] publicly; mental processes may exist, but their nature rules them out of scientific consideration. The "behaviorists" in political science and many logical positivists in philosophy have followed a similar line. But we can study self-observation, and we must include it in any reasonably complete account of human behavior. Rather than ignore consciousness, an experimental analysis of behavior has put much emphasis on certain critical issues.*

Right! But Skinner does not go far enough. As I (A.E.) have

noted in a special review of his book in the journal *Behavior Therapy*, he does not sufficiently emphasize self-reinforcement:

> *Ironically enough, Skinner himself has rarely gotten reinforced for his views on freedom and dignity; nor have I often gotten reinforced for my opposing views that man can largely control his own emotional destiny, in spite of many of the environmental influences that impinge on him. Yet both Skinner and I pigheadedly stick to our largely unreinforced views. Why? . . . [Skinner] leaves out some salient information about humans: (1) Pure free will does not exist, but this hardly means that individuals can make no choices. (2) Behavior gets shaped and maintained by its consequences partly because the "inner man" (or the individual) feels and perceives the consequences of behavior and, at least to some degree, decides to change. (3) The "inner man" defines some consequences as "desirable" or "undesirable." As noted above, Skinner gains the opposition of the majority of psychologists for his views, defines his own conclusions as "good" and "reinforcing," and chooses to see their opposition (social disapproval) as not particularly penalizing. Another thinker, with Skinner's views, might well choose to construe his peers' disagreement as too negatively reinforcing to buck; and he might consequently change his views, stop expressing them, depress himself about social disapproval, or commit suicide. (4) Although Skinner's "orneriness" has some prior environmental determinants, he probably also exercises some elements of "free choice." He himself mentions "the interaction between organism and environment," implying that the former significantly interprets and manipulates the latter, as well as the latter shaping and maintaining the former. A comprehensive, therapeutic view of humans gives some degree of strength and autonomy to both the organism and the environment—as, I think, Skinner does, too, but as some of his extreme statements appear to belie.*

In general, you may wage the most effective kinds of counterattacks against your needless and inappropriate anxieties along the following lines:

1. Track your worries and anxieties back to the specific beliefs of which they consist. Usually, you will find that you keep explicitly or implicitly telling yourself: "Doesn't it emerge as terrible that—?" and "Wouldn't it seem awful if—". Forcefully ask yourself: "*Why* would it emerge as so terrible that!—?" and "*Would* it really seem so awful if—?" Certainly, if this or that happened it

might well prove inconvenient, annoying, or unfortunate. But can you, really, ever find empirical evidence that anything that might happen to you turns *terrible* or *awful*? For, honestly, you don't mean (*do* you?) by these terms that if something happened it would seem *very* bad or even *100 percent* bad. You mean that it would prove *more* than bad—and how, ever, can *that* happen?

2. When a situation actually involves danger—as when you start to fly in a rickety old airplane—you can sensibly (a) change the situation (for example, don't take the trip) or (b) accept the danger as one of the unfortunate facts of life (thus, accept the fact that you may die in the rickety plane; that this would prove most unfortunate if you did; and that life, to have full satisfaction, may have to include considerable risk-taking). If you can minimize a danger, act to reduce it. If you cannot, or you would find it more disadvantageous to avoid it than to risk it, then you have less choice and you'd *just better* accept it. No matter how you slice it, the inevitable remains inevitable; and no amount of worrying will make it less so.

3. If a dire event may occur, and you can do no more to ward it off, then *realistically* weigh the chances of its occurring and *realistically* assess the calamity that will befall you if it actually does occur. Although another world war *may* occur tomorrow, will it *likely* come about? If it does occur, will you probably get maimed or killed? If you die, will it *really* prove much more catastrophic than your peacefully dying in bed ten or twenty years later?

4. You'd better use both verbal *and* active depropagandization to overcome a specific anxiety. First realize that *you* created the anxiety by your internal sentences and challenge and dispute them. Also, push yourself to *do* the thing you senselessly fear and keep repeatedly (and promptly and vigorously!) *acting* against this fear.

Thus, if you avoid riding on buses, realize that your over-concern has roots in your own negative propaganda: in your telling yourself that buses prove dangerous, that horrible things will happen to you in a bus, that if anything dreadful did happen on a bus you couldn't stand it, and so on. And contradict this nonsense by showing yourself that buses provide unusual safety; that very few people get injured while riding on them; that if an unpleasant event occurs on a bus, you can handle it. Preferably, force yourself, over and over again, to keep riding on buses and to keep showing yourself, while riding, rational beliefs about bus-riding. The more you do the things you senselessly fear *while* contradicting your self-imposed anxiety, the quicker and more thoroughly your needless panics will vanish.

5. Most anxieties related to the dread of making public mis-takes, or antagonizing others, of losing love. Always suspect that

some dire fear of disapproval lies behind your seemingly more objective fears, and continually and powerfully challenge and fight this fear by showing yourself that disapproval may bring disadvantages—but only self-defined "horror."

6. Convince yourself that worrying about many situations will aggravate rather than improve them. If, instead of telling yourself what "awfulness" would reign if something obnoxious happened, you tell yourself how silly, senseless, and self-defeating you will act if you *keep worrying* about this "awful" thing, you will have a much better chance of short-circuiting your irrational anxieties. Don't, however, blame or condemn yourself *for* your senseless worrying.

7. Try not to exaggerate the importance or significance of things. Your favorite cup, as Epictetus noted many centuries ago, merely represents a cup which you like. Your wife and children, however delightful, remain mortals. You need not take a negativistic, defensive "so-what" attitude and falsely tell yourself: "So what if I break my cup or my wife and children die? Who cares?" For you'd better care for your cup and your wife and children, in order to lead a more zestful and absorbing life. But if you exaggeratedly convince yourself that this remains the *only* cup in the world or that your life would turn out completely useless without your wife and children, you will falsely overestimate their value and make yourself needlessly vulnerable to their possible loss.

Remember, in this connection, that to enjoy an event wholeheartedly does *not* mean that you must catastrophize its absence. You may enjoy your cup, your wife, and your children wholeheartedly and truly care for them. But their sudden removal, although certainly a distinct loss and something that you may considerably *regret*, need not prove *calamitous.* This loss, however difficult, merely removes *something* that you ardently desire and love—it does not remove *you.* Unless, of course, you *insist* on identifying your*self* with the people and things you love; and that kind of identification goes with emotional disturbance.

8. Distraction, as we noted in the last chapter, may temporarily dissipate groundless fear. If you worry about a plane's falling, forcing yourself to concentrate on a magazine or a book may give you some respite. If you fear that you speak poorly, vigorous focusing on the content of your talk rather than on the reactions of your audience will often calm your fears. For deeper and more lasting removal of anxieties, however, a thoroughgoing philosophic approach, along the lines previously noted in this chapter, will prove much more effective.

9. Tracking your present fears to their earlier origins, and seeing how though they *once* seemed fairly appropriate they *no longer* hold water, often serves as a useful anxiety-reducing tech-

nique. As a child, you normally feared many things, such as staying in the dark or fighting with an adult. But you now have grown up. Keep showing yourself this and demonstrating that you can easily take certain chances now that you might have wisely avoided some years ago.

10. Don't make yourself ashamed of still existing anxieties, no matter how senseless they may seem. Certainly it seems wrong, meaning *mistaken,* for a grown person like you to retain childish fears. But *wrong* or *mistaken* does not mean *criminal* or *damnable.* And if people dislike you because you show anxiety, too bad—but hardly devastating! Admit, by all means, that you feel needlessly fearful; forthrightly tackle your silly worries; but don't waste a minute beating yourself over the head for making yourself anxious. You have much better things to do with your time and energies!

11. No matter how effectively you combat your anxieties, and temporarily eradicate them, don't feel surprised if they return from time to time. Humans fear again what they have once feared, even though they generally no longer remain afraid of this thing. If you once had a fear of high places and you conquered it by deliberately frequenting such places, you may still, on occasion, feel afraid when looking down from heights. In these circumstances, merely accept the returned fear, actively work against it again, and you will quickly see, in most instances, that it returns to limbo.

Always remember, in this connection, that you remain mortal; that humans have innate limitations; that they don't *completely* overcome groundless fears and anxieties; and that life continues as a ceaseless battle against irrational worries. If you fight this battle intelligently and unremittingly, however, you can *almost* always feel free from *almost* all your needless concerns. What more can you ask?

16 *ACQUIRING SELF-DISCIPLINE*

The easy way out usually comes off as just that—the easy way out of the most rewarding *life*. Yet you may have no trouble swearing by Irrational Idea No. 7: *The idea that you can more easily avoid facing many life difficulties and self-responsibilities than undertake more rewarding forms of self-discipline*. This idea proves fallacious in several significant respects.

First of all, the notion that the easiest way out of life difficulties constitutes the best way leads, at the very most, to the avoidance of action at the exact moment of decision—and not to ease during the moments, hours, and days that follow this decision. Augie Mallick, for example, kept convincing himself that it would prove terrible if the woman he had known for several years rejected his physical overtures. Every time he thought of putting his arm around her or holding her hand, he would feel overwhelmed by his fear of rejection and would take the "easy" way out by drawing away from her. At the exact moment of his withdrawal, he sighed with relief. But for the rest of the night with her, and often for many nights following, he loathed himself and suffered the torments of the damned for his one moment of "ease." For he realized that avoidance of fearful and difficult circumstances usually, in the long run, brings on far greater conflicts and self-annoyances.

By avoiding certain difficulties of life, moreover, you almost always tend to exaggerate their pain and discomfort. If Augie Mallick does take a chance, puts his arm around his friend, and actually gets rejected by her, will this rejection actually hurt him as much as, in imagination, he thinks it will? If he keeps getting rejected, will he *still* feel just as hurt? If he does get hurt, will his whole world fall apart? Almost certainly, if he keeps trying, the hard way, to win the favor of this woman, he will find the answer to those questions a pretty solid no.

Let us assume, again, that Augie tries, meets rejection, and gets hurt (or, more accurately, hurts himself by over-emphasizing the necessity of his getting accepted). Even so, will his self-hurt, following rejection, feel worse than his self-hurt following his not *trying*? Probably not.

Still again: If Augie tries and fails, he will almost certainly *learn* something by his failure, while if he never tries, he will learn little. If he does things the hard way, the woman he admires may ultimately accept him. And if she doesn't, the knowledge he acquires from getting rejected may help him succeed with some other woman.

In the normal course of events, if Augie keeps trying, even against odds, he will ultimately succeed with *some* woman. While if he gives up and foredooms himself to celibacy, his life will amount to a classic example of nothing ventured, nothing gained. But if he does venture, he will obtain some kind of satisfaction. We achieve few of life's outstanding gratifications without risk-taking. Augie, in terms of time and energies expended, has his choice of: put up or shut up. And the less he puts up, the less he will fulfill his aliveness.

Similarly with the more negative side of the coin of self-discipline. If Janice, who wants to lose weight, refuses to go through the continued difficulties of dieting, she will seemingly take the "easy" way out. But while she still enjoys her eating, will she also "enjoy" lugging around twenty extra pounds, losing attractive males to slimmer and trimmer women, feeling tired and "blah" much of the time, and risking several ailments that often go with an overweight condition?

The story, then, unwinds with nauseating similarity when you take the "easier" or unselfdisciplined way out of life difficulties and responsibilities. Either your "easier" way proves, in the long run, actually harder. Or it continues to seem easier—less consuming of time and energy—but also turns out considerably less rewarding.

Take, by way of example, the case of Elmer Pinkham, a bright and potentially capable law school student who came to see me (R.A.H.) some years ago. He got addicted to the easy-way approach to life and knew all the angles of work avoidance. Instead of buckling down to his studies, he spent considerable time learning the peculiarities of his professors—what they liked and did not like—so that he could induce them to give him good grades in spite of his continual goofing.

At the time Elmer came to see me he felt involved with a fellow student but found the going rough. "Sally," he said, "acts like a great kid, but also like a very dependent character. I just can't have an ordinary affair with her—she's moved in. I mean completely moved in. I just can't get anything done anymore. Not that I do much studying anyway; but with her around, I do absolutely none. We just make love, period. And I mean period! And she gives me a pain in the hindquarters as well, since she wants me at her beck and call every single moment of the day and night and I can hardly go to the john without her tagging along. Other girls, whom I would like to see, too, from time to time, remain absolutely out with Sally camping on my tail."

"If you find your relationship with Sally interfering with your long-term plans to finish school and pass your bar exam and with your desire to have more time to yourself, why don't you either change the relationship with her or drop it?" I asked.

"I can't change it," Elmer replied. "Sally will remain Sally. She clings like a baby. She leaves no other way to relate to her. And I couldn't drop her—I just couldn't face her tears and her hysteria. Why, she'd wail around for weeks. And with some of the things she knows about me, how I cheated on some of my law exams and that sort of thing, she might cause trouble, too. I just couldn't go through the trouble of facing her and getting her to leave me."

"But with things this way, you say she proves much more of a bother than a pleasure. And, granted that you might find it difficult to get rid of her, don't you think you'd think it worth it in the long run?"

"Yeah, I suppose so. But I wouldn't want to do it that way. I'd rather half keep her, you know. She does damned well in bed! And if I could only have less of her and not have her around all the time, that I'd like. But how can I have it that way?"

"You mean: How can you eat your cake and have it?"

"Well, you might put it that way. But maybe I can. Maybe I can find an angle I could work so that I could still have Sally, sort of on a part-time basis and not feel bothered by her so much and kept from seeing other women sometimes."

"I can see you've already figured something out. Something real cute, no doubt. Now, what plan do you have?"

"Well, Doc, like this. I thought that if you would call Sally in and tell her you have diagnosed my problems and all that jazz and that you think it necessary that she stop living with me, but just come around a couple of times a week, and stop getting so sticky with me, you know—. Well, I thought you could fix it up with her so that I wouldn't have to give her up, not go through getting her all upset like, yet could keep the best part of our relationship going."

"You want me to help you do things the easy way with Sally, so that you won't have to face any responsibilities or difficulties and yet get exactly what you want. And you want me to sell Sally a bill of goods, so that she'll accept half a loaf while you have your usual loaf and a half."

"Well, it would work out easier on Sally that way, too, wouldn't it? She wouldn't get hurt or anything and would understand my position. You could easily arrange it, from your side. You must include such things in your day's routine."

"It may surprise you to know," I said, "that my routine tends to run along other lines than acting as a kind of psychotherapeutic con man, easygoing fix-it expert, and emotional blackmailer. On the contrary, I help people to face and do things the hard way—because in the long run that way generally brings inner security and happiness. If I did what you want me to do, I would deprive you of the glorious opportunity to buckle down, for perhaps the first time in your life, to solve this difficult situation and gain some confidence that you actually *can* face and resolve tough situations that you encounter. I would also thus connive to help Sally avoid making her own difficult decisions about whether to accept you on your terms or go on behaving as a big baby, as she does now. So my answer: a flat no. I intend to do you the service of forcing you, if possible, to face life this time, so that you may learn how to cope with it and with yourself for a change and how to modify some of your obviously self-defeating, short-range hedonism."

"I feel surprised at your attitude," Elmer said. "You have a reputation as a liberal among psychologists. I've heard this from several people at the university. And yet you keep giving me that old character-building song and dance. That old crap about 'chin up, sweet, clean, puritanical bird in the hand of God; work hard, act like a good Christian, and you'll get a crumb from Jesus in the hereafter!' "

"You have the privilege of distorting what I say, if you wish. I *do* say, however: The line of least resistance that you keep continually taking, in your schoolwork, in your relations with Sally, and in some other aspects of your life, will not, almost certainly, bring you what you really seem to want (and what you beautifully hide from yourself): namely, work-confidence and truly rewarding relationships with others. Whether you like it or not (and I think you don't), you will not get maximum enjoyment until you learn to face the realities and difficulties of this world, figure out the best way of meeting instead of avoiding them, and act courageously and decisively about them. This may sound to you like a philosophy of puritanical punishment, work for work's sake, and character-building for your heavenly salvation. But no. It just remains one of the hard and cold facts of this highly unheavenly world."

"Maybe so, but I think I can do better than that. And I think I'll find another therapist with less austere ideals. There must exist an easier road to happiness than the one you insist upon."

I heard no more from Elmer. For all I know, he still keeps shopping for the easy way of life and a less austere therapist to help him climb its roads. I would wager, however, that life will someday catch him up on his short selling of it and himself. At that time, if he has not softened himself up too much to tackle his basic problems, he may return for some serious therapy. I'll probably remain at the old stand, with my "character-building" approach to life; and I shall, if he wants me to, gladly welcome him back.

If avoidance of life's difficulties and self-responsibilities leads, in most instances, to less rewarding activities and decreasing confidence, acceptance of the "harder" way usually makes greater sense. More specifically, this involves the following kinds of activities:

1. Although we do not recommend your taking on of needless tasks and responsibilities, which may even prove masochistic, you can identify truly desirable activities—and then unrebellingly and promptly perform them. Desirable life tasks usually include: (a) tasks aiding survival, such as eating, defecating, and building a shelter from the cold; and (b) tasks not strictly necessary for survival but that you usually must do to obtain desired goals—for example, brushing your teeth to prevent decay or commuting in order to live in the country and work in the city.

2. Once you view a goal as necessary for your survival or desirable for your happiness (and not because *others* think you should attain it), you can obtain self-discipline by vigorous self-propagandization and vigorous action. In particular, you can first ferret out and forcefully attack your main *un*disciplining internal verbalizations: the nonsense that you keep telling yourself along the lines of "I can more easily do what I have done in the past." "I don't believe that I *can* discipline myself," and "Why should I *have* to do these unpleasant things to get the pleasant results I desire?" Instead, try to acquire a philosophy represented by these kinds of sentences: "I'll find it definitely harder and less rewarding, especially in the long run, to do things the 'easy way.' " "I *do* have the ability, as a human, to discipline myself, even though it proves difficult to do so." "Whether I like it or not, I'll find *no* way to get the results I desire than by performing some unpleasant and time-consuming requisites."

3. Face the fact that, because you remain a fallible human, you often will have great difficulty getting started along a certain constructive line, and that normal principles of inertia will tend to hold you back and make starting a chore. *Expect* these problems to occur and prophylactically *accept* that you will often have to use *extra* push and *extra* energy to get yourself on the road to

self-discipline. Once you get going at brushing your teeth or getting up in the morning to travel to work, your task will tend to get easier and sometimes, even, enjoyable. But at the start it usually won't! Don't expect this. Easy or not, keep convincing yourself that, if you want to obtain certain results, no way normally exists *but* discipline. Sad—but true!

4. Once you start on self-discipline, you can often make things easier for yourself. Put yourself on a regular schedule or program: Give yourself some sub-goals on any major project that you undertake. Work on a piece-rate basis (for example, force yourself to write so many pages or do a certain minimum number of exercises a day). Give yourself some intermediate rewards for your disciplining (permit yourself to go to a movie *after* you have completed this much studying or that much housecleaning for the day). Although RET made use of self-reinforcing or self-management principles from its earliest beginnings, it more specifically does so today. Frequently, following B. F. Skinner, David Premack, and Lloyd Homme, the rational-emotive therapist will show people how to use contingency management—e.g., how to reward themselves with a high-frequency behavior (such as reading or eating good food) only after they have performed a low frequency behavior (such as studying). You can use this RET technique to help discipline yourself.

5. Guard against leaning over backward toward *too much* self-discipline or doing things the *too* hard way to achieve some magical rewards for your self-punishment. Most kinds of rigid adherence to rules, on the one hand, or inflexible rebelliousness against them, on the other hand, tend to throw away the baby with the bathwater and stem from emotional disturbance. Overdisciplining yourself can prove just as self-defeating as avoidance of necessary discipline.

In sum: it *can* prove difficult for you to keep fighting against your normal tendencies to give up easily on hard tasks, to put off till tomorrow what you'd better do today, and to slacken self-discipline long before it automatically develops its own momentum and begins to maintain itself. All right, so it proves hard. But you'd better resort to discipline if you intend to face many responsibilities, if you want to achieve long-range hedonism. *Your* goals and desires require continual self-discipline. Tough! But how else can you get by as a *human*?

Oscar Jimson kept taking the self-defeating alternative when he first came to see me (A.E.). Oscar, a young graduate student of psychology, seemed one of the brightest clients I ever had, but kept refusing to do his Ph.D. thesis. He also stymied all the important things he eagerly looked forward to doing in his chosen field by what he called "my goddamned natural laziness." "Can I," he asked, "have such a biological makeup that I *can't* discipline myself as others more easily can?"

I didn't get so easily sold on his biological hypothesis. "I doubt it," I said. "Especially since in other aspects of your life you seem to do remarkably well about self-discipline."

"You mean in my teaching?"

"Yes. You told me that in the classes you teach, you work very hard at preparing your lessons and really put considerable time and effort into them. And you take great pride in working so hard and proving such a good teacher."

"Right. I do work hard in that area."

"Then where arises this concept of 'natural biological laziness'? Obviously, if you can work hard at preparing your teaching, you can work just as hard at writing your thesis."

"But I find that different. In my class, I get an immediate amount of feedback or reward. My students love me and respond favorably to the work I do in their behalf."

"No doubt. And I feel sure you merit their approval. You give them something few other teachers do and they appreciate it."

"They really do."

"Great. But you still prove *my* point—that when you *want* to do hard work, and when your reward for doing it immediately follows, you have no trouble disciplining yourself. When, however, your reward remains remote—when the finishing of your Ph.D. thesis seems a year or two away, and your professors won't give you much of a pat on the head until after that year or two, then you idiotically tell yourself: 'Oh, I just got born lazy. I can't discipline myself.' You actually mean: 'I need immediate approval so desperately that I *won't* discipline myself until I have a guarantee that I'll get it.' Quite a different picture, yes?"

"What you say sounds true. But do I make that the only reason why I refuse to work on my thesis—because I demand immediate love satisfaction before I'll do anything?"

"No, probably not. There usually exist other reasons why a person, even one as bright as you, will senselessly refuse to discipline himself in certain areas."

"And which of them seem to apply in my case?"

"Well, first of all, the general principle of inertia. It *does* seem hard for people, even unusually sane people, to force themselves to get going and keep going on a long-term project like a Ph.D. thesis when they know perfectly well that quite a period of time will elapse before they finish it and before they reap the rewards of their labor. Little children, you will note, prove difficult to motivate for any long-range project, no matter how much good they would reap from persisting at it. And most adults all their lives retain much of this childish trait."

"So I remain childish—eh?"

"Yes; but not necessarily in any unusual or abnormal sense. You just have a lot of *normal* childishness in you, and you feel *normally* reluctant to give it up. Perhaps *that* constitutes your 'natural laziness.' "

"Yes. But don't we all have some degree of this kind of thing? And why does mine amount to more than somebody else's?"

"Well, for one thing, like so many highly intelligent individuals, you've had it a little *too* good academically most of your life. As a bright person, you've found that you could get along very well, especially during grade school and high school, with much *less* work than the average child has to do to keep up with his subjects."

"You seem right about that. I practically did no work at all during grade school and high school and still kept near the top of my class. And in college, I still found things easy."

"Exactly. So you didn't *need* to acquire good habits until, quite recently, you got into graduate school. And now, seeing that you have keener competition, and theses just don't write themselves, you'd better develop better work habits. But having gotten along so well with a minimum of scholastic effort, you probably think it highly *unfair* that you can no longer do so. So we come to the next point; your *rebelling* against doing the thesis. You don't think you should *have* to exert yourself so much."

"Well, it *does* seem tough, doesn't it? I never *did* have to do this kind of thing before."

"Yes, it does seem tough. So it does! But you'd still better do it—to get the rewards that *you* now want. And no amount of childish rebelling will make it any easier. Quite the contrary: as you recently have seen."

"True. The more I goof, the more I fall behind, and then the harder it gets to catch up. Besides, my profs at school have gotten more than a little disgusted with me—and that doesn't help at all."

"It never will. Not only will your kind of dillydallying encourage others, such as your professors, to feel disgusted with you. But it will tend to have a similar effect on you."

"I'll get disgusted with me, *too*?"

"You don't have to; in fact, you never have to down yourself, your personhood, about *anything*. But you will tend to doubt, as you put off the work, whether you really *can* do it."

"Mmm. I see what you mean. Again, you've got me. I have to admit that as I've kept putting off my dissertation I think more and more, 'Maybe I can't do it. Maybe it just does not comprise my kind of task. Teaching—yes. And passing courses. But maybe this kind of thing just goes beyond me.' "

"Par for the course, those kinds of thoughts. First you refuse to buckle down to the job—because of the normal inertia and the abnormal childish habit patterns we've discussed. Then, instead of getting the immediate approval you greatly crave and which you work your head off to achieve through teaching, you get criticism from your professors. Then you say to yourself, 'You know, maybe I *can't* discipline myself,' or 'Maybe I *can't* do this kind of a project.' Then, because of your inordinate fear of failure, and your unwillingness to put your own negative hypothesis to the test, you run further away from working on the thesis rather than facing it. You then engender still more professiorial displeasure and self-disgust. Finally, you really get caught up in the worst kind of a vicious circle and where you originally childishly rebelled against doing the work, now you feel terribly *afraid* to try it. End of the line—and practically the end of your career—if you don't stop this nonsense and cut this vicious circle."

"You make it sound real disturbed, my behavior."

"*Doesn't* it seem so?"

"Well—. What can I say?"

"Whatever you say won't change things very much and make your behavior saner. The real point: What will you now *do*?"

"About my natural inertia, my childish rebellion, my inordinate demands for immediate approval, and my thinking that I *can't* do the thesis, merely because I've not tried to buckle down to do it?"

"Yes. You summarize the case very nicely. Now what will you *do* about it?"

"I suppose if I told you that I'll stop this behavior and get right down to work on the thesis, you wouldn't believe me?"

"No—not till you actually started to work. But I wouldn't disbelieve you, either. For one thing, I know perfectly well that any person who works as well as you do in regard to your teaching *can* work just as well on a project like a Ph.D. thesis. So the question remains not whether you *can*, but whether you *will*? And maybe, now that you've seen *how* inconsistent and self-defeating you remain by not working on your dissertation, maybe you will."

"Goddammit, I *hope* I will."

"Hope sounds like a very nice sentiment; but not firm enough. You'd better get *determined* to overcome your childish rebelliousness and fear of failure. *Actively* determined. Which means actively ferreting out and vigorously disputing the antidisciplinary nonsense that you've fed yourself for all these many years."

"Right again! *Action* appears the real keyword. We'll see!"

And we did. Oscar Jimson got his thesis topic approved within the next few weeks, quickly buckled down to do his research on it, and a year later emerged as a newly fledged Ph.D. in experimental psychology. He still makes a fine teacher; and, in addition, acts as one of the most all-around self-disciplined men I know in his field. Whenever I meet him at psychological conventions these days, he facetiously stands at attention, gives me a Prussian Army salute, and exclaims: *"Action! Work! Self-discipline!"* Only he doesn't really sound so facetious.

17 REWRITING YOUR PERSONAL HISTORY

Perversely enough, one of the most important psychological discoveries of the past century, emphasized by both the psychoanalytic and the conditioned response (or behaviorist) schools of thinking, has proved most harmful to many individuals: the idea that humans remain most importantly influenced, in their present patterns of living, by their past experiences. People have used this partially sage and potentially helpful observation to create and bolster what we call Irrational Idea No. 8: *The idea that your past remains all-important and that because something once strongly influenced your life, it has to keep determining your feelings and behavior today.*

Often, in the course of one of my typical working days, I (A.E.) see about twenty individual and another twenty group therapy clients; and most of them, to one degree or another, believe that they *have* to behave in a certain disturbed way because of previous conditioning or early influences. A forty-year-old highly attractive divorcée, for example, tells me: "I couldn't possibly get more active in meeting men, as you keep trying to induce me to do, when I've never done anything of the sort before in my life." A young wife says that she would rather have her husband lose fifty thousand dollars in a business venture than get fired again—because she feels certain he would not find satisfactory employment in view of the fact that he has had so many poor jobs before. A remarkably good-looking, well-educated, and bright young man of twenty-two confesses that he can't imagine himself getting a satisfactory woman friend again if his present one leaves him, because "I have gotten conditioned from childhood to fear that I don't have sufficient worth to go out and get anyone I want. So how can I ever expect to do this?"

So it goes, through most of my working days, with innumerable clients indicating that the unkind, heavily sunk-in ravages of their past lives cannot possibly change in the present or future—unless I somehow magically help them to undo this pernicious influence. To which I normally respond:

"Rubbish! Whatever early conditioning or pernicious influences you experienced during your childhood, their effects don't linger on, today, just *because* of these original conditions—but because you still *carry* them on, because you still *believe* the nonsense with which you originally got indoctrinated. Now when will *you* dispute your own often-repeated beliefs and thereby *un*-condition yourself?" And the battle of therapeutic de-indoctrination continues merrily apace, until (usually) I win or (sometimes, alas) the client flees from me and the work he or she has to undertake to eliminate his exaggerated view of pernicious past influences.

Like these clients, most people in our society appear to believe that because something once significantly affected their lives, or seemed at one time appropriate or necessary, this thing must remain important forever. Thus, they believe that because they once had to obey their parents they still, as adults, should do so. Or because they have previously felt victimized by their environment, they still have to feel this. Or because they once held superstitions, they must continue to believe in their early acquired nonsense.

A strong belief in the enormous significance of the past proves irrational for several reasons:

1. If you still let yourself feel unduly influenced by your past experiences, you commit the logical error of overgeneralization. Because a thing holds true in *some* circumstances hardly proves it equally true under *all* conditions. Because your father may have acted unkindly during your childhood and you had to fight against his exploiting you does not mean that *all* men act equally unkindly and that you have to keep guarding yourself against them.

Because you once felt too weak to stand up against the domination of your mother hardly means that you must *always* remain that weak.

2. By allowing yourself to remain too strongly influenced by past events, you cease to look for alternative solutions to a problem. Only one possible solution to a difficulty rarely exists. If you remain flexible in your thinking, you will keep casting around till you find a better one than seems immediately apparent. But if you believe that you must remain unduly influenced by your past

experiences, you will tend to think mainly in terms of prior, and usually quite inadequate, "solutions."

3. Many aspects of behavior appropriate at one time turn decidedly inappropriate at another. Children, in particular, often devise various methods of solving their problems with their parents—such as wailing, balking, or having a temper tantrum when they want their own way. These later prove ineffective, since other adults will not respond to such devices unless employed by children. If you stick, therefore, to problem-solving devices that proved effective in the past, you will often find them highly inefficient in the present.

4. If you remain notably influenced by your past, you will maintain what the psychoanalysts call transference effects— meaning that you will inappropriately transfer your feelings about people in your past life to those with whom you associate today. Thus, you may self-defeatingly rebel against your boss's orders today because they remind you of your parents' high-handed orders of twenty years ago. Such transference relationships often turn out unrealistic and unrewarding.

5. If you unchallengingly continue to perform in a certain way because you have done so in the past, you will fail to gain many new experiences that might well prove exceptionally enjoyable. Thus, if you continue to devote yourself to sports mainly because you enjoyed having them in your early teens, you may never try artistic pursuits and may never discover that they can bring you more satisfaction than sports. Or if you refuse to try for a job as an accountant because you once lost a similar job, you may never get competent enough to retain and enjoy another accounting position.

6. Unquestioningly accepting the influences of the past renders you unrealistic, since the present does *not* remain the past but significantly differs from it. Riding in a Model T Ford on today's superhighways would prove dangerous because the old road and traffic conditions no longer exist. Treating your wife the same way that you treat your mother, when she definitely does *not* exist as your mother, may easily bring trouble.

In sum: Although the past, as the psychoanalysts and the behaviorists have clearly seen, indubitably exists and moderately influences people to repeat old patterns of behavior, it doesn't *have* to wield an enormous influence. You *can* change human nature, no matter how long a past condition of behaving has existed—otherwise we, like our ancestors, would still live in caves.

Your basic personality, moreover, has *not* got so inalterably set by your past experiences that you need a "deep" analysis of many years to restructure it. If, with the help of any effective therapeutic procedure, with participation in an intensive program of psychological reading, lectures, and group involvement, and with (above all) continual self-questioning and challenging of your own basic assumptions and philosophies, you will keep working hard at changing your "basic nature," you can often achieve remarkable results within a few months' to a few years' time.

True, most people more or less resist making drastic changes in themselves. Because largely, as we have shown throughout this book, they keep *reinforcing* their old beliefs—telling themselves, over and over, that blacks *do* no good, or that failing at a job *does* prove terrible, or that the world *should not* force them to bake their cakes before they can eat them. But this fact, rather than proving that "human nature" cannot change, really signifies just the opposite. Precisely *because* we keep reliving our past mistakes as a result of *our* self-sentences, we can normally change these mistakes through our other self-sentences. Just as our present behavior largely stems from our thinking about past experiences, our future activities will follow our present performances. And we, by determined thinking and practice, can enormously regulate and control our activities of today.

Harold Stover came to therapy with a quick and vicious temper which, he said right at the start, he just had to get rid of if he wanted to marry the girl of his dreams. "You've got to help me, Dr. Harper," he pleaded. "Because Grace says that if I fly off the handle once more in her presence she'll make that it, and get rid of me. She said that you helped her immensely, a couple of years ago, when she kept getting angry at her boss. And unless I let you help me, too, she will have had it."

"Well, I can only do my best," I said. "Or, rather, help you do your best. But, first of all, tell me a little about how your temper originated."

Harold then told a fairly typical tale of how, since early childhood, he had raised hell when even the slightest thing went wrong. And with some encouragement, too, since he remembered his mother proudly telling some guests that from his early nursing days he would howl with rage if she tried to get him to do anything he didn't want. "Harold had his own mind at birth," she fondly remembered. And it appeared that somehow this only child of hers, who insisted on having his own way at all times, appealed to the mother.

Under these conditions, as we might expect, his mother's evaluation of his temper tantrums as natural, inevitable, and vaguely cute got adopted by Harold himself. He looked upon his temper as a normal and effective means of getting what he wanted from his mother and others, especially women, whom he found sufficiently intimidatory. When Grace refused intimidation and frankly told him that he could split unless he stopped acting like a big, churlish child, he realized that he had reached the end of the temper tantrum line and that he would do better casting about for more suitable means of continuing life's journey.

I didn't find it hard to show Harold the origins of his tantrums, and he soon quite agreed he'd better not blame himself for having developed the way he did, since his mother had so obviously trained him that way, and he'd do himself no good, anyway, by self-recrimination.

"But where do I go from here?" Harold asked. "How do I get over this stuff, now that I know how it arose? Won't anything that goes back practically to birth, and has remained so deeply a part of my behavior pattern over so long a period of time, prove practically impossible to get rid of?"

"No," I replied. "True, considering how long you have had your childish temper tantrums—or how long, really, you have thought it perfectly *good and proper* to have them—you will have a *difficult* time in fighting them. So you'll find it difficult. But not half so difficult· as if you *don't* fight to get rid of these self-defeating reactions."

"But how? *How* do I fight them out of my system?"

"The same way, basically, as you put them *into* your system."

"But didn't we just get finished saying, a while ago, that my mother put them into my system, by rewarding me for having the tantrums, and thereby conditioning me to keep having them?"

"No, not exactly—although it may seem like that. Actually, your mother rewarded you, all right, for having your fits of temper. But also, and more importantly, you *accepted* and *kept looking for* further rewards. You didn't only say to yourself: 'Ah, there goes Mother again, indicating that I can have my temper tantrums; so I might as well continue having them.' You also said: 'Ah, Mother allows herself to feel intimidated by my tantrums. And Father goes along for the ride as well. And Florence, the maid, lets me get away with the same kind of thing. Now let me see: Whenever I want anything that they at first won't give me, I'll look for people like Mother and Father and Florence and yell my head off until they give it to me. I know that this will make me something of a bother to these people, but why should I care about that when I keep getting what I want? For I find it really terrible, really horrible, not to get what I want. And I would much rather get it, even if I have to keep bothering people, than not get it. And if some people won't give me what I want when I scream and yell, then to hell with them. I'll just find other people who *will* give me what I want.' Didn't you keep saying to yourself something along these lines?"

"Come to think of it, you hit it remarkably close. For I do remember, now that you've mentioned it, that I once had quite a lot of friends. As a small child, I made myself one of the most popular boys in my neighborhood. But when I found out that some of them wouldn't stand for my temper tantrums, and wouldn't let me have my way when I went into a fit, I somehow cut them off and wound up having a bunch of toadies who would keep giving in to me. And I must admit, now that I think of it again, that these toadies didn't include some of the brightest and most able kids on the block. But I stayed with the toadies anyway, to keep getting my way."

"You willingly sacrificed some of your brightest and most able friends to keep getting your immediate wants fulfilled. And haven't you retained that pattern up to now—giving up long-range goals or more able friends to surround yourself with toadies who quickly gratify you, just as your parents and maid originally gratified you at a moment's squawk?"

"Yes, I guess I have. But I still don't see how to get out of this pattern of behavior."

"As I said before—the same way you got into it. For if your dedication to tantrums stems largely, as we now see, not from *others' training*, but from *your* having trained yourself to take the easier and shorter-range hedonistic way, you can now train yourself *not* to have these temper fits, and to favor long-range hedonistic aims."

"Just as *I* said to myself, 'Well, go ahead, Harold, have your fits and blackmail others to do your bidding,' I can now say to myself, 'Stop the nonsense, Harold, and get what you really want out of life—longer-range and more deeply satisfying goals like winning Grace, for example—by behaving like an adult and *not* having any more fits.' Can I do it that way?"

"Yes. And just as you, partly as a rationalization for keeping your present goal of immediate gratification instead of longer-range goals, now keep telling yourself: 'How can I ever expect to change, to lose my tantrum habit, when it goes back to birth and represents an inextricable part of my personality?' so you can tell yourself, instead: 'No matter how long I've had this childish habit, nor how many people I've cajoled into going along with it, I *now* defeat my own best ends, so I'd better work my backside off, *against* my habit and *for* myself, to behave differently.' "

"You seem to keep saying that I'd better stop viewing it as terrible to lose out on some immediate pleasure: that I can stand such a loss; and that, for my greater good I'd just *better* change my ways."

"Yes, and make more of a *philosophic* than a *motor* change in your habits. And I feel sure that if you accept this adult philosophy, you can easily act maturely from here on in."

"But suppose I try what you say, and all goes well for a while, and then I fail, and have another real fit of temper?"

"Suppose you do. As long as you do not use your slip to 'prove' to yourself that you *must* have temper tantrums, and you definitely *can't* change, it will remain just that: a minor slip. And you will soon give up your tantrums again, until your relapses become fewer and fewer."

"As long as I stick to the present and keep working for a different future, I can forget about the long negative conditioning of the past?"

"Right. As long as, every time you slip back into a fit of temper, you say to yourself: 'Well, there I go again. I told myself some nonsense to make myself slip. Now let's see what I said. And how can I use this relapse to help myself avoid another temper outburst *next* time?' If you calmly, interestedly look at your slips, and your internalized sentences that cause them, your negative conditioning of the past will turn into the positive conditioning of the present and you solve your problem."

So it proved. Six weeks later Harold reported: "Would you believe it? Grace and I actually got engaged. You'll get a formal announcement just as soon as they get printed. And *she* did the pushing. 'Look, darling.' I said, when she suggested it the other night, 'I know that I haven't had any temper outbursts for the last six weeks now, and I feel glad for your sake and mine that I haven't. But how do you know I won't have one again tomorrow?' 'I don't know that you won't have one tomorrow again—though I doubt that you will,' Grace replied. 'But I didn't object so much to your outbursts as to the little-boy, you've-got-to-give-me-exactly-what-I-want attitude that caused them. And *that*, your attitude, has changed remarkably since you've gone to talk with Dr. Harper. And I feel sure that *that* won't change back to the old attitude very quickly. If it does,' and she smiled in her inimitable manner at this point, you know how she smiles, Doctor, 'well, I can always divorce you.' "

Grace and Harold did marry; his new grown-up attitude did not change back to the old little-boy ones; and they still manage to stay out of the divorce court. There seems every reason to believe that they will.

You, like almost any other intelligent and hardworking person, can overcome the influence of your past if you try some of these techniques:

1. Accept the fact that your past significantly influences you in some ways. But accept, also, the fact that *your present constitutes your past of tomorrow*. You cannot today make a single right-about-turn into an entirely different person. But you can *start* changing yourself significantly today so that *eventually* you will act quite differently. By *new* thinking and experiencing in the present, and by accepting your past as a *handicap* rather than a *total block*, you may radically change your tomorrow's (or the day after tomorrow's) behavior.

2. Objectively *acknowledging* your past errors, instead of

moralistically *damning* yourself for them, you can learn to *use* your past for your own present and future benefit. Instead of automatically repeating mistakes because you *once* made them, you can calmly *observe* and *question* these misdeeds. You can periodically review many of your customs and habits, in fact, to separate the wheat from the chaff and (if desirable) change your life accordingly.

3. When you find yourself strongly bound by some past influence that defeats your current goals, you can persistently and forcefully fight it on both verbal and action levels. Thus, if you keep acting like a little child toward your mother and fail to do what you really want to do, you can keep convincing yourself: "I do *not* have to continue to act this way. I *no longer* remain a child. I can speak up to my mother and tell her what I actually want to do. She has no real power over me anymore and cannot hurt me or prevent me from doing what I want unless I let her. I do not want to contribute to hurting her needlessly; but neither do I want to hurt myself. I once thought disaster would ensue if I stood up to her. Rubbish—it won't!" You can thus tackle any irrational influences from the past. Show yourself their foolishness: how they harm rather than help you; how you would get much better results if you removed them.

4. As ever, to effect a solid change in yourself, you'd better accompany your counter-propaganda with action. Deliberately *work* against the influences of the past: *force* yourself, for example, to act toward your mother in a more adult fashion, to risk her disapproval, to say and do things that you previously would have felt petrified to do. If you never in all your life talked to a stranger in a bus, went to a party alone, kissed a girl on your first date, or did similar things that you would like to do, *force* yourself, give yourself absolutely no peace, until you try and try again these terribly "fearful" acts. No nonsense! Don't just think: *act*! You can overcome years of past fright and inertia by days or weeks of forced practice today.

5. You can help yourself to act against the influences of the past by using self-management schedules. Every time you do talk to a stranger on a bus, for example, let yourself smoke or read the newspaper that day; every time you fail to take advantage of such an opportunity, refuse to let yourself smoke or read the newspaper that day. Reinforce yourself for combating your past; exact a swift penalty for foolishly going along with it.

6. Use rational-emotive imagery. For ten minutes a day *vividly* imagine yourself speaking to strangers. Let yourself feel anxious or ashamed. Then change your feeling to one of concern but *not* panic by changing your ideas about the "horror" of looking bad to these strangers. Steadily *practice* feeling concerned instead of anxious in this vividly fantasized "dangerous" situation.

7. Remember, above all, the past *has* passed. It has no magical, automatic effect on the present or future. At most, your past habits make it harder for you to change than to remain stationary. Harder but not impossible. Work and time; practice and more practice; thinking, imagining, and doing—you can use these as the unmagical keys that will unlock almost any chest of past defeats and turn them into present and future successes.

18
ACCEPTING REALITY

Let's face it: Reality often stinks. People don't act the way we would like them to act. This doesn't seem the best of all possible worlds. Even half-perfect solutions to many serious problems and difficulties just do not exist. Moreover, society often gets worse: seems *more* polluted, economically unfair, burdened with ethnic prejudices, politically oppressive, violence-filled, superstitious, wasteful of natural resources, sexist, and ultraconformist.

But you *still* don't have to feel desperately unhappy. Unkind reality doesn't depress millions of humans. What does? Their unthinking addiction to Irrational Idea No. 9: *The idea that people and things should turn out better than they do and that you must view it as awful and horrible if you do not find good solutions to life's grim realities.* An idiotic idea—for several reasons:

1. No reason exists why people *should* turn out any better than they do, even when they act very badly. Your grandiosity gets you to tell yourself, "Because I don't *like* people to behave the way they do, they *shouldn't*." Similarly, although you might find it lovely if things and events did *not* occur the way they do, they frequently *will*. Again, no reason exists why they *should*, *ought*, or *must not* happen, just because you (and others) *desire* them to occur differently.

2. When people behave other than the way you would like, they usually do not affect you too perniciously unless you *think* they do. If your wife acts nastily or your friends unfriendly, their behavior may well prove annoying; but rarely as bothersome as

you, by your low frustration tolerance, may *make* it. Similarly, when things or events go wrong, that seems unfortunate, and may affect you adversely. But not as adversely as when you think—or as you make it by telling yourself—"Things *shouldn't* occur this way. I can't stand it!"

3. Assuming that people actually harm you and events really go poorly, your upsetting yourself about this will still do no good. On the contrary, the more upset you feel, the less likely you will help change people or things for the better. Thus, if you incense yourself because your mate acts irresponsibly, the chances increase that he or she, feeling angry at your criticism, will act even more irresponsibly.

4. As Epictetus pointed out two thousand years ago, although we do have the power to change and control ourselves to a considerable degree (if we work hard and long enough at modifying our own beliefs and actions), we do not have a similar power to control the behavior of others. No matter how wisely you may counsel people, they remain independent entities and may—and, indeed, have the right as individuals to—ignore you completely. If, therefore, you get unduly aroused over the way others act, instead of paying more attention to how you respond to their actions, you upset yourself over an outside event beyond your control. This seems akin to tearing your hair because a jockey, a prizefighter, or an actor does not perform the way you would like. Very silly business indeed!

5. Upsetting yourself about other people and events will usually sidetrack you from your logical main concern: the way *you* behave, the things *you* do. If you control your own destiny, by the proper cultivation of your own emotional garden, the most harrowing things that happen will not perturb you too much and you may even help change people and things for the better. But if you unduly upset yourself over outside happenings, you will inevitably consume so much time and energy that you will have little left for the proper cultivation of your own garden.

6. The notion that an absolutely right or perfect solution to any of life's problems exists has little probability since few things remain all black or all white, and normally many alternative solutions prove viable. If you compulsively keep seeking for the absolutely best or perfect solution, you will tend to stay so rigid and anxious that you will tend to miss some highly satisfactory compromises. Thus, if you have to see the absolutely best TV program aired at a given time, you will probably keep anxiously turning from one channel to another and will end up seeing *none* of the programs.

7. The disasters that you imagine will occur if you do not quickly get a perfect and absolutely "right" solution rarely actually occur—except by arbitrary definition. If you *think* it

catastrophic to make a wrong decision—to marry the wrong person, for example, and wind up with a divorce—you will most likely
bring disaster on your head when you discover your mistake.
If you think it regrettable and unfortunate, but *not* catastrophic,
to make exactly the same wrong decision, you will bear your
mistake well—and perhaps even learn by it.

8. Perfectionism, almost by definition, turns into a self-
defeating philosophy. No matter how close you may come to
running the perfect race, living with someone who displays flaw-
less behavior, or arranging events so that you absolutely know
their outcome, you will never really achieve your perfectionist
goals. For humans do *not* behave like angels; events *don't* occur
with certainty; decisions do *not* turn out correctly at all times.
Even if you temporarily achieve perfection, your chances of remaining at this ultimate peak approximate zero. Nothing remains
perfectly static. Life *equals* change. Whether you like it or not,
you'd better accept reality the way it occurs: as highly imperfect
and filled with most fallible humans. Your alternative? Continual
anxiety and desperate disappointment!

Take the case of Laura. Laura came from a close-knit family.
Although her father favored her over her two sisters and two
brothers, she felt that her mother preferred them. Then her father
died during her twentieth year, and left a large amount of insur-
ance to his wife. One of Laura's main problems, and one which she
brought up continually during the early sessions of therapy, involved
her great anxiety about her mother's ability to manage this sum.
According to Laura, her mother kept extravagantly spending it.

Said I (A.E.) after hearing a number of Laura's complaints
and seeing that she probably intended to keep making them:

"Why do you fret so much about what your mother does
with this money, anyway? After all, *she* has the money. Your
father *did* leave it to her. And she *has* a perfect right to do with it
what she likes—to throw it down the sewer, if that pleases her."

"Yes, I realize that, of course," Laura replied. "But you see,
my mother always had my father to look after money matters
before. Now she doesn't and she doesn't know how to say no to
my greedy brothers, sisters, and in-laws."

"Do you want some of the money yourself, for some special
purpose?"

"No, I do all right. I have a good job and opportunities for
advancement. And my fiancé does fine, too, and comes from a
well-to-do family. So I don't want a cent of her money for myself.
Not a cent."

"Then where does your problem lie? Why don't you just
forget about what your mother does with her money and go
about your own business? Apparently she hasn't asked any
advice from you. And if she wants to give all the money to

your brothers and sisters and their families, she has that privilege."

"But how can she behave that way—throwing away the money like that, when she may need it later? And giving all of them everything they want! Why, in no time at all she'll have no money!"

"Perhaps so; but that remains *her* problem. Besides, you have already called to her attention the fact that you think she keeps spending too much too fast, haven't you?"

"Oh, yes. I spoke to her as soon as I saw, a few weeks after my father's death, what she kept doing."

"And she said?"

"To mind my own goddamn business!"

"Well?"

"But how *can* she do this? She acts terribly wrongly! Can't I do something to stop her?"

"Let's assume, for the moment, that she behaves wrongly or stupidly to spend the money—"

"Oh, she does; she does!"

"Well, I don't know that everyone—especially your brothers and sisters—would agree to that. But let's assume it—that almost any sane and objective person would agree with you. So? So she behaves wrongly. But hasn't your mother the democratic right to do wrong? Will you take away that right from her?"

"But—! But does she do *right* to act wrong?"

"No, obviously not. If she acts wrongly, she acts wrongly; and she can't at one and the same time also act rightly. OK: so she does wrong. But you still haven't answered my question: Doesn't every person, including your mother, have the right to do wrong? Or do you want to *force* them, if you can, to always act correctly?"

"What do you mean?"

"Well, let's put it this way: It certainly seems desirable, you and I will agree, that humans act well instead of badly, that they make fewer rather than more mistakes. And if your mother behaves wrongly about her spending this money—as we assume for the sake of discussion that she does—then it would prove highly desirable if she stopped behaving that way, and refrained from spending the money the way she does spend it. But let's suppose that she acts wrongly, dead wrongly, about the spending, and that she just won't *stop* doing so—she will continue to spend the money badly, to squander it on your brothers and sisters and their families."

"But *should* she?"

"Ah, why *shouldn't she*? Why *shouldn't* she act badly, if she does, and continue to behave wrongly if she wants to do so? Why shouldn't she remain a fallible human, like all of us, and make one mistake after another? Would you want her, really expect her, to operate as a saint?"

"No, I wouldn't."

"You *say* you wouldn't; but do you really *mean* what you say? For here your mother acts completely wrongly according to your hypothesis. And you insist that she not do wrong, that she only do right. But she does act wrongly about spending and seems determined to continue doing so. Now it seems to me that she'd have to turn into something of a goddess, in these circumstances, not to do wrong—or to stop doing wrong when she wants to keep doing it. You really mean, of course, that you *demand* that she do things *your* way rather than *her* way. And even more than that, you demand that she *want* to do things your way rather than hers. And you give her no democratic right whatever to want to do things *her* way—however wrong, according to you, me, and the world that way may seem."

"But I still say: *Should* a person act wrongly, when she can just as well behave better?"

"A rhetorical question. Because, obviously, if people *could* easily behave well, they probably would. And when they do wrong about something, it means either that they want to do right, but somehow can't, or that they don't even want to do right—and therefore certainly won't."

"I—I really don't know what to say."

"Well, think about it a little more, and you'll see that what I say rings true, and that you just haven't looked at it. Suppose, for example, that you acted like your mother, kept doing something wrong—say, spending a lot of money rather recklessly and foolishly."

"I'd act wrongly if I did—just as wrongly as she does."

"All right, let's suppose you did. But the real point: Wouldn't you have a *right* to do wrong—to make your own mistakes? Suppose your mother came to you, in those circumstances, and advised you to stop spending the money the way you kept doing, and suppose you thought over her advice, but still decided to go on spending your money foolishly. Again: Wouldn't you have the *right* to do things your way instead of hers, and make your own mistakes?"

"I see what you mean now. Even though I acted stupidly, I'd have a perfect right, as a human, to do what I wanted, and perhaps by doing it to prove my behavior stupid."

"Exactly. For don't forget that people like your mother practically never *think* they act wrongly when they make their mistakes. Later, perhaps, they realize it. But not at the time they make them. Now, how else can they learn *except* by making errors and finally proving they have behaved wrongly?"

"I guess so. There doesn't seem any other way, actually, that they can learn how wrongly they act, does there?"

"No, not for all practical purposes. They *could* see their

errors merely from someone's pointing them out. But if they don't, then what else can they do but make their mistakes and *then*, in retrospect, see that they did?"

"But how wasteful that people have to act that way first and *then* see their errors!"

"Yes—but humans behave that way. Much of the time they *first* make their mistakes and *then* recognize them. As saints, they doubtless would behave differently. But sainthood or angelhood doesn't seem their lot—fallibility does! Besides, look at the advantages of their fallibility and of our permitting them to have it."

"What advantages?"

"Well, for one thing their fallibility leads them to have experiences, and often quite valuable experiences, that otherwise, if more cautious and less fallible, they might never have. Memoirs would seem dull reading if people behaved as infallibly as you would like!"

"Oh, I think we could make *that* sacrifice to create a better world!"

"Maybe so. But listen to an even more important point. If people make fewer mistakes the way *you* want to force them to do—by not only bringing their errors to their attention but damning and punishing them for such errors—would you want to live in the fascist-type world that you would then create? If you, for example, really could and did force your mother to stop her rash spending, how do you think she and millions of others like her would *enjoy* your rule? How would you, for example, enjoy people like your mother telling you what kind of a job you could work at, whom you could marry, and just how much money you could spend each week?"

"I don't suppose I'd enjoy it at all."

"I don't suppose you would. And yet doesn't your proposal amount to that—a small group of 'correct' and presumably infallible people having the power to tell a much larger group of 'incorrect' and fallible people exactly how to run their lives? Would you really want to live in this kind of dictatorial and fascistic society?"

"You keep saying that allowing people to make serious mistakes and to defeat your own ends constitutes the price we have to pay for democracy."

"Well, doesn't it?"

"Hmm. I never thought about that."

"As I said before: Think it over. Besides, you'd better face another aspect of your problem with your mother."

"Which aspect?"

"Simply that although you set up the situation as if she hurts herself, with you on the outside merely watching her self-defeating game, we have to suspect that really, underneath, you may feel that she keeps hurting *you* by refusing to play *your* perfection-seeking game."

"You think that I really want her to love me as much as my brothers and sisters and that I keep using her spending as an excuse to force her to do so?"

"Certainly a possibility. Surely, from your standpoint, a less than perfect family circle has existed, especially since your father's death, as he mainly cared for you. Now under the guise of helping your mother spend her money better, you may try to get your *own* way, break up some of her closeness with the other family members, and achieve the 'ideal' situation that *you* think should exist. Then, when you cannot attain this 'ideal' and achieve more of your mother's love, you refuse to accept reality and start wailing about *her* wrongdoings."

"But wouldn't it seem natural for me to want to get closer to my mother and to get back some of the love she's kept from me all these years?"

"Yes, it seems natural for you to *want* to do so. But, if so, you use distorted and ineffective means of achieving your desires. If you truly accepted the reality of her favoring your brothers and sisters, and tried to change this reality—say, by acting exceptionally nicely to her yourself—you would follow a sane enough program. But instead you deny the reality that you consider so unfair and imperfect—pretend that your mother's favoritism of the other family members does *not* trouble you—and then keep flaying your mother on a supposedly different issue. And your sharp criticism of her, of course, will only help *preserve* the poor reality that you want to change."

"By bothering her about the spending of the money, the way I do, I just keep antagonizing her further and giving her good reason for favoring the others. You mean that?"

"Exactly that. By refusing to face and put up with the grim reality of your family life, and by telling yourself much of the time, 'She behaves unfairly! She *shouldn't* act this way!' you induce yourself to act in the very manner that will almost certainly help perpetuate and aggravate this unpleasant reality. While, on the other hand, if you accepted, for the present, the ungracious position your mother puts you in, you might well, as an intelligent and hardworking person, do something to correct it."

"My, you've certainly given me a lot of food for thought in this session! I'd better think over carefully what we've talked about and see whether I really have kept doing what you say and have covered up my own perfectionism and refusal to accept reality by keeping after Mother about her spending."

"By all means think about this carefully and see whether you do not find that some of the hypotheses I have suggested accurately fit your situation."

Laura did think things over; concluded that even though she still considered her mother mistaken about the money, she mainly felt upset for other reasons. For the first time she began to accept, quite democratically, her mother's right to make her own mistakes and errors. Within the next several months, her relations with her mother enormously improved and some of the mother's reckless spending, possibly because of these improved relations, did stop. More importantly, Laura went back to living her own life more effectively and began to get along better with her fiancé, whose imperfections she had previously covertly simmered about, but whom she could now accept in a more uncritical manner.

Some general rules for combating your perfectionism and grandiosity and learning to accept reality even when it shows some of its most unpleasant aspects:

1. When people act badly in relation to you or to themselves—as they often do in this world—ask yourself whether you should *really* excite yourself about this. Do you actually *care* what these people do? Do their actions truly *affect* your life? *Will* these people change, no matter how much effort you spend helping them? Do you *want* to spend sufficient time and energy to help them? Do you actually *have* it available to spend? Unless you can answer questions like these with a resounding yes, hadn't you better stay somewhat aloof from others' errors and shortcomings and merely offer them, especially when asked, moderate advice and help?

2. Assuming that you do consider it highly worthwhile to get involved with helping others change, try to do so in an unfrantic way. If you really want people to change for their own (or even your own) good, you will almost always prove most helpful by adopting permissive, uncritical, and accepting attitudes. Do your best to see things from *their* frames of reference, rather than your own. Firmly reject, if you will, their self-defeating *behavior* but do not reject *them*.

3. Even when people act nastily to you, or actually harm you, don't condemn them or retaliate. Whether you like it or not, they do act the way they do; and you think childishly when you believe they *shouldn't*. The more you deal with their nastiness objectively, the better an example you may set them. Also, the more constructive a plan you may devise to induce them to stop acting that way and the less you will annoy yourself because of their behavior. If, when faced with difficult people (or things or events), you keep telling yourself how terribly and awful they remain, you will only make your situation more difficult. If you tell yourself, instead, "This situation stinks—tough! So it stinks," you will at least prevent yourself from feeling angry about annoyances and you can act more effectively to make the situation less stinking.

4. Ceaselessly fight your own perfectionism. If, as an artist or a producer, you would like to work on a near-perfect *work* or *product*, fine. But *you* will never exist as perfect; nor will anyone else you know. Humans remain thoroughly fallible; life essentially uncertain. The quest for certainty and perfection involves (a) the childish fear of living in a highly uncertain and imperfect world; and (b) the conscious or unconscious drive to excel all others, to be King or Queen of the May, and thus "prove" your absolute superiority over everyone else. You won't live with minimal anxiety and hostility until you fully accept, as Hans Reichenbach shows, that you live in a world of probability and chance, and unless you accept yourself because you *exist* and not because you exist as "better" than anyone else.

5. Since no perfect solutions to problems and difficulties emerge, you'd better accept some compromises and *reasonable* solutions. The more you keep your eyes open for alternative answers to a given problem, the more likely you'll find the best *feasible* answer to it. Impulsive and impatient choices often prove ineffective. Think about, consider, and compare the different alternatives open to you. Try *objectively* to see various sides of an issue, with a minimum of prejudices and preconceptions. In the final analysis, however, you'd better make some kind of a plunge. Make this plunge *experimentally*, with the full knowledge that it *may* work out well—and it may *not*. If you fail, you'll find it unfortunate, but rarely catastrophic. And failure doesn't have anything to do with your intrinsic value *as a person* (if such value actually exists). Humans mainly learn by doing and by failing—a truth about (highly uncertain and imperfect) reality that you can accept.

6. Assuming that you can choose nonperfectionistically among several alternatives, you can still leave the door open to taking *other* choices in the future. For the best alternative that you may take today may not remain so tomorrow. Your own desires, outside conditions, and other people with whom you get involved all may significantly change; and you can take these changes into account in your choice among alternatives. You can adopt what George Kelly calls an outlook conducive to "a program of continuous construct revision." Or, as Alfred Korzybski would put it, your life plan$_1$ may not stay the same as your life plan$_2$; and you'd better differentiate between your own preferences and goals, as well as the most feasible methods of achieving them, at one point in time or another.

19 OVERCOMING INERTIA AND GETTING CREATIVELY ABSORBED

There seems no easy way out of life's difficulties and responsibilities. Yet millions of civilized people believe heartily in Irrational Idea No. 10: *The idea that you can achieve maximum human happiness by inertia and inaction or by passively and uncommittedly "enjoying yourself."* This notion appears irrational for several reasons:

1. Humans rarely feel particularly happy or alive when inert, except for short periods of time between their exertions. Although they get tired and tense when ceaselessly active, they just as easily turn bored and listless when they constantly rest. Passive "enjoyments," such as reading, play-going, or watching sporting events, remain entertaining and relaxing when engaged in fairly regularly. But a steady and exclusive diet of this kind of "activity" tends to pall and to lead to feelings of ennui and alienation.

2. Most intelligent and perceptive people seem to require vitally absorbing activity to stay maximally alive and happy. Perhaps less intelligent people can sit in the sun day after day and need no other occupation for their full enjoyment. But highly intelligent adults rarely remain enthusiastic and gratified for any length of time unless they have some rather complex, absorbing, and challenging occupations or avocations.

3. To some degree, human contentment seems almost synonymous with absorption in outside people and events, or what Nina Bull calls goal-orientation. Fascinatingly enough, some inappropriate negative emotions (such as intense anxiety and guilt) as well as certain inappropriate positive emotions (such as egomania or

erotomania) prove highly absorbing and exciting, save some people from boredom and apathy, and consequently may perpetuate themselves in spite of their severe disadvantages. People with such emotions *actively* participate in life; and therefore resist giving up their feelings of anxiety or mania. Intense absorption seems to remain the common denominator of practically all forms—including disturbed forms—of aliveness.

4. What we usually call *loving* or feeling *in love*, as opposed to desiring *to get loved*, constitutes one of the main forms of vital absorption. In fact, the three main forms of vital absorption comprise: (a) loving, or feeling absorbed in other people; (b) creating, or getting absorbed in things; and (c) philosophizing, or remaining absorbed in ideas. Feeling inert, passive, or inhibited normally keeps you from getting absorbed in any of these three major ways—and hence from truly living. Living essentially means doing, acting, loving, creating, thinking. You negate it by prolonged goofing, loafing, or lazing.

5. Although, as we pointed out previously in our chapter on self-discipline, many or most people find it *initially* harder to get themselves into vitally absorbing activities, and *at first* easier to sit on their backsides and do little or nothing, when they fight against this initial difficulty and propel themselves into activity they come to enjoy these actions (and sometimes, also, their results) far more than they would continue to enjoy prolonged inactivity. The game normally *does* prove worth the candle—if you keep playing it long enough.

6. People who lead a lazy, passive existence and who keep saying that "nothing really interests me very much" almost always (consciously or unconsciously) defend themselves against irrational fears, especially the fears of failure. Viewing failure with horror, they avoid activities they would really like to engage in; and after sufficient avoidance, they conclude, in all sincerity, that they have no interest in these activities. They thus cut off one potential piece of their life space after another and may end up disinterested in everything. In some respects, these apathetic, listless, and bored individuals feel even more unhappy than actively anxious and hostile people: who at least, as we indicated a few paragraphs back, get *absorbed* in their fears and hatreds.

7. Work confidence seems intrinsically related to activity. You know you *can* do something you would like to do because you have already proven, by your past behavior, that you *have* done it or something akin to it. A girl who never tried to walk would hardly acquire confidence in her ability to walk—or to swim, or ride, or do almost any other kind of muscular activity. This doesn't deny that in our society we get drilled into the dire need to succeed at tasks and projects; we do. And much of our "pride" or "self-confidence," therefore, actually consists of *false*

pride and *false* confidence: born of this dire need to succeed.

We'd better make the point here that I (A.E.) also make in *Reason and Emotion in Psychotherapy* and *Growth Through Reason:* You obtain work confidence or love confidence by proving, in action, that you can achieve at work or win at love. You can enjoyably have these feelings: since if you know that you can do well at achievement or love, you will feel motivated to strive for future rewards in these areas. You'd better not confuse work confidence and love confidence, however, with *self*-confidence, which really exists definitionally and describes an undesirable state.

For if you say, "I feel confident that I can do well in school or in my job," you make a verifiable statement that you can empirically validate by demonstrating that, most of the time, you *do* perform well in school or on your job. But if you say, "I have great self-confidence," you strongly imply that (1) you do practically everything well, (2) you therefore exist as a great or good *person*; and (3) you consequently have the right to continue to exist and enjoy yourself. You cannot really prove these hypotheses, especially the last two.

You had better, then, by all means strive for work or love confidence but *not* for self-confidence. If self-confidence (or, better, self-acceptance) exists at all, you have it simply because you choose, decide, opt, to have it. You never have to *earn* it in any way.

Even with a minimum of social upbringing, a human develops as the kind of animal who had better accept certain challenges and at least *try* various tasks to have confidence that he can perform them. And the philosophy of inertia and inaction, especially when motivated by fear of failure, blocks the development of work confidence and love confidence.

8. You require action, as we have stressed throughout this book, to break the pattern of your own self-defeating behavior. If you have almost any habit pattern that sabotages your health, happiness, or relations with others, and you want to change it, you usually have to work forcefully against this habit, with both verbal-propagandistic and activity-deconditioning approaches. Human growth and development take time and effort. The more inert and inactive you remain, the more you will tend to block your own strongest desires, to sabotage your own healthy ends.

9. Inertia has a tendency to perniciously accumulate. The more you refrain from doing some activity—especially out of anxiety—the more you get used to *not* doing it. It then feels harder and harder to do. The more, for example, you keep from doing the writing or the painting that you keep telling yourself you really want to do, the more difficult you eventually find it to get down to work. And, as noted above, you frequently lose

interest in it entirely. Humans easily get habituated to doing both good and bad acts. A little inertia, when excused and coddled, therefore tends to lead to more inertia—and so on, almost ad infinitum.

Let us take, as a case in point, the condition of compulsive homosexuality, which literally tens of thousands of males get addicted to every year, largely because it originally seems an "easy" way out for them—considering how difficult we often make it for the young male to fulfill himself sexually with the young female. Recent studies show that fixed or exclusive homosexuality may include biological as well as psychological factors and doesn't always indicate emotional disturbance. Other studies also indicate that nonsexual disturbances, including extreme compulsiveness, may involve a biological predisposition as well as an acquired (environmentally learned) conditioning. So we'd better ignore neither the innate nor the learned tendencies of humans to behave in any "normal" or "abnormal" manner.

Even if humans biologically tend—meaning, *find it easy*—to behave in a certain way, compulsive individuals strongly *incline to*, and don't *have to* perform, uncontrollably—just as compulsive overeaters *tend to* but do not *have to* stuff themselves.

Jack M., a compulsive or obligatory homosexual, came to therapy at the age of twenty-five. Since fifteen, he had an exclusively homo-erotic background. He had felt attracted to girls earlier but had not had the courage to date any of them, for fear that they would look askance at his pimply face and his long, gangly body. And he had found easy solace in older homosexual males, who accepted him with his 'ugliness' and even made most of the overtures themselves.

After ten years of highly promiscuous homosexual behavior, including one arrest and a recent attempt to blackmail him at the school for boys at which he taught, Jack decided he'd better attempt to "go straight." And he came to see me (A.E.) with the knowledge that I, unlike a good many therapists, strongly felt that compulsive homosexuals definitely could change.

At first, Jack worked hard at therapy. He agreed that he'd better make some drastic changes in his thinking; and he did not resist the homework assignments (a common part of rational-emotive therapy) which involved his forcing himself to make dates with women. When, however, it came to carrying out the second part of these assignments—making some sexual overtures to the females he dated—Jack started to balk and to bring forth various excuses. He kept going with one particular woman, Tammie, who responded well if he tried to kiss or pet her; but he rarely tried.

"It seems to me," he said in the course of our seventh session, "futile to kiss and pet until I feel a strong urge to do so. Otherwise, it will just feel artificial and mechanical."

"With that kind of attitude," I said, "you'll probably wait forever. For how can you possibly, with your long-standing homosexual background, strongly *want* to kiss Tammie (or any other female)? How, for that matter, could you strongly want to eat oysters until you first tried them, several times perhaps, and finally *knew* that you enjoyed them?"

"But I could strongly *want* to try oysters for the first time, to *see* if I might like them."

"Exactly! If you had no silly fear of oysters, you probably *would* want to try them for the first time, to see if you could cultivate a taste for them. But you *do* have a silly fear of females. And while you have this fear, why should you *want* to kiss or pet them?"

"All right: but how do I get over my fear?"

"Just as you would get over your fear of oysters, if you had one. First, by convincing yourself that oysters don't exist as terrible, awful, and death-dealing. And, second, by forcing yourself to keep trying them until you *proved*, in action, that nothing horrible occurs when you eat them. Or until you proved that you really don't *prefer* oysters, but that you no longer feel horrified or terrified by the mere thought of eating them."

"So I can tell myself that I *won't* find it terrible to kiss females, and keep kissing and kissing and kissing them?"

"Right. For no matter how much you do the first part of this depropagandizing—the part where you keep seeing that kissing women does *not* prove terrible—nothing will probably happen until you also try the second part. Every time you get a chance to kiss Tammie and don't do so, you actually repropagandize yourself with your fears: tell yourself that it *would* turn out awful if you kissed her. Or, in other words, you keep saying to yourself, by your inactivity, 'This fear of kissing Tammie may seem like nonsense *in theory* but it sure as hell conquers me *in action*. Boy, how difficult to overcome!' And by repeating to yourself how difficult it remains, you actually keep *making* it more difficult to give up."

"According to your way of looking at it, then, I'd better keep subjecting myself to actions that counteract my fears of women before I can really expect to *believe* the absurdity of these fears. Right?"

"Right!"

"But I just *can't* go ahead and kiss Tammie, feeling the way I do. If I forced myself to do so, against my own fundamental tastes, I'd have such a disgreeable experience that it might well hinder rather than help me get heterosexually interested."

"Why should it? If you had a fear of swimming, but showed yourself many times that no real danger existed and that in a shallow pool you couldn't possibly drown, and if you then plunged in, would your swim feel so unpleasant that you'd never go in the water again? Or would you, once you plunged, *see* what you had theoretically but ineffectively tried to tell yourself—that the pool *proves* shallow and that you *can't* possibly drown?"

"I guess I'd soon see swimming as *un*dangerous. But have you a fair analogy? In swimming, I'd only have to plunge into the water. But in trying to behave heterosexually, I have to go through a complicated set of thoughts, feelings, and actions that don't seem *me.*"

"True. But in swimming, too, you would have to undergo a complicated set of thoughts, feelings, and actions before you could swim well. For plunging into the water only involves the *first* step. After that, you have to get used to the feel of the water, learn not to swallow too much of it, practice moving your arms in coordinated ways, see that you breathe properly while you swim, and so forth. You have perhaps a hundred different thoughts, feelings, and acts while swimming that you probably never before had while, say, walking, riding, or dancing. And these movements and these feelings *comprise 'you'* as you practice them. You *grow* to like them after a time. Many of them, in fact, you grow to like only *after* you have developed proficiency at them—maybe weeks or months later. Thus, although you at first may dislike using the breaststroke in swimming, because you started with a crawl stroke, once you have tried and have gained proficiency at the breaststroke you may come to prefer it. Your liking and doing a fine breaststroke then *constitutes* part of your swimming personality. Whereas at first you found it foreign, you later may feel it more natural."

"It all sounds easy, the way you put it. But *how* can I bring myself to kiss Tammie when I really don't want to do so?"

"Very simply: by forcing yourself. Just as you would force yourself to plunge into the swimming. And by, as I said before, fighting against your present nonsense: your telling yourself that it would prove horrible if she rejected your kiss, or indicated that she didn't like it, or let you have some sex satisfaction and *then* rejected you. Plunging means plunging—there seems no other way."

"Even against my own *feelings*?"

"*Especially* against your own feelings. For your feelings mainly consist of arbitrary fears. You don't even *know* it would feel unpleasant to kiss Tammie: rarely having tried! But what you really oppose, and have no so-called *feeling* for, doesn't seem to involve kissing so much as the idea of your *having* to take the bull by the horns, *having* to work at conquering your fear and your inertia. Don't you really have feelings against *that*?"

"Well, yes: now that you mention it. I *don't* like the idea of having to go to all this goddamn trouble to enjoy myself, if I ever actually do succeed in enjoying myself, with a woman when, as you well know, I already get a heck of a lot of enjoyment out of men."

"Ah, you see! You would like to change, to enjoy hetero-sexuality—*if* doing so involved little or no work. But since it *does* take pain, and *does* require all kinds of effort and practice, and since you already can enjoy yourself sexually with males without this kind of effort and practice, you don't see why you should have to change. That appears exactly why so few homosexuals overcome their fear of heterosexuality—and why so few hetero-sexuals overcome their anxiety about homosexual activity: because they want to do so magically, without work, without practice."

"But they can't, can they?"

"No, not very often. No magic exists. No easy way! And people find it tough to conquer their tendency to give in to inertia and self-defeating habits. Really tough! In your case, either you can force yourself to kiss Tammie, and to keep kissing her till you *learn* to enjoy it. Or else you can remain compulsively homo-sexual, with obvious disadvantages, for the rest of your life."

"So, no matter how I feel about kissing her, I'd darned well better try it."

"Yes. Don't stress how you feel about kissing Tammie, but how you feel about *yourself.* If you really accept yourself and want to get over this self-imposed limitation, you will try kissing Tammie, just as you would try swimming if you irrationally feared it. Only, kissing and copulating with females will probably prove even more enjoyable, once you have tried it, than swimming!

Jack, for once, did try. The very next date he had with Tammie, he avoided going out with her (which previously he felt only too eager to do) and instead stayed home and forced himself, literally forced himself, to try some petting. Much to his surprise, he discovered that her body felt softer and nicer to touch than that of most of the males with whom he had previously had sex. And she, this time, put *him* off, saying that she didn't feel she knew him well enough to go as far as he wanted to go. He could hardly wait to date her again. In his therapy session that followed this first strong attempt at sex with a woman, he said:

"Let me admit it: I quickly could see my wrongness—and your rightness. My negative feelings about kissing Tammie entirely resulted from my fear and resentment. I could see that when I first put my arm around her, I almost died a thousand deaths, fearing that she would push me away or, worse yet, make a laughing remark, like I used to hear my sisters make when they told each other how stupid and silly most of their boyfriends seemed and how they just couldn't stand their kisses or caresses. But I pushed ahead anyway. I could almost hear you saying to me: 'See! You *do* have anxiety. What do you mean you have no *feeling* for kissing her?' And I said to myself: 'Damn right, I feel *terror*! But I won't feel it forever. Screw it all, I won't! And I kept my arm around her, and drew her to me, though my heart kept beating like a goddamn drum or something. And before I knew it, much to my surprise she had turned her face up and obviously wanted me to kiss her. Imagine!—*wanted* an old faggot like me to kiss her! 'Well,' I said to myself, 'Here I feel scared as hell that she'll reject me and dump me out of the window and she really wants it, *she really honest-to-blazes wants it*!' I didn't hesitate after that. I just grabbed her and got the sweetest, juiciest kiss I never knew even existed before. 'Hell,' I said to myself again, 'so I've fought against *this* all these years, and keeping myself from getting it. Hell, hell, hell!' That did it. No more of that crummy panic and fighting for me. I know the game hasn't ended and I've got a long, long way to go yet. And I know I'll still have to force myself at times. But once that initial old inertia starts to go—just as you said it would—things can get awfully jumping enjoyable!"

Jack kept going. Within the next year he had several affairs, with Tammie and two other women. He enjoyed all of them immensely, got engaged to Tammie, and looked forward to marrying her. His sexual interest in males considerably diminished and he felt sure that whatever interest he had, he could control, or occasionally act out uncompulsively. His work (as a draftsman) also improved considerably. He saved money for the first time in his life. And he found himself much less resentful toward both males and females.

"How can I take the time," he said at one of his last therapy sessions, "to hate others and make up excuses for their holding me down when I keep so busy, these days, caring for Tammie, devoting myself to my work, and doing everything possible to plan for my marital and vocational future? Damn inertia and passivity! Too bad I haven't got more time to find other interesting projects to sink my teeth into!"

In many important respects, then, it would appear that action, particularly when it takes the form of creative, intensely absorbing activity, proves one of the mainstays of happy human living. If you (consciously or unconsciously) believe otherwise and live by a philosophy of inertia and inaction, you will sabotage your own potential satisfaction. More specifically, the kinds of actions you can take to help bring about fuller living can include:

1. You can attempt to get vitally absorbed in some persons or things outside yourself. Loving persons rather than things or ideas has distinct advantages: since other people can, in their turn, love you back and beautifully interact with you. But loving some long-range activity or idea—such as getting vitally attached to an art or a profession—also has its great rewards, and in some respects may prove more durable, varied, and involving than loving another person. Ideally, you can love both persons and things. But if you

get, especially at a certain period of time, thoroughly absorbed in one *or* the other, you may still thoroughly enjoy yourself.

2. Try to find some persons or things in which you can honestly get absorbed for *their own* sake and not for "ego-raising" reasons. It may seem fine and noble if you love your own children; or your orphaned younger brother. Or if you get devoted to one of the helping professions, such as teaching, psychology, or medicine. But you have a perfect right, as a human, "selfishly" to devote yourself to the most attractive person in town or to an avocation, such as coin collecting, which has relatively little social value. You probably won't love anyone or anything very deeply unless you follow the courage of your own convictions and do not try to win the approval of others by getting interested in what you think *they* would like you to love.

3. In devoting yourself to any field of endeavor try to choose a challenging, long-range project or area rather than something simple or short-ranged. Most highly intelligent individuals will not for very long remain highly absorbed in simply making a sexual conquest, stamp collecting, playing checkers, or weight lifting: for they can master these pursuits in a length of time and then often find them boring and unchallenging. Rather, try to select a goal such as writing a fine novel, making an outstanding contribution to physics, or achieving and retaining a high-level love relationship. This kind of pursuit may well remain intriguing for some time to come.

4. Don't expect vital absorptions to develop quickly. Because of inertia, fear of failure, or ignorance of the true depths of a given subject, you may at first have to push yourself, experimentally and forcibly, into a certain field of endeavor, and make yourself stick at it for a reasonable length of time, before you really begin to get absorbed in and fascinated by it. Before you conclude that you definitely do not enjoy your relationship with a given person or your preoccupation with a given project, give it an honest, fairly prolonged try. Then, if you still don't feel enamored, you can look around for a different kind of absorption.

5. Think about varying your interests and having some minor side projects going, even if you get absorbed in some major endeavor. Especially do so if your main involvement may not last forever. Wisely have some alternate involvements available. Humans dote on variety as well as on sustained goals; and you can easily go stale if you only concentrate on one pursuit. If, therefore, you vary your reading, your hobbies, the orginizations to which you belong, and your circle of friends, you may remain more vitally alive than if you routinely keep doing the same thing over and over.

6. You can combat inertia and inaction by tracking down your own irrational anxieties and hostilities that lie at their source.

If you remain self-defeatingly inert, you probably keep convincing yourself of some nonsense—such as "I find it easier and better to let others do things for me than to do them myself" or "Wouldn't it prove terrible if I risked writing that novel and miserably failed?" You can force yourself to *see* that you keep saying these self-sabotaging sentences and challenge, question, and dispute them, most vigorously and consistently, until you change them for saner, motion-impelling verbalizations.

7. It takes more than self-talk. In the final analysis, you often would better literally force yourself, propel yourself, push yourself, into action. Often, you can make yourself—yes, *make yourself*—undertake specific *acts* of courage: beard an employer in his office, ask a very attractive person to dance, take your idea for a book to a publisher. And keep forcing yourself into action long enough and often enough until the action itself proves easier and easier, even enjoyable.

8. As George Kelly has shown, you can deliberately adopt a different role for a period of time and force yourself to live up to this assumed role. If you habitually act shyly and retiringly, and for a week can act as one of the most outgoing and assertive individuals you know, you may find it relatively easy, after acting out that role, to behave less inhibitedly. The more you force yourself to do a thing that you feel "sure" you cannot do, the more you may prove your "certainty" mythical and show yourself you *can* do this thing.

J. L. Moreno and Fritz Perls have made much of role-playing in psychotherapy. George Kelly particularly emphasizes it as an assignment to do in between therapy sessions. In RET, we specialize in giving our clients risk-taking, shame-attacking, routine-changing homework assignments. Try some regular role-playing for yourself, particularly in the form of assertion training, where you push yourself to do "daring" things you normally refuse to do.

20 *LIVING RATIONALLY IN AN IRRATIONAL WORLD*

As we have noted throughout this book, you could hardly conceive of a more irrational world than our present society. In spite of the enormous advances in technical knowledge made during the last century, and the theoretical possibility that all of us could live in peace and prosperity, we actually hang on to the brink of local strife, world war, economic insecurity, political skulduggery, organized crime, pollution, ecological bankruptcy, business fraud, sexual violence, racial bigotry, labor and management inefficiency, religious fanaticism, and other manifestations of idiocy and inhumanity.

On a more personal scale, conditions appear equally bad or worse. None of us—no, not a single, solitary one of us—fails to have intimate encounters, almost every day of our lives, with several individuals (bosses or employees, husbands or wives, children or parents, friends or enemies) who behave stupidly, ignorantly, ineffectually, provocatively, frustratingly, viciously, or disturbedly. Modern life, instead of seeming just a bowl of cherries, often more closely resembles a barrel of prune pits.

Nevertheless, in today's world you do not *have* to feel depressed. Fortunately enough, along with your endowment with a fair share of inanity and insanity, you *also* have a remarkable capacity for straight thinking. And, as we noted in the opening pages of this book, if you intelligently organize and discipline your thinking and your actions, you can live a decidedly self-fulfilling, creative, and emotionally satisfying life *even* in our highly unsatisfactory world.

We can summarize the main practical points that we have made in this volume as follows:

Your desires and emotions do not consist of mysterious, uncontrollable forces that drive you to do their bidding. Although they have deep biological and learned roots, and therefore remain partly beyond your *immediate* control, they directly relate to your thinking and imagining and consequently largely stay within your *eventual* control. Where the wishes and feelings of lower animals and of young children almost entirely depend upon their inborn urges and the influences of their surrounding environment, you, as a human adult, can uniquely alter your own emotional responses and considerably control your destiny.

Your thinking remains intimately related to your perceiving, moving, and desiring and does not have a pure and independent existence. Although you cannot maintain perfect control over it, you can—by observing, analyzing, questioning, and changing the internalized sentences of which it largely consists—significantly modify and regulate your thought process. At the same time, by controlling a considerable amount of your thinking, you can also learn to change and regulate much of your emoting.

Emotional disturbance or neurosis essentially consists of letting your emotions run away with you: of feeling hysterically overconcerned about certain people and things, on the one hand, or of acting defensively underconcerned, on the other hand. While you, like other humans, probably have a biological disposition to disturb yourself, you also learn to think in an ignorance-based or irrational manner. Although potentially capable of thinking straighter and of more effectively controlling your behavior, you get habituated to thinking irrationally and to engaging in self-defeating behavior.

If you would control your emotions and keep yourself from leading a self-downing, neurotic existence, you'd better discard the major irrational ideas that you (and millions of your fellow members of this society) developed early in life. These ideas, which once might have seemed appropriate (in view of your helpless state as an infant and child) mainly resulted from (1) your early inability to think straight (particularly your childish insistence on immediate gratification rather than on future gains and your inability to accurately distinguish real from imagined dangers); (2) your dependence as a child on the planning and thinking of others; (3) the superstitions and prejudices inculcated in you by your parents; and (4) the indoctrinations by the mass media of your culture.

Although, as you grew older, you probably challenged and disputed your irrational premises to some extent, you also held on tenaciously and defensively to many of them, and have kept reindoctrinating yourself until the present. This *re*propagandizing—

which unconsciously but forcefully goes on day after day—mainly serves to keep your original irrationalities alive, in spite of the devastating results which they continue to have. But by closely observing your beliefs and by making yourself fully aware of your reindoctrinating processes, you can learn to dispute and counter-attack the irrational ideas you now perpetuate.

At the same time, because your irrational thinking has (over the years) led to pernicious forms of action or inaction (to lashing out at others impulsively or anxiously refraining from doing what you really want to do in life), you'd better *actively* as well as *thinkingly* challenge your hostile or inhibited ways of behaving. Thus, you can literally *force yourself* to give up childish impulse gratification (such as lying, stealing, attention-getting, or addiction to drugs or alcohol) or to do the things you senselessly fear (such as socializing, dating, or going for job interviews).

This kind of double-barreled, simultaneous attack on your deeply ingrained irrational ideas and self-defeating behavior can prove truly effective. For vigorous thinking about your emotional upsets or inhibitions will serve to pave the way to appropriate action or restraint; and forceful counteraction against your anxieties and hostilities will serve as the best form of depropagandization of the silly ideas that lie behind them. You will find thinking *and* doing *equally* desirable in attacking your oldest and deepest self-defeating tendencies.

Some of the major irrational ideas which you can strongly and persistently challenge, as well as forcefully propel yourself to act against, include these:

1. Dispute the belief that you must feel loved or accepted by every significant person for almost everything you do. Instead, try to stand on your own two feet; keep the approval of others as a *desirable* but not *necessary* goal; seriously and self-correctively consider other people's criticisms of your traits without concurring with their negative evaluations of *you*. Mainly strive to do what *you* really enjoy rather than what *other people* think you ought to do.

2. Give up the notion that you must act quite competently, adequately, and achievingly. Try to *do* or to do *well* rather than to do *perfectly*. Try to better your own performances rather than those of others. Strive, if you will, to perform better at art, ball playing, or business than you do now. But do not delude yourself that you will prove a better *person* if you achieve your goal. Strongly desire and work for success in your chosen fields. But accept failures as undesirable but not awful—as having nothing whatever to do with your intrinsic value as a human.

3. Get rid of the idea that you can label certain people bad, wicked, or villainous and that *they* deserve severe blame or punishment for their sins. Accept your own and others' wrongdoings

objectively: as misdeeds to learn from and to try to correct in the future. Fully acknowledge your and others' fallibility and make due allowances for the possibility—indeed, the practical certainty—of your and their continuing to make numerous errors and mistakes. Learn to distinguish between your having *responsibility* for your actions (which you frequently do) and deserving damnation for these actions (which you do not). See that when you condemn yourself or others you act perfectionistically and grandiosely, and that you thereby usually help to perpetuate rather than correct your or their misdeeds. Don't confuse people with their deeds, a *person who acts badly* with a *bad person*. As L. S. Barksdale has noted, although you can sensibly rate an individual's *acts*, can you ever legitimately rate *that which acts*?

4. Combat the idea that you must view it as terrible, horrible, and awful when things do not go the way you would like them to go. When conditions seem undesirable or obnoxious, determinedly try to change them for the better. When, for the moment, you cannot change them, accept them (and wait and plan for the time when you can). The greater your loss or frustration, the more philosophic you can make yourself in regard to it: the more you can see it as undesirable—but not as unbearable nor intolerable.

5. Reject the hypothesis that human misery gets externally caused and that you have little or no ability to control your depression or self-pity. Instead, realize that you create most of your own misery with your own irrational thinking, your self-propagandization; and that you can minimize your despair or anger by changing your thinking or your self-talk. If you ferret out your own irrational *shoulds*, *oughts*, and *musts* and replace your childish demands and whinings with realistic preferences, you need rarely make yourself anxious or upset.

6. Rid yourself of the idea that if something may prove dangerous or fearsome, you must get terribly occupied with and upset about it. Seriously question the real dangers accompanying the things you fear and determine the actual probabilities of their occurring or leading to dreadful consequences if they do occur. If you would live fully and creatively, accept certain inevitable dangers and risks that go with life. Most of your overconcern stems from your definitions—follows from your own awfulizing internalized sentences—and can get dealt with by observing and disputing your definitional assumptions, especially your assumptions that you must always please others and achieve outstandingly.

7. Stop trying to run away from many life difficulties and responsibilities. Short-range hedonism, or the insistence on immediate gratifications, proves a senseless philosophy in most instances. You can change it for a harder-headed, longer-range approach to pleasure and enjoyment. Determine what you'd really

better (not must!) do—and then, no matter how unpleasant these things, unrebelliously and promptly perform them. Although acquiring a considerable degree of self-discipline may seem unduly difficult, in the long run you will find the "easy" and undisciplined way harder, less rewarding, and often self-sabotaging.

8. Surrender the idea that the past remains all-important and that because something once strongly affected your life it must do so indefinitely. While considering your past history seriously and doing your best to learn valuable lessons from it, realize that your present constitutes tomorrow's past, and that working to change the present may enable you to create a radically better future. Continual rethinking of your old assumptions and reworking of your past habits can help minimize most of the pernicious influences from your childhood and adolescence.

9. Give up the notion that people and things should happen differently from the way they do and that life turns awful and horrible if good solutions to its grim realities don't quickly appear. Whether you like it or not, reality *exists* and you'd better accept its existence before you set about changing it. At times, wisely accept compromise and reasonable rather than perfect and certain solutions to life problems.

10. Dispute the idea that you can achieve maximum human happiness by inertia and inaction or by passively and uncomittedly "enjoying yourself." Strongly try to get absorbed in some persons or things outside yourself—involvements that truly interest you, rather than those that mainly bring you approval. In devoting yourself to any endeavor, try to choose a challenging, long-range project. Force yourself, by specific acts of courage, to take risks, to act against your own inertia, to make yourself committedly *alive.*

Summing up. While taking good care to avoid needlessly and gratuitously hurting others, consistently try to remain *you.* On the one hand, devote yourself self-interestedly to those pursuits likely to bring *you* the greatest satisfaction in your relatively brief span of life; and, on the other hand, absorb yourself in people and things outside yourself because *you* truly enjoy them. Your paramount absorption can unashamedly consist of the fulfillment of your own desires, your morality of enlightened self-interest. If you attain true self-interest, you will normally have a considerable degree of what Alfred Adler calls social interest because (1) your own interest, when you choose to live in a social group, involves consideration of other members of your group; and because (2) when you possess rational self-interest (rather than irrational self-centeredness), you normally find pleasure in helping and caring for some other humans.

These, then, seem some of the most essential rules for a sound and intelligent life—a life based on knowledge and reason and dedicated to the proposition that through your reasoning powers you may best achieve a highly satisfying emotional existence. Will following these rules absolutely ensure your living a maximally creative and happy life? Not necessarily; because, as we have several times noted in this book, some important intra- and interpersonal factors remain beyond your control.

Accidents and physical ailments do occur. Environmental conditions sometimes bring severe frustration. War and famine, pestilence and destruction, still, even in this relatively enlightened age, show their ugly fangs. But the human spirit, when freed of ignorance and cant, has remarkable resiliency. However bowed and bent it may temporarily seem, it still may throw off its unthinking and conventionalist chains, and rise above some of the nastiest handicaps.

You, as a human, potentially have that spirit. If you resolutely strive to think, fight, and act, you can probably use it to good effect. If, after making a concerted effort to question your own basic premises and to propel yourself to act against your self-defeating habit patterns, you still find yourself beset by intense feelings of anxiety or hostility, you probably could use professional help. By all means, in these circumstances, go for intensive therapy—even a little of which may prove enormously helpful.

If you do not feel too emotionally blocked or upset to benefit from the rational approach to living that we have outlined in this book, then try to see what you can do by working, working, and (yes, everlastingly) working at it. Good luck—and good reasoning!

21 RATIONAL-EMOTIVE THERAPY OR RATIONAL BEHAVIOR TRAINING UPDATED

As promised in the introduction to this book, we now will indicate, in more detail than in some of the previous examples, some of the major additions and refinements to rational-emotive therapy. I (A.E.) originated this system around the early part of 1955 and gave a first paper on it at the 1956 meetings of the American Psychological Association in Chicago. Since that time, RET has gone through many minor and some major changes, originated by myself and some of my main collaborators over the years—especially Dr. Robert A. Harper, Dr. H. Jon Geis, Edward Garcia, Dr. William Knaus, Dr. John M. Gullo, Dr. Paul A. Hauck, Dr. Donald H. Meichenbaum, Dr. Janet L. Wolfe, Dr. Arnold A. Lazarus, Dr. Aaron T. Beck, and (most notably) Dr. Maxie C. Maultsby, Jr. It has taken on various other names than RET—such as rational therapy (RT), semantic therapy, cognitive-behavior therapy (CBT), and (quite popularly) rational behavior training (RBT). We (and others) consider it an intrinsic part of the new movement favoring cognitive-behavior therapy; and we feel delighted that those behavior therapists who also employ cognitive methods tend to use RET, or something quite close to it, along with more orthodox forms of behavior modification.

Can we briefly list some of the major changes and revisions in RET that have taken place since its inception? We certainly can! For example:

COMBATING ABSOLUTISTIC THINKING. RET deals with all kinds of irrationalities, illogicalities, superstitions, and unrealistic statements that people devoutly believe and use in a self-defeating way. But we note with increasing clarity, as the years go by, that although exaggerated, illogical, or invalidly based thinking frequently leads to some degree of emotional disturbance, absolutistic or magical thinking tends to bring about even more pernicious results and lies at the root of more serious and pervasive disturbance. Thus, if you strongly believe, "I'd better do perfectly on my job, else I'll probably get fired," you will tend to feel somewhat anxious and insecure. For how can you expect to do *perfectly*? And your statement, "I'll probably get fired," in all likelihood remains false; but your belief in it will help you feel overconcerned rather than merely concerned.

If you dogmatically believe, "I *must* do perfectly on my job, else I'll *certainly* get fired, and that would prove *awful!*" you get yourself into even greater emotional trouble. Because: (1) Although you can give no reason why you *must* do perfectly, believing that you must will tend to drive you up a wall: make you *frantic* about doing perfectly and help you do more *im*perfectly. (2) The belief that you will *certainly* get fired if you act imperfectly on your job will tend to make you even more anxious—and, again, remains not only highly improbable but utterly unprovable. (3) Your conviction that getting fired would prove *awful* greatly increases the pain you attribute to losing your job and tends to make you still more frantic—and, ironically, afraid of the *awfulness* you have invented but cannot empirically substantiate.

We have constantly found, in our clinical practice, that virtually all feelings of what we call emotional disturbance stem from *must*urbation: from three kinds of devout *shoulds*, *oughts*, or *musts* that humans invent and then plague themselves with: (1) "I *must* do well, and *must* turn into a *horrible person* if I don't"—leading to feelings of inadequacy, worthlessness, insecurity, self-damnation, anxiety, and depression. (2) "You *must* treat me kindly, fairly, and considerately; and you rate a *rotten individual* if you don't!"—leading to feelings of anger, resentment, hostility, and overrebelliousness. (3) "The universe *must* make things easy for me, give me what I want without too much trouble or annoyance; and I *can't stand* it when this terrible universe doesn't!"—leading to feelings of low frustration tolerance, avoidance, self-pity, and inertia. None of these *must*urbatory beliefs or premises appear empirically confirmable. All prove dogmatic and absolutistic. Each leads to almost inevitable emotional upsetness and to self-sabotaging behavior. All result in forms of acute or chronic whining. And whining about your own, others', or the worlds' failings constitutes the main element of what we usually, and perhaps euphemistically, call neurosis or emotional disturbance.

RET therapists and students, such as those we train at our clinic and our workshops at the Institute for Advanced Study in Rational Psychotherapy in New York City (and at our other branches in other regions), learn to zero in quickly on any implied or stated absolutes—*shoulds, oughts, musts, needs, necessities, got to's, supposed to's,* or *have to's*—that they use to disturb themselves and actively and vigorously to dispute these *musts.* RET also teaches self-upsetting people to discover their other illogicalities and irrationalities and to uproot and surrender them. But it especially shows them how, most of the time, they tend to have clear-cut *musts*; and it gives them the slogan "Cherchez le *should*! Cherchez le *must*!" (Look for the *should*! Look for the *must*!) to help them almost immediately find the main philosophic source of their "emotional" problems and to undo this absolutistic source.

GIVING UP SELF-RATING.   In early writings on RET, such as *How to Live with a Neurotic* and the first edition of *A Guide to Rational Living,* we taught people not to evaluate themselves or their egos in terms of any of their performances or accomplishments—not to think, for example, "I can call myself good because I treat others well," or "I rate as bad because I let myself keep acting incompetently"—but to base their "goodness" or "human worth" solely on the fact of their aliveness, their existence. Thus, they could legitimately tell themselves, "I exist as good because I have life."

This seemed a very practical solution to the problem of human worth, since people whom we got to adopt it thereafter tended to accept themselves merely because they remained alive, and practically never downed themselves nor considered themselves valueless. Unfortunately, as noted in later RET writings (particularly *Reason and Emotion in Psychotherapy*), this "solution" didn't always hold up too well, since some bright clients would object: "What *makes me* 'good,' just because I have aliveness? Why couldn't I just as legitimately say, 'I rate as bad because I remain alive?' "

Well, they seemed right! The more we thought about it, the more we could see that calling oneself good because one had aliveness merely amounted to a tautology: it remained true by definition but could not get confirmed empirically. It worked. But it appeared a highly inelegant solution to the problem of human worth. Discussing the matter more thoroughly in a paper honoring the philosopher Robert S. Hartman, I (A.E.) concluded that the whole concept of human value remains a sort of Kantian thing-in-itself; it probably never can get empirically validated; and we can well dispense with it in psychology and philosophy. I said, in other words, that humans really seem to have no "worth" or "value," except by somewhat arbitrary definition; and they don't have to rate, value, measure, or evaluate "themselves," their "essence," or their totality at all. When they give up such evaluating, self-rating, or ego measurement, they practically eliminate their most serious "emotional" problems.

RET now teaches, in other words, that if you *insist* on evaluating yourself totally, or having a "self-image," or rating your "worth" as a human, then you'd better use a "solution" such as the one we gave in the original edition of this *guide*. Say, "I like myself [or, better, accept myself] simply because I exist, because I remain alive." That kind of solution still seems practical or pragmatic and will get you into virtually no emotional difficulties. It works!

More elegantly (and with less philosophical argument), however, you can refuse to rate "yourself," your "humanity," your "ego" at all! You can say: "I seem to exist—that remains empirically provable. I also can continue to exist, if I choose to do so. While remaining alive, I to some extent have the choice of minimizing my pain and maximizing my (short- and long-range) pleasure. OK: I therefore *choose* to remain alive and to enjoy myself. Now let me see how I can most effectively achieve these goals!"

With this sort of philosophy, you can avoid rating yourself, your totality, your human worth, at all. "You" don't get rated as good, bad, or indifferent. "You" have no image of yourself. But "you"—or your organism—definitely exists; and this organism chooses to remain alive and to seek enjoyment rather than needless pain. Consequently, because you *want* (not *need*) to continue to exist joyfully, you value and disvalue many or most of your traits, deeds, acts, and performances. Any act, for example, that leads to your premature demise or that enables you to live but to have pain or joylessness, you evaluate as "bad." And any act that leads to a long and pleasant life, you tend to evaluate as "good." Ratings and measurements of your *behaviors* continue to exist and to have importance. But ratings and measurements of your *self*, your *humanity*, your *totality*, your *ongoingness*, your *you-ness*, go by the board.

Will you find this nonevaluation of self difficult to achieve? Indeed you will, in most instances. For RET assumes that your "normal" human condition involves not merely rating your acts, deeds, and traits but imagining a "self" or "ego" and rating *it*. So you'll probably have great trouble making yourself into a person who doesn't rate yourself. But try it! We think you definitely (though not *perfectly*) can do this. And accomplishing this difficult feat—which we explain how to do in this revised edition of the *Guide* and in other writings on RET (such as *Growth Through Reason, How to Master Your Fear of Flying, Executive Leadership*, and *Humanistic Psychotherapy: The Rational-Emotive Approach*) can prove fun!

DOING HOMEWORK ASSIGNMENTS. Right from the start, RET emerged as a cognitive-behavior system of therapy, since it held that humans rarely change themselves considerably unless they not only rethink their self-defeating philosphies but *act* against these irrational beliefs. Although what we now call behavior therapy did not really exist at this time, RET clearly stated some of its outstanding theories and practices. For it gave clients cognitive, imaginative, emotive, and activity homework assignments. It persuaded them to *work* against their fears; to *practice* new kinds of thinking; to deliberately *stay* in obnoxious situations at times, while showing themselves that they *can* stand such situations. It also employed techniques of self-management —or what the famous psychologist B. F. Skinner calls operant conditioning: inducing clients to use rewards or reinforcements when they did sensible things and penalties (though not self-damnation!) when they acted foolishly.

Since RET's early days, then, we have developed and systematized homework assignments. In recent years, we have tended to increase this emphasis and have particularly pioneered in the use of *in vivo* (alive) desensitization. Thus, if clients feel afraid to encounter others socially, we frequently recommend that they do a graduated series of assignments in this respect: first, merely attend a social gathering; second, make sure they talk to one or a few people at such a gathering; third, really try to get to know someone there; fourth, make an appointment to meet this person on the outside; fifth, try to see this person steadily; etc.

In using self-management or operant conditioning, we follow some of the rules laid down by B. F. Skinner, David Premack, Lloyd Homme, and others and reinforce and penalize not only behaviors but thoughts, emotions, and homework assignments. Thus, if our clients refuse to do their disputing of their irrational beliefs, we can let them set themselves a reinforcement (such as sex, food, music, or companionship) when they do regular disputing and a penalty (such as cleaning the house, writing a long report, or sending a contribution to a cause they despise) when they don't do this kind of disputing. Self-reinforcement or contracting gets used very frequently in RET.

COMBATING SELF-DAMNATION.   From the start, as we showed in the first edition of the *Guide*, RET has stressed the importance of people's refraining from blaming themselves (and others) for their poor performances. It does so now as much as ever! But we have realized that the use of the word *blame* has limitations. For when we say, "Don't blame yourself for doing badly," you can interpret our statement to mean, "I'd better not say that I did badly, since I really acted pretty well." But, probably, you didn't act *well*, and you *did* act badly. So you thus lie to yourself. Or, instead, you may admit that you have done badly and say to yourself: "Oh, well, I guess I acted poorly. But why need I take my mistake seriously? It really doesn't matter very much that I made it." In this case, you will probably not make strong efforts to correct your mistake or to avoid making it again in the future.

We really would like you, of course, to fully acknowledge that you have made some kind of error, if you actually have acted badly; realize that you handicap yourself if you keep acting in that manner; and work as hard as you can to minimize or eliminate this kind of poor behavior in the future. We therefore, in RET, now tend to try to convey to people: "Yes, you acted poorly, and will keep getting unfortunate results if you continue to act that way. But don't, under any conditions, berate *yourself*, your entire personhood, for making such errors. Don't *damn* or *devil-ify* yourself in any way, no matter how many times or how seriously you err. Your *acts* may prove foolish or reprehensible; but *you* cannot justifiably get damned, downed, or devil-ified (made into a devil or demon) for performing them."

Instead of *self-blaming*, therefore, we now tend to use the terms *self-downing*, *self-damning*, and *self-denigrating* in RET. For people falsely tend to believe that you *should* get blamed for doing a bad act; when they would really mean, if they spoke more accurately, that *the act* but not *you* rates as blameworthy. Since *downing*, *damning*, and *devil-ifying* have stronger and more magical connotations than *blaming*, and since RET particularly opposes any flagellating of the *person* (truly a magical concept), we now tend to use these terms instead of the less rigorous term *blaming*.

DISCRIMINATING INAPPROPRIATE FROM APPROPRIATE EMOTIONS.   In the first editions of *How to Live with a Neurotic* and *A Guide to Rational Living*, we erroneously stated and implied that you could legitimately feel sorry, sad, or unhappy but that if you experienced these feelings very strongly you behaved neurotically. We now realize that this distinction has little legitimacy: since even your exceptional sorrow or displeasure may prove appropriate, assuming that you have some unusually strong wants or preferences and that these keep getting thwarted. Thus, if you get stranded on a desert island and the only other human with you utterly refuses to talk with or to relate to you in any way, you certainly could *appropriately* feel very frustrated and unhappy about this rejection.

Extreme sorrow and unhappiness, however, do *not* equal depression, despair, shame, or self-downing. And it still remains legitimate to disciminate between the former negative feelings, on the one hand, and the latter, on the other hand. Even 99 percent unhappiness may not equal 1 percent depression. The two feelings tend to rest in two different emotional continua; and although depression would rarely exist without concomitant frustration, sorrow, or unhappiness, the latter can easily exist without the former. Moreover, whereas frustration, sorrow, and unhappiness frequently emerge as quite appropriate feelings—assuming that you desire something very much and get deprived of it—depression, despair, shame, and self-downing (as well as hostility, rage, and feelings of low frustration tolerance) practically never appear appropriate and had best get eliminated.

Do we merely quibble in this connection? We think not. If we bother to define our terms rigorously—which we'd better do in the fields of psychology and psychotherapy—frustration, sorrow, and sadness seem to arise when you strongly *prefer*, *desire* or *want* something and your preferences get blocked. Thus, if you say, "I greatly prefer to succeed in school," and you fail miserably, you then normally conclude, "I find it most unfortunate that I have failed to get what I want, succeeding in school. Now let me see whether I can succeed next time; or, if I can't succeed at all, let me see how I can feel reasonably happy without the advantages of a school degree." As a result of these observations and evaluations, you will then tend to feel frustrated, sorry, and sad—and sometimes very much so.

Depression, despair, shame, and self-downing, however, arise from a *different* or *extra* set of beliefs; namely: "I absolutely *must* succeed in school." And, when you don't succeed, you then logically—because of this silly *must*—conclude: "I find it *awful* that I have failed! I *can't stand* my failure! I will *always* keep failing. I rate as a *rotten person* for failing so miserably!" With these highly irrational, absolutistic beliefs, you *make* yourself depressed, despairing, ashamed, and self-downing. Such emotions, although quite genuine and authentic, normally harm you, and therefore we can call them *inappropriate*, *illegitimate*, or *self-defeating*.

The fact that you "naturally" or "humanly" feel depressed (at point C, your emotional and behavioral Consequences), when beset with obnoxious stimuli or Activating Experiences (at point A) does *not* make this feeling "normal" or "healthy." Nor does the fact that you easily create such feelings, by firmly and strongly believing (at point B, your Belief System) that the Activating Experiences *should* or *must* not exist, mean that you have no control over your irrational beliefs and cannot stop yourself from believing them. You *can* see, acknowledge, and minimize them. And, if you don't, you will continue to create and strongly have these inappropriate feelings: inappropriate because depression, for example, usually involves extreme unhappiness, inertia, the conviction that you can't change and that conditions must remain horrible, and interference with energies and time that you might otherwise employ to change your depression-creating beliefs and the obnoxious activating events that you wrongly think "caused" them.

RET, then, has a clear-cut theory of appropriate and inappropriate, rational and irrational, thoughts, feelings, and behaviors. It starts with the premise that virtually all humans strongly desire to stay alive and to feel relatively happy and free from pain. If they have these basic values (which they choose and *need* not have), it then labels as irrational any thought, idea, attitude, belief, or philosophy that seriously sabotages these values; and, similarly, it labels as inappropriate any feeling or behavior that seriously interferes with the achievement of these values. Rational ideas, conversely, aid the chosen human values of survival and happiness; and appropriate feelings and behaviors similarly aid your staying happily alive. By clearly differentiating what you choose as your basic values and how you rationally abet and irrationally interfere with their attainment, you encourage appropriate rather than inappropriate emoting and behaving.

USING EMOTIVE AND AFFECTIVE METHODS. From its inception, RET always held to a cognitive-emotive-behavioristic theory and practice. Virtually all psychotherapies do this, but RET does so in a more explicit, determined manner than do many of the other systems. We first called it rational therapy (RT) to emphasize perhaps its *most* distinctive element: its persuasive, teaching, logical, philosophic aspects. But by the time we got around to writing the first edition of the *Guide* we had already changed the name to rational-emotive therapy (RET), to indicate that it didn't consist *only* of a cognitive approach but had important emotive and behavioral aspects as well.

Over the years, we have tended to emphasize and utilize the emotive aspects of RET more than we did at the very beginning. We deliberately show for clients what Carl Rogers calls unconditional positive regard, or complete acceptance of them as persons, no matter how inadequately or immorally they act. We employ a good many of the affect-arousing exercises used by encounter groups or individual therapists—and in this respect have invented some special risk-taking, shame-attacking, and personal encountering exercises. Not only do we help people acknowledge or get in touch with their "negative" feelings—such as those of anxiety, guilt, and hostility—but we specialize in helping them *strongly*, *vehemently*, and *powerfully* think, emote, and act against these feelings when they lead to harmful results. We allow ourselves, as therapists, to have warm, loving feelings toward some of our clients, as long as we do not thereby sidetrack them from unconditionally accepting themselves and giving up their dire *needs* for our (or anyone else's) approval or love. We use, as we have always used, strong and direct confrontational methods, especially in some of our group therapy procedures, and do not hesitate to show clients that they lie to themselves or that some of their ideas amount to arrant nonsense. We often help clients to push themselves into emotional involvements with others, including involvements with other members of their regular or marathon groups. We quite consciously employ, at times, supportive methods of individual and group therapy.

The main difference between RET and other therapies that use emotive and affective approaches involves the purpose for which these methods get employed. Rational-emotive therapists frequently do the same emotive things that other kinds of therapists do. But we usually do them to help people *get* better rather than merely or mainly *feel* better: to help them change their fundamental philosophic premises and make themselves relatively unsettable (but *not* unemotional!) about practically *anything* that may occur to them in the present or future. We rarely use emotive exercises or techniques simply because they evoke feeling, because they abreactively unblock repressions, because they lead to pleasurable sensations, or because they "work." We use them, rather, as part and parcel of long-range cognitive and training processes: to help people to make major philosophic reconstructions. We consistently employ but take care not to deify human emotions.

USING IMAGINATIVE TECHNIQUES. As noted above, RET has always used activity, *in vivo* homework assignments: getting people to act against their anxieties, obsessions, compulsions, inhibitions, and other disturbances. In the original edition of the *Guide* we also referred occasionally to imaginative techniques: such as fantasizing yourself as able to do something and thereby changing your outlook and helping yourself do this desired thing. Since that time, encouraged partly by the work of Joseph Wolpe, Arnold Lazarus, Thomas Stampfl, and Joseph Cautela, we have made much greater use of imaging techniques in RET. In particular, Dr. Maxie C. Maultsby, Jr., originated the technique of rational-emotive imagery; and I (A.E.) have helped develop this method into one of the most frequently used and effective methods in our RET and RBT therapeutic bag. In the leaflet on rational-emotive imagery (REI) published by the Institute for Advanced Study in Rational Psychotherapy, Dr. Maultsby and I outline it as follows:

> Would you like to think more rationally and make yourself less emotionally upset? Try these techniques of rational-emotive imagery (REI).

NEGATIVE IMAGERY

> Picture to yourself or fantasize, as vividly and intensely as you can, the details of some unpleasant Activating Experience (A) that has happened to you or will likely occur in the future. As you strongly imagine this event, let yourself feel distinctly uncomfortable—for example, anxious, depressed, ashamed, or

hostile—at C (your emotional Consequence). Get in touch with this disturbed feeling and let yourself fully experience it for a brief period of time. Don't avoid it: on the contrary, face it and feel it!

When you have actually felt this disturbed emotion for a while, push yourself—yes, *push* yourself!—to change this feeling in your gut, so that instead you *only* feel keenly disappointed, regretful, annoyed, or irritated but *not* anxious, depressed, guilty, or hostile. Don't think that you can't do this—for you can. You can, at almost any time you work at doing so, get in touch with your gut-level feelings and push yourself to change them so that you experience different feelings. You definitely have the ability to do this. So try, concentrate—and do it!

When you have let yourself, pushed yourself *only* to feel disappointed or irritated, look at what you have done in your head to *make yourself* have these new, appropriate feelings. You will note, if you observe yourself clearly, that you have in some manner changed your Belief System (or Bull Shit!), at B, and have thereby changed your emotional Consequence, at C, so that you now feel regretful or annoyed rather than anxious, depressed, guilty, or hostile. Let yourself clearly see what you have done, what important changes in your Belief System you have made. Become fully aware of the new Beliefs (B) that create your new emotional Consequences (C) regarding the unpleasant Activating Experience (A) that you keep imagining or fantasizing.

If your upsetting feelings do not change as you attempt to feel more appropriately, keep fantasizing the same unpleasant experiences or events and keep working at your gut until you *do* change these feelings. Don't give up! *You* create and control your feelings. You *can* change them.

Once you succeed in feeling concerned rather than anxious, disappointed with your behavior rather than ashamed of yourself, or displeased with others' traits rather than hostile to them for having such traits, and once you see exactly what Beliefs you have changed in your head to make yourself feel badly but not emotionally upset, keep repeating this process. Make yourself feel disturbed; then make yourself feel displeased but not disturbed; then see exactly what you did in your head to change your feelings; then practice doing this, over and over again. Keep practicing, until you can easily, after you fantasize highly unfortunate experiences at A, feel upset at C, change your feelings at C to one of disappointment but not upsetness, and see what you keep doing at B to change your Belief System that creates and maintains your feelings. If you keep practicing this kind of rational-emotive imagery (REI) for at least ten minutes every day for the next few weeks, you will get to the point where whenever you think of this kind of unpleasant event, or it actually occurs in practice, you will tend to easily and automatically feel displeased rather than emotionally upset.

Illustrative Example: At A, the Activating Experience or Activating Event, let us suppose that you have failed to do a job well and your supervisor or boss has severely criticized you for this failure. You feel depressed or self-downing about this (at C, your emotional Consequence) and you want to get over this disturbed feeling.

Let yourself strongly, vividly fantasize the details of your failing and getting criticized (of its actually occurring in the past or its happening in the future). Let yourself feel, as you intensely picture this failure and criticism, depressed or self-downing. Feel this! Get keenly in touch with your emotions of depression and worthlessness! Keep in touch with them for a short period of time.

Now push yourself—yes, *push* yourself—while keeping this same unfortunate set of conditions vividly in your mind to make yourself feel *only* disappointed and concerned. If you have trouble doing this, keep persisting until you succeed. You *can* fantasize failure and make yourself feel *only* concerned and disappointed *rather than* depressed and worthless. Do this!

When you have begun to feel *only* concerned and disappointed (and *not* depressed and worthless), look for what you have started telling yourself, in your head, to *make yourself* have these new, appropriate feelings. You will find that you probably have started telling yourself something like: "I guess it doesn't prove *awful* for me to fail and get criticized, even though I *do* find it unfortunate and highly inconvenient. The world will hardly come to an end if my supervisor or boss keeps criticizing me, even though I don't like this and wish I could make him or her stop. I *can* stand failing, although I'll never want to fail. While my acts seem bad and deplorable, they hardly make me a *rotten person*."

While you still vividly imagine your failing and getting severely criticized, keep practicing telling yourself these kinds of rational beliefs. And keep *feeling* the appropriate emotions of disappointment, regret, concern, and displeasure—and *not* depression or worthlessness.

POSITIVE IMAGERY

If you would employ positive imagery and thinking, picture to yourself or fantasize, as vividly and intensely as you can, the details of some unpleasant Activating Experience (A) that has happened to you or will likely occur in the future. If you want to do so, you can picture the situation at A at its very worst—the worst that you ever experienced it or will probably ever experience it in the future. Let yourself feel distinctly uncomfortable—for example, anxious, depressed, ashamed, or hostile—at C (your emotional Consequence). Get in touch with this disturbed feeling and let yourself fully experience it for a brief period of time.

As you feel upset at C, notice what you keep telling yourself at B (your Belief System or Bull Shit) to *make yourself* feel disturbed. When you clearly see these Beliefs, Dispute them (at D), as you would in the usual kind of Disputing that rational-emotive therapy (RET) or rational behavior training (RBT) teaches you to do.

Now, as you see these irrational Beliefs and vigorously Dispute them, strongly fantasize how you would feel and behave *after* you started giving them up and *after* you started believing, instead, rational Beliefs about what keeps happening to you at A. Intensely picture yourself (1) disbelieving your irrational Beliefs and believing your rational ideas about obnoxious events that may occur at A; (2) feeling appropriately displeased or disappointed rather than inappropriately depressed or hostile at C; and (3) acting in a concerned instead of an upset manner at E.

Keep practicing this procedure, so that you first imagine something unfortunate or disadvantageous; then make yourself feel depressed, hostile, or otherwise disturbed about your image. Then see what irrational Beliefs you hold to create your disturbance; then work on changing these Beliefs. Then strongly picture yourself disbelieving these ideas and feelings and acting in accordance with your new rational philosophies; and wind up by actually feeling only concerned and displeased rather than depressed or hostile.

Illustrative Example: At A, the Activating Experience or Activating Event, let us suppose (once again) that you have failed to do a job well and your supervisor or boss has severely criticized you for this failure. You feel depressed or self-downing about this (at C, your emotional Consequence) and you want to get over this disturbed feeling.

Let yourself strongly, vividly fantasize the details of your failing and getting criticized (of its actually occurring in the past or its happening in the future). Let yourself feel, as you intensely picture this failure and criticism, depressed or self-downing. Feel this! Get keenly in touch with your emotions of depression and worthlessness! Keep in touch with them for a short period of time.

Now actively look for the irrational Beliefs (at B) with which you keep creating your disturbed feelings, and make sure that you find them. Don't give up easily! Assume that your feelings get created by your own Beliefs and persist until you discover these Beliefs—especially the *shoulds, oughts,* and *musts* they almost invariably include.

You will probably find that your irrational Beliefs follow these lines: "I find it *awful* to fail and get criticized! If my supervisor or boss keeps criticizing me, my job will end, the whole world will practically end for me, and I'll never get a good job again or find happiness at work. I can't *stand* failing and getting criticized! If I keep failing like this, that proves me a thoroughly rotten person who remains incapable of succeeding at practically anything!"

Get yourself to see your own irrational Beliefs very clearly. Then vigorously, persistently Dispute them (at point D), until you see that you don't *have* to believe them and that you *can* give them up and feel much better about the obnoxious things, the failing and getting criticized, happening to you at A. Picture yourself, as vividly as possible, actually holding a radically different philosophy about your failing. Such as: "I don't have to find it *awful*, but merely inconvenient and disadvantageous, to fail and get criticized. If my supervisor or boss keeps criticizing me, I probably won't lose my job but will merely keep getting criticized for not doing it well enough. If I somehow do lose my job, I'll probably get another good one again, and may even learn considerably from this bad experience. Although I'll never *like* failing and getting severely criticized, I certainly can *stand* it! Even though I keep failing, that only proves me a person with flaws, who cannot do as well as I'd prefer to do but who never turns into a rotten person, utterly incapable of succeeding at anything."

As you picture yourself believing this, also see yourself, as vividly as you can: responding appropriately to a critical supervisor or boss; looking around for better solutions to your problems of failing; seeing the possible loss of a job as a problem to get solved rather than as a catastophe; and accepting yourself fully, no matter how poorly you do in job situations. Keep practicing these positive thoughts and images, until you easily and automatically begin to feel disappointed, concerned, and displeased rather than depressed and self-flagellating.

SELF-REINFORCEMENT

As noted above, if you use either negative or positive rational-emotive imagery, you will probably find it useful to spend at least ten minutes a day practicing one or both of these forms of REI for a period of two or three weeks. You may find them particularly useful if you expect an unpleasant or risky situation to occur—such as taking a stiff examination of some kind—and you fear you will get anxious or depressed when it does occur. If for several days or week before its transpiring, you vigorously employ these REI methods, you may find that you easily meet the situation, when it does occur, without the feelings of anxiety or depression you would usually experience.

If you frequently avoid homework assignments, such as REI, and you want to encourage yourself to carry them out, you may use operant conditioning or self-management methods (originated by B. F. Skinner, David Premack, Marvin Goldfried, and other psychologists). Select some activity that you highly enjoy and that you tend to do every day—such as reading, eating, television viewing, masturbation, or social contact with your friends. Use this activity as a reinforcer or reward by *only* allowing yourself to engage in it *after* you have practiced REI for at least ten minutes that day. Otherwise, no reward!

In addition, you may penalize yourself every single day you do *not* use REI for at least ten minutes. How? By making yourself perform some activity you find distinctly unpleasant—such as eating something obnoxious, contributing to a cause you hate, getting up a half hour earlier in the morning, or spending an hour conversing with someone you find boring. You can also arrange with some person or group to monitor you and help you actually carry out the penalties that you set for yourself. You may of course steadily use REI without self-reinforcement. But you will often find it more effective if you use it along with rewards and penalties that you execute right after you practice or avoid practicing this rational-emotive method.

PRACTICING DISPUTING IRRATIONAL BELIEFS, RET, in general, teaches people to seek out, discover, and dispute their irrational beliefs. To give them concrete practice at doing this, however, we use, at the Institute for Advanced Study in Rational Psychotherapy in New York City, a specific Disputing Irrational Beliefs (DIBS) instruction sheet. This DIBS sheet, which I (A.E.) have written, goes as follows:

If you want to increase your rationality and reduce your irrational beliefs, you can spend at least ten minutes every day asking yourself the following questions and carefully thinking through (not merely parroting!) the appropriate answers. Write down each question and your answers to it on a piece of paper; or else record the questions and your answers on a tape recorder.

1. WHAT IRRATIONAL BELIEF DO I WANT TO DISPUTE AND SURRENDER?
   ILLUSTRATIVE ANSWER: I must receive love from someone for whom I really care.
2. CAN I RATIONALLY SUPPORT THIS BELIEF?
   ILLUSTRATIVE ANSWER: No.
3. WHAT EVIDENCE EXISTS OF THE FALSENESS OF THIS BELIEF?
   ILLUSTRATIVE ANSWER: Many indications exist that the belief that I must receive love from someone for whom I really care remains false:
   a. No law of the universe exists that says that someone I care for *must* love me (although I would find it nice if that person did!).
   b. If I do not receive love from one person, I can still get it from others and find happiness that way.
   c. If no one I care for ever cares for me, I can still find enjoyment in friendships, in work, in books, and in other things.
   d. If someone I deeply care for rejects me, that will seem most unfortunate; but I will hardly die!
   e. Even though I have not had much luck in winning great love in the past, that hardly proves that I *must* gain it now.
   f. No evidence exists for *any* absolutistic *must*. Con-

sequently, no proof exists that I must have *any-thing*, including love.

g. Many people seem to exist in the world who never get the kind of love they crave and who still lead happy lives.

h. At times during my life I know that I have remained unloved and happy; so I most probably can feel happy again under nonloving conditions.

i. If I get rejected by someone for whom I truly care, that may mean that I possess some poor, unloving traits. But that hardly means that I rate as a rotten, worthless, totally unlovable individual.

j. Even if I had such poor traits that no one could ever love me, I would still not have to down myself and rate myself as a lowly, bad individual.

4. DOES ANY EVIDENCE EXIST OF THE TRUTH OF THIS BELIEF?

ILLUSTRATIVE ANSWER: No, not really. Considerable evidence exists that if I love someone dearly and never get loved in return that I will then find myself disadvantaged, inconvenienced, frustrated, and deprived. I certainly would prefer, therefore, not to get rejected. But no amount of inconvenience amounts to a *horror*. I can still *stand* frustration and loneliness. They hardly make the world *awful*. Nor does rejection make me a turd! Clearly, then, no evidence exists that I *must* receive love from someone for whom I really care.

5. WHAT WORST THINGS COULD *ACTUALLY* HAPPEN TO ME IF I DON'T GET WHAT I THINK I MUST (OR DO GET WHAT I THINK I MUSTN'T)?

ILLUSTRATIVE ANSWER: If I don't get the love I think I must receive:

a. I would get deprived of various pleasures and conveniences that I might receive through gaining love.

b. I would feel inconvenienced by still wanting love and looking for it elsewhere.

c. I might *never* gain the love I want, and thereby continue indefinitely to feel deprived and disadvantaged.

d. Other people might down me and consider me pretty worthless for getting rejected—and that would prove annoying and unpleasant.

e. I might settle for pleasures other than and worse than those I could receive in a good love relationship; and I would find that distinctly undesirable.

f. I might remain alone much of the time: which again would prove unpleasant.

g. Various other kinds of misfortunes and deprivations might occur in my life—none of which I need
define as *awful, terrible,* or *unbearable.*

WHAT GOOD THINGS COULD I MAKE HAPPEN IF I DON'T
GET WHAT I THINK I MUST (OR DO GET WHAT I THINK I
MUSTN'T)?

a. If the person I truly care for does not return my
love, I could devote more time and energy to
winning someone else's love—and probably find
someone better for me.
b. I could devote myself to other enjoyable pursuits
that have little to do with loving or relating, such
as work or artistic endeavors.
c. I could find it challenging and enjoyable to teach
myself to live happily without love.
d. I could work at achieving a philosophy of fully accepting myself even when I do not get the love I
crave.

You can take any one of your major irrational
beliefs—your *shoulds, oughts,* or *musts*—and spend at
least ten minutes every day, often for a period of several
weeks, actively and vigorously disputing this belief.
To help keep yourself devoting this amount of time
to this DIBS method of rational disputing, you may
use operant conditioning or self-management methods
(originated by B. F. Skinner, David Premack, Marvin
Goldfried, and other psychologists). Select some activity that you highly enjoy and that you tend to do
every day—such as reading, eating, television viewing,
masturbation, or social contact with your friends. Use
this activity as a reinforcer or reward by *only* allowing
yourself to engage in it *after* you have practiced DIBS
for at least ten minutes that day. Otherwise, no
reward!

In addition, you may penalize yourself every
single day you do *not* use DIBS for at least ten minutes. How? By making yourself perform some activity
you find distinctly unpleasant—such as eating something
obnoxious, contributing to a cause you hate, getting up
a half hour earlier in the morning, or spending an hour
conversing with someone you find boring. You can also
arrange with some person or group to monitor you and
help you actually carry out the penalties and lack of
reinforcements that you set for yourself. You may of
course steadily use DIBS without any self-reinforcement.
But you will often find it more effective if you use it along
with rewards and penalties that you execute right after

you practice or avoid practicing this rational-emotive method.

EMPLOYING EDUCATIONAL TECHNIQUES. RET has always primarily followed an educational rather than a psychodynamic or a medical model of psychotherapy. It holds that humans *naturally* and *easily* think crookedly, emote inappropriately, and behave self-defeatingly; and that consequently it seems best to use all possible educational modes of dramatically, strongly, and persistently *teaching* them how to do otherwise.

Our strong emphasis in RET, therefore, rests on employing a large variety of effective educational measures. We use a great deal of bibliotherapy, and get most of our clients to read some RET pamphlets and books, such as *How to Live with a Neurotic*, this *Guide*, and *Humanistic Psychotherapy: The Rational-Emotive Approach*. We give them Homework Report sheets to fill out in between group or individual sessions and to go over (and have corrected) during the sessions. We encourage them to tape-record many of their sessions on a cassette recorder and to listen to the recordings several times before the next session. We get them to use, at times, cards with rational statements, to carry around with them or stick on their mirrors; and diagrams and drawings outlining RET principles. We have games and procedures they can use to keep up on RET theory and practice. We teach them exercises that they can employ within and outside of sessions. We distribute tape recordings of rational-emotive talks, interviews, and seminars that people can listen to, so that they can get some of the RET ideas more completely. We have some video tapes and movie films of RET talks, interviews, and therapy sessions.

In many ways, then, we employ educational procedures. And we believe that the future of psychotherapy in general, and of RET in particular, may well lie in the development of even better methods of emotional education, so that "disturbed" and "nondisturbed" individuals can learn how to think more straightly about themselves and the world at virtually all age levels: literally from the cradle to the grave. We even suggest that, ultimately, the terms *emotional education* or *tolerance training* may replace the term *psychotherapy*.

GATHERING RESEARCH DATA. When RET originated, we based it on the small amount of research in cognitive-behavior therapy that existed in the middle 1950's. And that amounted to little more than a hill of beans! Since that time, what we might well call a massive amount of research studies have appeared to substantiate RET theory and practice. I (A.E.) have gathered these materials for the last several years and hope to publish, in the future, a large bibliography of articles and books on rational-emotive and cognitive-behavior therapy.

One part of this bibliography includes several hundred studies that strongly support RET theory: particularly, the theory that if we subtly or honestly induce subjects to change their beliefs, attitudes, opinions, or philosophies, they will at the same time almost automatically make significant—and often highly dramatic—changes in their emotions and their behaviors. Many prominent experimental, social, and clinical psychologists have published confirmatory studies of this nature—including Gerald Davison, Jerome Frank, Richard Lazarus, O Hobart Mowrer, Donald Meichenbaum, Stanley Schacter, and Stuart Valins.

Another part of the RET bibliography includes scores of clinical assessment studies, almost all of which tend to show that rational-emotive procedures, or other allied cognitive-behavior therapy methods, help people significantly more than nontherapeutic control procedures; and that RET produces clinical results as good as or better than various other kinds of therapy, such as client-centered and classical behavior therapy. Validation studies of this kind have resulted from the experiments of many researchers, including D. E. Burkhead, A. Ellis, W. R. Maes and R. A. Heimann, Donald Meichenbaum, Maxie C. Maultsby, Jr., K. L. Sharma, G. L. Taft, Larry Trexler, and Harvey Zingle.

Because RET theory and practice gets presented in specific and concrete terms, and we usually ask for clear-cut definitions of the phrases we use, psychological researchers find it attractive to test. We can therefore confidently predict that an increased number of studies of its theoretical and clinical aspects will continue to get turned out. To which we say: great! In the final analysis, any system of therapy that does not attract and pass the test of rigorous experimentation hardly seems worth advocating. We look forward to the continued testing of RET procedures in every feasible way! Meanwhile, why don't *you* proceed to test it on *you*?

REFERENCES

Items preceded by a check (√) may prove of particular help to readers interested in additional reading in the area of rational living. Items preceded by an asterisk (*), published or distributed by the Institute for Rational Living, Inc., 45 East Sixty-fifth Street, New York, N.Y. 10021, U.S.A., can normally get ordered from the institute. The institute will continue to make available these and other materials, as well as to present talks, seminars, workshops, and other presentations in the area of human growth and rational living. Those interested can send for its current list of publications and events.

√Adler, Alfred. *Superiority and Social Interest.* Edited by H. L. and R. R. Ansbacher. Evanston, Ill.: Northwestern University Press, 1964.

√————. *Understanding Human Nature.* New York: Greenberg, 1927.

√Alberti, R. E., and Emmons, M. L. *Your Perfect Right: A Guide to Assertive Behavior.* San Luis Obispo, Cal.: Impace, 1971.

√Ansbacher, H. L., and Ansbacher, R. R. *The Individual Psychology of Alfred Adler.* New York: Basic Books, 1956.

√Ard, Ben N., Jr. *Treating Psychosexual Dysfunction.* New York: Jason Aronson, 1974.

√————. *Counseling and Psychotherapy.* Palo Alto, Cal.: Science and Behavior Books, 1966.

√Ard, Ben N., Jr., and Ard, Constance C., eds. *Handbook of Marriage Counseling.* Palo Alto, Cal.: Science and Behavior Books, 1969.

Arnheim, R. *Visual Thinking.* Berkeley, Cal.: University of California Press, 1969.

Arnold, Magda. *Emotion and Personality.* New York: Columbia University Press, 1960.

√Bach, George R., and Deutsch, Ronald M. *Pairing.* New York: Avon, 1973.

√Bach, George R., and Wyden, Peter. *The Intimate Enemy.* New York: Avon, 1971.

Bannister, D., and Mair, J. M. M. *The Evaluation of Personal Constructs.* New York: Academic Press, 1968.

√Barksdale, L.S. *Building Self-esteem.* Los Angeles: Barksdale Foundation, 1974.

✓ Beck, A. T. *Depression*. New York: Hoeber-Harper, 1967.
✓ ————. "Cognitive Therapy." *Behavior Therapy* 1 (1970): 184-200.
✓*Bedford, Stewart. *Instant Replay*. New York: Institute for Rational Living, 1974.
✓ Berne, Eric. *What Do You Say After You Say Hello?* New York: Grove Press, 1973.
✓ Bone, Harry. "Two Proposed Alternatives to Psychoanalytic Interpreting. In *Use of Interpretation in Treatment*, edited by E. Hammer, pp. 169-96. New York: Grune & Stratton, 1968.
✓ Bourland, D. David, Jr. "A Linguistic Note: Writing in E-Prime." *General Semantics Bulletin* 32, 33 (1965, 1966): 111-14.
✓ ————. "The Semantics of a Non-Aristotelian Language." *General Semantics Bulletin* 35 (1968):60-63.
————. "The Un-isness of Is." *Time*, May 23, 1969, p. 69.
Bull, N. "An Introduction to Attitude Psychology." *Journal of Clinical & Experimental Psychopathology* 27 (1960):147-56.
Burkhead, David E. "The Reduction of Negative Affect in Human Subjects: A Laboratory Test of Rational-Emotive Therapy." Ph.D. thesis, Western Michigan University, 1970.
✓ Burton, Arthur, ed. *Operational Theories of Personality*. New York: Brunner Mazel, 1974.
✓ Casler, Lawrence. *Is Marriage Necessary?* New York: Human Science Press, 1973.
✓ Cautela, Joseph R. "Treatment of Compulsive Behavior by Covert Sensitization." *Psychological Record* 16 (1966):33-41.
Cobb, Stanley. *Emotions and Clinical Medicine*. New York: Norton, 1950.
✓*Criddle, William D. "Guidelines for Challenging Irrational Beliefs." *Rational Living* 9(1) (Spring, 1974):8-13.
✓*Danysh, J. *Stop Without Quitting*. San Francisco: International Society for General Semantics, 1974.
✓ Davison, Gerald C., and Neale, John M. *Abnormal Psychology: An Experimental-Clinical Approach*. New York: Wiley, 1974.
Davison, Gerald C., and Valins, Stuart. "Maintenance of Self-attributed and Drug-attributed Behavior Change." *Journal of Personality and Social Psychology* 11 (1969):25-33.
Dewey, John *Human Nature and Conduct*. New York: Modern Library, 1930.
DiLoreto, Adolph. *Comparative Psychotherapy*. Chicago: Aldine-Atherton, 1971.
Dorsey, John M. *Illness or Allness*. Detroit: Wayne State University Press, 1965.
✓* Ellis, Albert. *The American Sexual Tragedy*. New York: Twayne, 1954. Rev. ed., New York: Lyle Stuart and Grove Press, 1962.
✓*————. *The Art and Science of Love*. New York: Lyle Stuart, 1960. Rev. ed., New York: Lyle Stuart and Bantam, 1969.
✓*————. "Cognitive Aspects of Abreactive Therapy." *Voices: The Art and Science of Psychotherapy* 10(1) (1974):48-56. New York: Institute for Rational
✓* Living, 1975.
✓*————. *Disputing Irrational Beliefs (DIBS)*. New York: Institute for Rational Living, 1974.
✓*————. "Emotional Education at the Living School." In *Counseling Children in Groups*, edited by Merle M. Ohlsen, pp. 79-94. New York: Holt, Rinehart & Winston, 1973. Reprinted: New York: Institute for Rational Living, 1974.
✓*————. *Executive Leadership: A Rational Approach*. New York: Citadel Press, 1972.
✓*————. *Growth Through Reason*. Palo Alto, Cal.: Science and Behavior Books, 1971. Hollywood: Wilshire Books, 1974.
✓*————. *Healthy and Unhealthy Aggression*. New York: Institute for Rational Living, 1974.
✓*————. *Homework Report*. New York: Institute for Rational Living, 1972.

✓*————. *How to Live with a Neurotic.* New York: Crown, 1957. Rev. ed., 1975.

✓*————. *How to Master Your Fear of Flying.* New York: Curtis Books, 1972.

✓*————. *Humanistic Psychotherapy: The Rational-Emotive Approach.* New York: Julian Press, 1973. New York: McGraw-Hill Paperbacks, 1974.

*————. *Is Objectivism a Religion?* New York: Lyle Stuart, 1968.

✓*————. "Is Psychoanalysis Harmful?" *Psychiatric Opinion* 5(1) (1968):16-124. Also: New York: Institute for Rational Living, 1969.

✓*————. "My Philosophy of Psychotherapy." *Journal of Contemporary Psychotherapy.* 6(1) (1973):13-18. Reprinted: New York: Institute for Rational Living, 1974.

✓*————. "The No Cop-out Therapy." *Psychology Today* 7(2) (July, 1973):56-52. Reprinted: New York: Institute for Rational Living, 1973.

————. "Outcome of Employing Three Techniques of Psychotherapy." *Journal of Clinical Psychology* 13 (1957):344-50.

✓*————. "Psychotherapy and the Value of a Human Being." In *Value and Valuation: Essays in Honor of Robert S. Hartman,* edited by J. W. Davis, pp. 117-39. Knoxville: University of Tennessee Press, 1972. Reprinted: New York: Institute for Rational Living, 1972.

✓ ————. "Psychotherapy Without Tears." In *Twelve Therapists,* edited by Arthur Burton, pp. 103-26. San Francisco: Jossey-Bass, 1972.

✓ ————. "Rational-Emotive Theory." In *Operational Theories of Personality,* edited by Arthur Burton, pp. 308-44. New York: Brunner Mazel, 1974.

✓ ————. "Rational-Emotive Therapy." In *Current Psychotherapies,* edited by R. Corsini, pp. 167-206. Itasca, Ill.: Peacock, 1973.

✓ ————. "Rational-Emotive Therapy." In *Four Psychotherapies,* edited by Leonard Hersher, pp. 47-83. New York: Appleton-Century-Crofts, 1970.

✓*————. *Reason and Emotion in Psychotherapy.* New York: Lyle Stuart, 1962.

✓*————. *The Sensuous Person: Critique and Corrections.* New York: Lyle Stuart, 1972. New York: New American Library, 1974.

✓*————. *Suppressed: Seven Essays Publishers Dared Not Print.* Chicago: New Classics House, 1965.

*Ellis, Albert, and others. *A Bibliography of Articles and Books on Rational-Emotive Therapy and Cognitive-Behavior Therapy.* New York: Institute for Rational Living, 1975.

✓*Ellis, Albert, and Gullo, John M. *Murder and Assassination.* New York: Lyle Stuart, 1972.

✓ Ellis, Albert, and Harper, Robert A. *Creative Marriage.* New York: Lyle Stuart, 1961. Hollywood: Wilshire Books, 1973 (under the title *A Guide to Successful Marriage*).

✓*Ellis, Albert; Krasner, Paul; and Wilson, Robert Anton. "Impolite Interview with Dr. Albert Ellis." *Realist.* 1960, No. 16. 9-11; 1960, No. 17, 7-12. Reprinted: New York: Institute for Rational Living, 1970.

✓*Ellis, Albert; Wolfe, Janet L.; and Moseley, Sandra. *How to Raise an Emotionally Healthy, Happy Child.* Hollywood: Wilshire Books, 1972.

English, H. B., and English, Ava C. *A Comprehensive Dictionary of Psychological and Psychoanalytical Terms.* New York: Longmans, Green, 1958.

✓ Epictetus. *The Works of Epictetus.* Boston: Little, Brown, 1899. *Also see* Hadas, Moses.

✓ Frank, Jerome D. *Persuasion and Healing.* Rev. ed. Baltimore: Johns Hopkins University Press, 1973.

✓ Frankl, Viktor E. *Man's Search for Meaning.* New York: Washington Square Press, 1966.

Freud, Sigmund. *Collected Papers.* New York: Collier Books, 1963.

Fromm, Erich. *The Art of Loving.* New York: Bantam, 1963.

✓*Garcia, Edward, and Pellegrini, Nina. *Homer the Homely Hound Dog.* New York: Institute for Rational Living, 1974.

Garmezy, Norman, and Neuchterlein, Keith. "Invulnerable Children: Fact and Fiction of Competence and Disadvantage." Mimeographed. Minneapolis, 1972.

Gillette, Paul, and Hornbeck, Marie. *Depression: A Layman's Guide to the Symptoms and Cures.* New York: Outerbridge & Lazard, 1973.

✓ Ginott, Haim G. *Between Parent and Child.* New York: Macmillan, 1965.

✓ Glasser, William. *Reality Therapy.* New York: Harper, 1964.

Goldfried, Marvin R.; Decenteco, Edwin T.; and Weinberg, Leslie. "Systematic Rational Restructuring as a Self-control Technique." *Behavior Therapy,* 5 (1974):247-54.

✓ Goldfried, Marvin R., and Merbaum, Michael, eds. *Behavior Change Through Self-control.* New York: Holt, Rinehart & Winston, 1973.

✓*Goodman, David, and Maultsby, Maxie C., Jr. *Emotional Well-being Through Rational Behavior Training.* Springfield, Ill.: Charles C. Thomas, 1974.

✓ Greenwald, Harold. *Decision Therapy.* New York: Wyden, 1974.

✓ ———. ed. *Active Psychotherapies.* New York: Atherton, 1967.

✓ Grossack, Martin. *You Are Not Alone.* Boston: Marlborough, 1974.

✓ Hadas, Moses, ed. *Essential Works of Stoicism.* New York: Bantam, 1962.

✓ Harper, Robert A. *The New Psychotherapies.* Englewood Cliffs, N.J.: Prentice-Hall, 1975.

✓ ———. *Psychoanalysis and Psychotherapy: 36 Systems.* Englewood Cliffs, N.J.: Prentice-Hall, 1959.

✓ Harper, Robert A., and Stokes, Walter S. *Forty-five Levels to Sexual Understanding and Enjoyment.* Englewood Cliffs, N.J.: Prentice-Hall, 1973.

Hartman, Robert S. *The Measurement of Value.* Carbondale, Ill.: Southern Illinois University Press, 1967.

✓*Hauck, Paul A. *Overcoming Depression.* Philadelphia: Westminster Press, 1973.

✓* ———. *Overcoming Frustration and Anger.* Philadelphia: Westminster Press, 1974.

✓ ———. *The Rational Management of Children.* New York: Libra, 1967.

———. *Reason in Pastoral Counseling.* Philadelphia: Westminster Press, 1972.

✓ Hayakawa, S. I. *Language in Action.* New York: Harcourt, Brace & World, 1965.

Herzberg, Alexander. *Active Psychotherapy.* New York: Grune & Stratton, 1945.

Homme, Lloyd. *How to Use Contingency Contracting in the Classroom.* Champaign, Ill.: Research Press, 1969.

✓ Horney, Karen. *Collected Writings.* New York: Norton, 1972.

Hoxter, A. Lee. "Irrational Beliefs and Self-concept in Two Kinds of Behavior." Ph.D. thesis, University of Alberta, 1967.

Jacobsen, E. *You Must Relax.* New York: Pocket Books, 1958.

Janov, A. *The Primal Scream.* New York: Dell, 1970.

✓ Johnson, Wendell. *People in Quandaries.* New York: Harper, 1946.

Jones, Richard G. "A Factored Measure of Ellis' Irrational Belief System, with Personality and Maladjustment Correlates." Ph.D. thesis, Texas Technological University, 1968.

Jung, C. G. *The Practice of Psychotherapy.* New York: Pantheon, 1954.

✓ Kelly, George. *Clinical Psychology and Personality.* New York: Wiley, 1969.

✓ ———. *The Psychology of Personal Constructs.* New York: Norton, 1955.

✓ Kiev, Ari. *A Strategy for Daily Living.* New York: Free Press, 1973.

✓*Knaus, William J. *Rational-Emotive Education: A Manual for Elementary School Teachers.* New York: Institute for Rational Living, 1974.

✓ Korzybski, Alfred. *Science and Sanity.* Lancaster, Pa.: Lancaster Press, 1933.

✓*Kranzler, Gerald. *You Can Change How You Feel.* Eugene, Ore.: author, 1974.

Laughridge, Stanley Theodore. "A Test of Irrational Thinking as It Relates to Psychological Maladjustment." Ph.D. thesis, University of Oregon, 1971.

✓ Lazarus, Arnold A. *Behavior Therapy and Beyond.* New York: McGraw-Hill, 1971.

Lazarus, R. S. *Psychological Stress and the Coping Process.* New York: McGraw-Hill, 1966.

✓*Lembo, John M. *Help Yourself.* Niles, Ill.: Argus Communications, 1974.

✓ Lewis, W. C. *Why People Change.* New York: Holt, Rinehart & Winston. 1972.

Lindner, Robert. *Prescription for Rebellion.* London: Gollancz, 1953.

✓ Low, Abraham A. *Mental Health Through Will-Training.* Boston: Christopher, 1950.

Lowen, Alexander. *The Betrayal of the Body.* New York: Macmillan, 1966.

✓ Lynn, John G. "Preliminary Report of Two Cases of Psychopathic Personality with Chronic Alcoholism Treated by the Korzybski Method." In *General Semantics.* New York: Arrow Editions, 1938. Reprinted: Lakeville, Conn.: Institute of General Semantics, 1970.

*MacDonald, A. P., and Games, Richard G. "Ellis' Irrational Values." *Rational Living.* 7(2) (1972): 25-28.

McGill, V. J. *Emotion and Reason.* Springfield, Ill.: Charles C. Thomas, 1954.

Maes, Wayne R., and Heimann, Robert A. *The Comparison of Three Approaches to the Reduction of Test Anxiety in High School Students.* Washington, D.C.: Office of Education, 1970.

✓ Marcus Aurelius. *"The Thoughts of the Emperor Marcus Aurelius Antonius.* Boston: Little, Brown, 1900. *Also see* Moses Hadas.

✓ Maslow, A. H. *Motivation and Personality.* 2d ed. New York: Harper, 1970.

✓ ———. *Toward a Psychology of Being.* Princeton: Van Nostrand, 1962.

✓ Masters, William, and Johnson, Virginia E. *Human Sexual Inadequacy.* Boston: Little, Brown, 1970.

✓*Maultsby, Maxie C., Jr. *More Personal Happines Through Rational Self-counseling.* Lexington, Ky.: Author, 1971.

✓*———. *Help Yourself to Happiness.* New York: Institute for Rational Living, 1975.

✓ ———. *How and Why You Can Naturally Control Your Emotions.* Lexington, Ky.: author, 1974.

✓*———. "Systematic Written Homework in Psychotherapy." *Rational Living.* 6(1) (1971): 16-23.

✓*Maultsby, Maxie C., Jr., and Ellis, Albert. *Technique for Using Rational-Emotive Imagery (REI).* New York: Institute for Rational Living, 1974.

✓*Maultsby, Maxie C., Jr., and Hendricks, Allie. *Five Cartoon Booklets Illustrating Basic Rational Behavior Therapy Concepts.* Lexington, Ky.: authors, 1974.

*Maultsby, Maxie C., Jr. and Hendricks, Allie. *You and Your Emotions.* Lexington, Ky.: University of Kentucky Medical Center, 1974.

✓*Maultsby, Maxie C., Jr.; Stiefel, Leanna; and Brosky, Lynda. "A Theory of Rational Behavioral Group Process." *Rational Living.* 7(1) (1972): 28-34.

Meehl, Paul E. *Psychologists' Opinions as to the Effect of Holding Five of Ellis' "Irrational Ideas."* Minneapolis: Research Laboratory of the Dept. of Psychiatry, University of Minnesota, 1966.

✓ Meichenbaum, Donald H. *Cognitive Behavior Modification.* Morristown, N.J.: General Learning Press, 1974.

✓ ———. *Cognitive Factors in Behavior Modification: Modifying What Clients Say to Themselves.* Waterloo, Canada: University of Waterloo, 1971.

✓ Merrill, M.G. "There Are No Absolutes." *ART in Daily Living* 1(4) (1972): 6-9.

Meyer, Adolf. *The Commonsense Psychiatry of Dr. Adolf Meyer.* New York: McGraw-Hill, 1948.

Mischel, W. "Toward a Cognitive Social Learning Reconceptualization of Personality." *Psychological Review* 30 (1973):252-83.

Moreno, J. L. *Who Shall Survive?* Washington, D.C.: Nervous and Mental Disease Publishing Company, 1934.

√*Morris, Kenneth T., and Kanitz, H. Mike. *Rational-Emotive Therapy.* Boston: Houghton Mifflin, 1975.

√ Mosher, Donald. "Are Neurotics Victims of Their Emotions?" *ETC.: A Review of General Semantics* 23 (1966):225-34.

Mowrer, O. H. "Preparatory Set (Expectancy)—A Determinant in Motivation and Learning." *Psychological Review* 45 (1938):62-91.

Orlansky, Harold. "Infant Care and Personality." *Psychological Bulletin* 46 (1949):1-48.

Paul, G. L. *Insight versus Desensitization in Psychotherapy.* Stanford: Stanford University Press, 1966.

Pavlov, I. P. *Essays in Psychology and Psychiatry.* New York: Citadel Press, 1962.

Peller, Lili E. "The Child's Approach to Reality." *American Journal of Orthopsychiatry* 9 (1939):503-13.

Perls, F. C. *Gestalt Therapy Verbatim.* Lafayette, Cal.: Real People Press, 1969.

√ Phillips, E. Lakin. *Psychotherapy.* Englewood Cliffs, N.J.: Prentice-Hall, 1956.

Premack, David. "Reinforcement Theory." In *Nebraska Symposium on Motivation*, edited by D. Levine. Lincoln, Neb.: University of Nebraska Press, 1965.

Rado, Sandor. *Adaptational Psychodynamics: Motivation and Control.* New York: Science House, 1969.

Rank, Otto. *Will Therapy and Truth and Reality.* New York: Knopf, 1945.

Reich, Wilhelm. *Character Analysis.* New York: Orgone Institute Press, 1949.

Reichenbach, Hans. *The Rise of Scientific Philosophy.* Berkeley: University of California Press, 1953.

Reik, T. *Listening with the Third Ear.* New York: Rinehart, 1948.

√ Rimm, David C., and Masters, John C. *Behavior Therapy.* New York: Academic Press, 1974.

Rogers, C. R. *On Becoming a Person.* Boston: Houghton Mifflin, 1961.

Rokeach, Milton. *Beliefs, Attitudes and Values.* San Francisco: Jossey-Bass, 1968.

√ ———. *The Nature of Human Values.* New York: Free Press, 1973.

√ Russell, Bertrand. *The Conquest of Happiness.* New York: Bantam, 1968.

Russell, Philip. "An Empirical Test of Rational-Emotive Therapy." M.A. thesis, University of Kentucky, 1972.

Salter, A. *Conditioned Reflex Therapy.* New York: Capricorn Books, 1949.

Schacter, Stanley. *Emotion, Obesity, and Crime.* New York: Academic Press, 1971.

Schultz, J. H., and Luthe, W. *Autogenic Training.* New York: Grune & Stratton, 1959.

Sewell, W. H.; Mussen, P. H.; and Harris, C. W. "Relationships among Child Training Practices." *American Sociological Review* 20 (1955):137-48.

Sharma, K. L. "A Rational Group Therapy Approach to Counseling Anxious Underachievers." Ph.D. thesis, University of Alberta, 1970.

√ Shibles, Warren. *Emotion.* Whitewater, Wis.: Language Press, 1974.

Shulman, Lee M., and Taylor, Joan K. *When to See a Psychologist.* Los Angeles: Nash, 1969.

Skinner, B. F. *Beyond Freedom and Dignity.* New York: Knopf, 1971.

Stampfl, Thomas, and Levis, Donald. 'Phobic Patients: Treatment with the Learning Approach of Implosive Therapy." *Voices* 3(3) (1967):23-27.

Sullivan, H. S. *Conceptions of Modern Psychiatry.* Washington, D.C.: William Alanson White Foundation, 1947.

Taft, G. L. "A Study of the Relationships of Anxiety and Irrational Ideas." Ph.D. thesis, University of Alberta, 1965.

✓ Thorne, F. C. *Principles of Personality Counseling*. Brandon, Vt.: Journal of Clinical Psychology Press, 1950.

Thorpe, G. L. "Short-term Effectiveness of Systematic Desensitization, Modeling and Behavioral Rehearsal, and Self-Instructional Training in Facilitating Assertive-Refusal Behavior." Ph.D. thesis, Rutgers University, 1973.

✓ Tillich, Paul. *The Courage to Be*. New York: Oxford, 1953.

✓ Tosi, Donald J. *Youth: Toward Personal Growth, a Rational-Emotive Approach*. Columbus, Ohio: Merrill Publishing Co., 1974.

Trexler, Larry D. "Rational-Emotive Therapy, Placebo, and No-Treatment Effects on Public-speaking Anxiety." Ph.D. thesis, Temple University, 1971.

Valins, Stuart. "Cognitive Effects of False Heart-rate Feedback." *Journal of Personality and Social Psychology* 4 (1966):400-8.

Valins, Stuart, and Ray, Alice A. "Effects of Cognitive Desensitization on Avoidance Behavior." *Journal of Personality and Social Psychology* 7 (1967):345-50.

Velten, Emmett C. "The Induction of Elation and Depression Through Reading." Ph.D. thesis, University of Southern California, 1967.

✓ Walling, Connie. "An Argument against the Desirability of Theoretically Presupposing Calm Indifference in Undesirable Life Situations." *ART in Daily Living* 1(2) (1972):3.

✓ Watzlawack, Paul; Weakland, John; and Fisch, Richard. *Change*. New York: Norton, 1974.

✓ Weekes, Claire. *Hope and Help for Your Nerves*. New York: Hawthorn, 1969.

✓ ———. *Peace from Nervous Suffering*. New York: Hawthorn, 1972.

Wiener, Daniel N. *A Practical Guide to Psychotherapy*. New York: Harper & Row, 1968.

Wiener, Daniel N., and Stieper, D. R. *Dimensions of Psychotherapy*. Chicago: Aldin, 1965.

Wolberg, Lewis R. *The Technique of Psychotherapy*. 2d ed. New York: Grune & Stratton, 1968.

✓ Wolfe, Janet L. "How Integrative Is Integrity Therapy?" *Counseling Psychologist* 3(2) (1973):42-49.

———. "Short-Term Effects of Modeling/Behavior Rehearsal, Modeling/Behavior Rehearsal—Plus—Rational Therapy Placebo, and No Treatment on Assertive Behavior." Ph.D. thesis, New York University, 1975.

———. "What to Do Until the Revolution Comes: An Argument for Women's Therapy Groups." Paper presented at Women's Conference, Madison, Wis.: November, 1973.

Wolpe, Joseph. *Psychotherapy by Reciprocal Inhibition*. Stanford: Stanford University Press, 1958.

Wolpe, Joseph, and Lazarus, Arnold. *Behavior Therapy Techniques*. New York and London: Pergamon Press, 1966.

✓*Young, Howard S. *A Rational Counseling Primer*. New York: Institute for Rational Living, 1974.

✓*———. *Understanding and Overcoming Anger*. New York: Institute for Rational Living, 1975.

Zimbardo, R. G. *The Cognitive Control of Motivation*. Chicago: Scott, Foresman, 1969.

Zingle, Harvey W. "Therapy Approach to Counseling Underachievers." Ph.D. thesis, University of Alberta, 1965.

TAPE RECORDINGS, FILMS, AND VIDEO TAPES

Ellis, Albert. *John Jones. Tape-recorded Interview with a Male Homosexual.* Philadelphia: American Academy of Psychotherapists Tape Library, 1964.

*————. *Rational-Emotive Psychotherapy.* Tape recording. New York: Institute for Rational Living, 1970.

*————. *Theory and Practice of Rational-Emotive Therapy.* Tape recording. New York: Institute for Rational Living, 1971.

✓*————. *Solving Emotional Problems.* Tape recording. New York: Institute for Rational Living, 1972.

✓*————. *A Demonstration with a Woman Fearful of Expressing Emotions.* Filmed demonstration. Washington, D.C.: American Personnel and Guidance Association, 1973.

✓*————. *A Demonstration with a Young Divorced Woman.* Filmed demonstration. Washington, D.C.: American Personnel and Guidance Association, 1973.

✓*————. *A Demonstration with an Elementary School Child.* Filmed demonstration. Washington, D.C.: American Personnel and Guidance Association, 1973.

✓*————. *How to Stubbornly Refuse to Feel Ashamed of Anything.* Tape recording. New York: Institute for Rational Living, 1973.

*————. *Rational-Emotive Psychotherapy.* Filmed interview with Dr. Thomas Allen. Washington, D.C.: American Personnel and Guidance Association, 1973.

*————. *Rational-Emotive Psychotherapy Applied to Groups.* Filmed interview with Dr. Thomas Allen. Washington, D.C.: American Personnel and Guidance Association, 1973.

————. *Recession and Depression: Or How Not to Let the Economy Get you Down.* Tape recording. Philadelphia: American Academy of Psychotherapists Tape Library, 1973.

✓*————. *RET and Marriage and Family Counseling.* Tape recording. New York: Institute for Rational Living, 1973.

✓ ————. *Twenty-five Ways to Stop Downing Yourself.* Tape recording. Philadelphia: American Academy of Psychotherapists Tape Library, 1973.

✓*————. *Twenty-one Ways to Stop Worrying.* Tape recording. New York: Institute for Rational Living, 1973.

✓*————. *Cognitive Behavior Therapy.* Tape recording. New York: Institute for Rational Living, 1974.

✓*————. *Rational Living in an Irrational World.* Tape recording. New York: Institute for Rational Living, 1974.

*————. *The Theory and Practice of Rational-Emotive Therapy.* Video tape recording. New York: Institute for Rational Living, 1974.

*Ellis, Albert, and Wholey, Dennis. *Rational-Emotive Psychotherapy.* Tape-recorded interview. New York: Institute for Rational Living, 1970.

✓ Harper, Robert A., and Ellis, Albert. *A Tape-recorded Interview.* Tape recording. Philadelphia: American Academy of Psychotherapists and Division of Psychotherapy of the American Psychological Association Tape Library, 1974.

Henderson, John; Murray, David; Ellis, Albert; Cautela, Joseph; and Seidenberg, Robert. *Four Psychotherapies. Tape-recorded Interviews with the Same Anxious Male.* Philadelphia: American Academy of Psychotherapists, 1973.

✓*Maultsby, Maxie C., Jr. *Overcoming Irrational Fears.* Tape cassette series. Chicago: Instructional Dynamics, 1975.

✓ ————. *A Rational Approach to Irrational Fears and Insomnia.* Tape recording. Lexington, Ky.: University of Kentucky Medical Center, 1973.

✓*Wolfe, Janet L. *Rational-Emotive Therapy and Women's Problems.* Tape recording. New York: Institute for Rational Living, 1974.

INDEX